Family life and illicit love in
earlier generations

Family life and illicit love in earlier generations

Essays in historical sociology

PETER LASLETT

*Fellow of Trinity College and Reader in Politics
and the History of Social Structure in the
University of Cambridge*

*Director of the Cambridge Group for the His-
tory of Population and Social Structure*

CAMBRIDGE UNIVERSITY PRESS

Cambridge
London   New York   Melbourne

Published by the Syndics of the Cambridge University Press
The Pitt Building, Trumpington Street, Cambridge CB2 1RP
Bentley House, 200 Euston Road, London NW1 2DB
32 East 57th Street, New York, NY 10022, USA
296 Beaconsfield Parade, Middle Park, Melbourne 3206, Australia

First published 1977

Photoset and printed in Malta by Interprint (Malta) Ltd

Library of Congress Cataloguing in Publication Data
Laslett, Peter.
Family life and illicit love in earlier
generations.
Bibliography: p.
Includes index.
1. Family — History. 2. Illegitimacy — Great
Britain. 3. Orphans and orphan asylums — Great
Britain. 4. Slavery—United States. I. Title.
HQ503.L375   301.42'09   76—21010
ISBN 0 521 21408 4 hard covers
ISBN 0 521 29221 2 paperback

Dedicated to my wife, Janet Crockett Laslett, in gratitude for what she has done in this book, and in the other writing we have undertaken together.

Contents

Introduction: the necessity of a historical sociology

The feeling which most of us have about the family is direct, spontaneous and often very powerful. It is strong enough, in fact, to sustain a fund of interest in all aspects of family life, including the family life of earlier generations, on the part of people for whom the past history of other things may have little value. Any writer on the subject out of the university, therefore, has both an advantage and a handicap. He can count on his possible readers' wanting to know what he has to say; but he must find it difficult to provide the information which he thinks they ought to have in a form acceptable to them.

'Acceptable' here means written in plain, readable prose. It means naming the names of the past people whose familial experience is being described, spelling out the resemblances with what goes on in the home in our own day, and lighting up the contrasts. Leafing over the pages of this book will soon show that a good part of the exposition is not in prose at all, but in figures, frequently in tables of figures and sometimes in graphs. Not much experience is actually described. Not many of those who took part in family life, or fell illicitly in love, have their names and ages written out. Not much is said about how different these things were in days gone by or how much the same. The reader may perhaps come to think he has been cheated of what he had a right to expect to be able to read.

This is especially a pity in the present case, because the facts and figures here set out could never have been assembled at all without the co-operation and the active help of hundreds of people who have demonstrated their interest in earlier family life in a practical way. No single scholar, no body of scholars banded together in an institution, could ever have recovered the hundreds of thousands, the millions even, of individual acts of procreation reported upon in chapter 3, which tries to write out the story of bastardy in England over the last four hundred years.

The job could only have been done as it was done in fact. That is to say, by the co-operative work of many persons willing to search out the recordings of baptisms, to note those marked 'illeg.', 'spur.', 'base', 'alias' or 'bastard', and then to report their findings systematically to the researcher. The creation of the file of one hundred English communities which has yielded standard samples for such things as three gene-

1

rational households, or the proportion of orphaned children living with their widowed mothers, was likewise made possible by the help of volunteers who found the documents, and also by the painstaking, repetitive, daunting work of those who did the analysis at Cambridge. Only because of the sustained effort and interest of these people could we begin to write upon such topics as comparative household composition, or the familial identity of the West, or about parental deprivation in the past as compared with parental deprivation in our own day.

I have done my best at the appropriate places to acknowledge all this help, and to make it clear how far this book is a work of collaboration, not of individual composition. But a debt acknowledged is not a debt repaid, and it remains to be seen whether the appearance as a book of a series of decidedly numerical studies, often couched in abstractions and only seldom engaged with personalities, will be taken as any kind of service in return. Even the foreign scholars who have exchanged evidence and results may feel they have a right to expect more of a connected study, solider and more advanced conclusions, perhaps more history and less social science, or the other way round. This brings us to the point where it may begin to appear why a book of this kind has to be written in this particular form. The reason is to be found in the clear and present necessity of a historical sociology.

'Sociology' has never been a popular word amongst historians, and perhaps not many of them would be prepared even now to accept the necessity of its existence. There are many reasons for this: the literary and humanist tradition of historical writing; its preoccupation with unique events, unique personalities, unrepeatable episodes and experiences; the status-ordering of faculties in universities, which has given to history a place in the First Division in some sort of succession to the Classics, and has relegated the social sciences, the 'soft sciences', to a lower division altogether. More interesting, perhaps, are the political reasons. Sociology and the social sciences generally have been regarded by those engaged in the celebration of the *status quo* as inevitably subversive, by those whose interest is in changing society as irremediably committed to the defence of the social order which exists.

This last is a dilemma from which the study of society may never escape, and perhaps ought never to try to do. It would not be difficult to demonstrate, however, that the writing of history can be subjected to the same sort of criticism, that its claim to objectivity appears to be more convincing only because its traditional methods have worked to obscure its final political tendencies. To acknowledge that history stands in need of sociology is to realize that this is how history will come to recognize its own position in the social world. Which implies an admission that history stands as much in need of a theory of itself as of any other form of generalization about social facts.

This may seem rather a portentous reflection in an introduction intended to explain or to justify a series of studies of the history of family life, with an excursus into sexual behaviour. Before we propose rather more specific reasons why history can be said to stand in need of the social sciences, we may consider why it is that the social sciences stand in need of history. This, so it seems to me, can be dealt with in a summary fashion and in terms of social welfare as well as of social theory. 'The value of historical sociology to the creation of policy in the present', it is said in chapter 5, 'is in denoting how far we differ from past people and how much we are the same. With respect to aging, it is maintained that we . . . shall have to invent appropriate social forms, for they cannot be recovered from our history . . . Our situation remains irreducibly novel: it calls for invention rather than imitation.'

The confident conviction that the historical record has a social use, in enabling us, as was insisted in *The world we have lost,* to understand ourselves in time, is close to the surface on other occasions. The situation of the black family in the United States as it was in the 1960s, a situation which was freely described as almost desperate by government advisors as well as by social investigators, looks rather different when historical sociology addresses itself to the situation of the black slave family. The ghetto in the contemporary American city no longer appears as the inevitable outcome of the situation on the slave plantation as it is described in the last chapter of this book. The problem of the parentally deprived child in the contemporary world, a world which believes itself to be peculiarly prone to the breakup of marriage, is likewise considerably changed. For it turns out, as chapter 4 attempts to show, that high industrial society in the twentieth century is not *more* likely, but *less* likely, to leave children without their natural parents than was pre-industrial England.

The discovery of a time dimension in areas where the passage of years had scarcely previously been noticed could be said to be part of the prospectus for a historical sociology. Some of these areas are already beginning to become familiar, as for example the history of illegitimacy, where the first long time series was arrived at almost a decade ago. Only in the last year or two, however, has it become apparent that the bringing forth of illegitimate children over this long stretch of time was to some extent the responsibility of an ongoing, descent-related sub-society, discernible in the same communities over several succeeding generations.

If this comes as a surprise, it is surely only because questions of this kind, questions of continuance over time, had never previously arisen in this area of enquiry. 'Perdurance' is a word for such a phenomenon, a noun which appears in the first sentence of our first chapter and a concept which occurs again and again thereafter. The details of the perduring sub-society of the illegitimacy-prone have, moreover, a significance for the general study of social wholes. For they can be said to bear upon the nature of social rules, rules of such fundamental importance as those which govern sexual behaviour, and upon the plural, the conflicting, character of social structures. This in its turn brings us up against the notorious limitations of a functional explanation and of theories of balance and self-regulation.

Or we might take turnover of population. This was the earliest topic to appear written up in the form which now seems to have established itself as usual for exercises in historical sociology, a form even at the outset necessarily subjected to figures, tables and numerical analysis. The slight sensation of shock felt by those who first found out, by doing the necessary sums, that there could be a turnover of nearly two-thirds of all persons in a pre-industrial English village within twelve years has been deliberately preserved in chapter 2. This fifteen-year-old discovery (the actual comparison of the two lists for Clayworth was made in 1961) may yet startle some readers.

Now that the facts of population turnover are becoming familiar, however, and falling into place, what begins to surprise us is how little we can know of social experience if something like this can have been overlooked entirely for so long. The figures for change of address, which used to be brought out to show how quickly everything happened in the advanced United States, how temporary everything is and how volatile in high industrial society, have lost their meaning, and for historical reasons. 'Lost' is not quite right. They have changed their meaning because at last a temporal landscape has been mapped out behind them.

The seven topics which occupy us here are of course only a selection from the possible subject matter of historical sociology. We may take another one at random, from political science. Patriarchal authority is widely believed to be the subjective-symbolic counterpart of political authority. How interesting it is to be informed, therefore, that in England, where political patriarchalism was codified in the 1630s by Sir Robert Filmer, paternal power was exercised over servants, over strangers to the family and to the kin, that is, very much more than it was exercised over kinsmen.

Familial authority, therefore, seems always to have been political authority in this sense in the English and Western European past, and political education, political socialization, quite literally patriarchal. It was a matter of positive inculcation by the catechizing priest, using rote learning and the rich array of samples of paternal authority contained in Holy Writ so as to condition the minds of the masses of illiterate English youth. The paradox that this situation should have been discovered in the country which was the first to develop representative institutions has already been noticed by political scientists.[1]

It can be shown in ways like these how the distorted picture which synchronic social science has brought about requires the therapeutic intervention of the historian or of the historian as sociologist. We do not understand ourselves because we do not yet know what we have been and hence what we may be becoming. This must change, is changing.

As we turn back to the necessity of a historical sociology for historians themselves, we may take note of two circumstances which bear upon the form of presentation adopted here. In the first place, because of the recent emergence of this line of study it is frequently appropriate to put forward a bold hypothesis and to support it with a body of miscellaneous early evidence. This means that a table of percentages gathered from a number of diverse places at different times is the easiest and perhaps the only economical form of demonstration. Chapter 1 is an obvious example, and stands in fact as the introduction to the intellectual themes of the volume as distinct from the methods which have had to be used to expound them. The field, I hope, is still novel enough and the topics sufficiently profitable to compensate the reader for the crudities he will encounter.

In the second place is the characteristic shared by all of the subjects dealt with here. They are to varying degrees demographic, to do with the family and the family group. It is significant in itself, of course, that in our generation preoccupation with population should be so strong. There are other reasons, as will become evident as we proceed, why demography should have become the first body of social scientific theory and technique to be used by those calling themselves historical sociologists. But it goes without saying that demography is not the only social science which they can learn to use, and that its dominance in these early stages has not been a necessary one. Economics was domesticated amongst historians two generations ago and its presence is taken for granted in these essays. But demography has proved to be remarkably fruitful in every direction.

Now demography is a tabular pursuit. Its prose is inevitably studded with digits and intercalated with tables. Although this should explain the frequent occurrence of figures and tables in each of our chapters, the population problems of our days are in no sense the final objects of the work. The example of illegitimacy should have made it plain that what must also interest the historical sociologist is the further

[1] See Laslett 1975 and especially G. J. Schochet, Patriarchalism, politics and mass attitudes in Stuart England', *Historical Journal*, XIII (1969): 413–41, with his recent monograph *Patriarchalism and political theory* (Oxford, 1975).

intellectual horizon, those general issues of social control, social development, social composition, which this new-found understanding of the
past can be made to open up.

Quantities are crucial here, just as they are with demography itself.
But quantification is an incident, a circumstance, never an end. As for the
computer, it should surely now no longer be necessary to lay it down
that this intricate, time-consuming, ingenuity-demanding, exasperating
and marvellously useful machine is an instrument only. It is hardly
ever mentioned in the course of this book, but much of the text depends
upon the computer's having played its part. With so much numerical
evidence to deal with, however else could we have done the work?

Ten years ago, in an attempt to map out the relationship of history
to the social sciences, as they then were, it was insisted that the interests of the historian must be wider and more diffuse than those of the
social scientist.[2] 'Deliberative societal history' was the unwieldy phrase
there used to describe the active component of historical sociology, and
this was only one of the activities of the writers of history, with their
immense and varied readerships and great range of intellectual responsi-
bilities. But restricted as this sector is, to lose command here might be
to yield strategic control of social history as a whole. There are those
who believe that the quantifiers are in a position to succeed to this particular command. And by quantifiers people from outside the realm of
historical study seem often to be meant.

To my mind, anyway, the notion of quantification, mechanical or
otherwise, as being in some way alien to the historian's accepted way
of doing his job or even as opposed to it, is entirely misconceived. Even
apposition seems wrong to me. Whenever a statement is made about a
plurality of persons and it is claimed that they are more this than that,
or mostly the one and not the other, or on average like this rather than
like anything else; whenever a proposition is made in social terms,
whether it is about votes, or prices, or length of life, or the number of
heirs likely to live long enough to succeed, or even about the distribution
of opinions, or preferences, or beliefs, then quantities are in question.
All historians deal in societies to some extent, even if their chosen subjects are individuals or states of mind, and therefore all historians deal
in quantities.

The important distinction, as Professor Michael Drake[3] so correctly

[2] See Laslett 1967b.

[3] In my view the most illuminating of the numerous works which have appeared
in recent years on quantification in history and in historical sociology are the course
books prepared by Michael Drake and his colleagues for the Open University course
D301, Historical Data and the Social Sciences, issued in 1974 by the Open University
Press, Milton Keynes.

insists, is between quantification which is implicit and quantification which is explicit. What must be seen apart are statements which are covertly numerical, whether or not the historian who uses them recognizes the fact, and statements which are overtly numerical, where the historian does his best to get usable figures and deals with them as figures should be dealt with, that is whenever possible statistically, mathematically. But he remains a historian still, even if he does his computation by machine.

This is not the end of the matter, of course. To guard against misunderstanding I should like to lay strong stress on two or three straightforward points. One is that the historical statements which are implicitly numerical are few and quite rare in much historical writing, although they are likely to be the key assertions when it comes to social change in the past. Another is that the question of which of these numerical statements can be appropriately and adequately dealt with statistically or mathematically has to be settled on every single occasion. Disagreement is very probable here, especially since, as in all social analysis, numerical or quasi-numerical indicators have to be used rather than the more exact numerical measurements of the physical sciences. A third point is that even when there is agreement as to the appropriateness of the indicators and even when it is also granted by everyone that the numerical analysis is itself properly suited to the issue and has been correctly carried out, the outcome is very unlikely to settle the issue with finality. Certainty is not to be secured simply by the adoption of the proper method for the task, and in any case the answering of one question, however important, always leads to the raising of other questions.

There is a fourth important point not quite distinct from those already set out, which has to be taken a little further. Historical documents which come in figures, or which can easily or unequivocally be made into figures, like series of prices paid, or lists of votes cast, or registrations of baptisms, marriages and burials, or even listings of inhabitants by household, are not because of that very fact more reliable in the results they yield than documents of other kinds. On the contrary. Because they are susceptible of quantification — by counting items, for example — completeness, exhaustiveness, is of much greater significance in documents of this kind than in those which describe or recount. But final completeness is extremely unlikely to be an attribute of historical documents, especially of those which come to us from traditional times, when numeracy as well as literacy was spread so thin throughout society.

Those who handle such 'statistical' sources, then, should pay heed when they are told, as they are repeatedly told, not to be deceived into supposing that evidence which comes in numbers is closer to the truth than evidence which does not. Nor must they fail in their professional duty, the particular obligation laid on historians, to be critical of their sources.

There are, nevertheless, features of such evidence which do distinguish it from evidence of other kinds, and which do make an agreed settlement of the issues in question considerably more likely. Because these sources are numerical, or can easily be made so, it is frequently possible for them to be so manipulated by the historian that he can estimate how far they are likely to be out, or incomplete: their degree of error. He does this first by common sense and secondly by statistical theory and statistical method. Estimation of degree of error cannot be carried out with anything like such confidence for documents which do not come in countable items. Moreover, the very unawareness of the composers of such lists of items of the purposes to which their work would finally be put insures against deception of a particular kind, the deception which comes from a desire to make a case.

In the prospectus for English historical demography composed at about the time when the numerical facts concerning turnover of population at Clayworth in the 1670s and the 1680s were coming to light, the following sentences were written about the conditions under which demographic evidence was created in that now so distant-seeming past.

'If we think of the educated priest, or the literate parish clerk scrawling out the words and figures in the appointed book after the baby had been borne from the font, or the body laid out on the floor of the grave, with the puzzled faces of the illiterate peasants crowding round him, we can see at once how far our purposes were from his mind. If he failed in his task at the time, because he was cold, or the sun had set and he had no light, or because he had something else to do, then it might lie upon his conscience, if he was a conscientious man. But whether or not a sense of duty in the mind of a priest, duty to his order or duty to his flock, was sufficient to keep him at his task of registration consistently enough to earn our praise so long after he is dead, it is impossible to imagine that he could ever have anticipated being judged on our criteria.'[4]

But this attribute of its sources is not the only virtue possessed by historical demography, and not the only reason why the results which

---

[4] Laslett, 'The numerical study of English society', introduction to E. A. Wrigley (ed.), *An introduction to English historical demography* (1966), p. 3. When men of the past themselves had the statistical attitude, or some approach to it, as when Gregory King writes out his tables, then this quality of *unanticipation* disappears, and it becomes very important to discover whether a particular case was being made out in the very act of recording. See Laslett 1973.

it has produced during the last decade seem to be such a strong persuasive towards accepting the necessity of a historical sociology by historians. The processes it deals in are universal, or as near universal as can be found amongst regularities in human behaviour. We are all born, we all die, and nearly all of us live long enough to get married. Both before and after marriage we tend to live in family groups. Every one of these things comes in figures to be counted. They belong, moreover, with the known, tested, reliable body of theory developed by demography, except only those numerical facts about the composition of families for which an allied, if as yet inchoate and dependent, kind of theory is now being developed. We can therefore make comparisons across cultures and over time in this area of human behaviour which are unequivocally quantitative. This is also true of another of the social sciences which has begun to enter into historical sociology.

This pursuit is econometrics. It is the econometricians who have tended to set up quantification in apposition to other historical methods, and it is they who incline to see their activity as different in kind from *traditional history* as it is coming to be called. In this way they have in a sense laid claim, from outside, to the central ground of the study of social change in the past. This thrust into historical territory has proceeded so far that it was possible to write as follows of the most ambitious publication so far issued by econometricians acting as historians.

'The most interesting aspect of this book is its implication for the future of the historian: humanist scholar or numerical technician? On this there seems to be one simple thing to be said. *Time on the Cross* is no treatise in higher mathematics, however skilful its authors, and however mystified the distinguished historians have been who have tried to review it in the United States. Throughout my life at the university, men have been calling for the merger of the disciplines. Now that the moment is come, it is not for the historian to draw back: unless, of course, he really believes that others better qualified than himself can now do that job better than he can.'[5]

This concluding judgement on a book which sought to upset the interpretation of a central theme in the political history of the United States as well as of the social development of its people, must be largely independent of how far its authors turn out to be right or wrong on any of the issues which they raise. From now on, anyone who wishes to make his own decision between North and South will have himself to be some-

[5] Laslett, broadcast review of Fogel and Engerman 1974, printed in *The Listener*, 4 July 1974. Some phrases of the original were omitted from the printed version, phrases which drew attention to the fact that the mathematics employed were well within the capacity of a beginning historian.

thing of an econometrician, or cliometrician, as he is now being called. In this sudden and imperative fashion the historian of the United States has been brought to admit to the necessity of a historical sociology.

If the English or indeed any Western European historian is disposed to think that no such imperative demand yet exists for him, he might reflect on the implications of the thesis of the first chapter of this book. There a particular view is taken of the Western family throughout its history. It is hinted again and again that the unique pattern of post-poned marriage, predominance of the simple family household, and so on has had considerable effects on European economic, social, political, cultural and even industrial life. Since Western European industrial-ization has within the last two centuries transformed the life of the whole world, it could be said that these familial characteristics existing in the past of Britain, the Low Countries, and the European North west as a whole, may have had a global significance.

But who can tell, without a set of sociological principles, how the form of the family affects economic change and activity? How can we argue from one phenomenon to another, or from a particular set of variables to a particular set of outcomes, unless we acquaint ourselves with all that is relevant in all the social sciences we can master? It is difficult to see how anyone could proceed at all from the position laid down in that chapter without a historical sociology.

The particular theory there briefly and boldly set down may like-wise be shown to be wrong. But it might still be true that a theory of this kind relating family life to social change would be the most promis-ing point of departure for the attempt to find out why the world in our day should be divided so fatefully between industrial and non-industrial societies.

Sociology has been used in this introduction to cover all the discip-lines banded together in the social sciences. This rough and ready pro-cedure is forced upon the social scientist working in past time because of what is so often called his interdisciplinary position. He finds him-self, as should be evident from the argument so far, having to take up the contents and techniques of many well-established traditions of study, and to do with them what he is able. But though this may make him an indifferent anthropologist on one page, an indifferent economist or social psychologist on another, it should not make him an indifferent user of figures. For the use of figures began its career in the analysis of social facts very early indeed in scientific time. It was an invention by the English which took place before ever societies began to be distinguished between the industrial and the non-industrial.

This is one reading, anyway, of the pioneering sociology of men like William Petty, John Graunt or Gregory King during the Scientific

Revolution of the seventeenth century. All these men, it may be noted, are to be described in the first place as demographers, but also as economists and even as econometricians, especially Gregory King (see Laslett 1973). This is not the occasion to try to understand why it was that such an early initiative was lost sight of in England, and why social science, under the guise of *political arithmetic*, was so little heeded by writers of history until so very recently. Suffice it to say that it is simply untrue to suppose that overt numerical argument, rigorous demonstration in figures, an insistence on finding numerical indicators where that was feasible and on setting out arguments in the form of tables where that was necessary, can appropriately be called newcomers to English or American intellectual culture.

A historical sociology is neither a novelty nor an inhumanity. It should have infused historical scholarship for the last three hundred years, and it must do so from now onward. To such weighty and unexpected conclusions can we be brought when we reflect on the strong feelings which we all seem to have about the family, its present and its past.

1. Characteristics of the Western family considered over time

Institutions and cultural complexes have to possess some persistence over time, some perdurance, if they are to be significant for the historian of social structure. The Western family pattern, like the European marriage pattern so brilliantly described over a decade ago by John Hajnal,[1] must be shown to have been present over many generations in order to qualify as a characteristic trait of Westernness.

This family pattern no longer singles out Western European culture as once it did — or did according to the view which I shall propound here. Indeed certain important features of it have ceased to exist altogether in the contemporary West, notably the servants, whose numbers used to be considerable. This is to be expected now that cultural and institutional convergence has become so conspicuous in high industrial society. It is in this way that a socialist Russia, a transformed Japan, and a country like Denmark may all finally come to resemble each other as they now are more than they resemble themselves as they previously were. Nevertheless, the data now coming into view suggest

[1] 'European marriage patterns in perspective', published in D. V. Glass and D. E. C. Eversley (eds.), *Population in history* (1965). The present chapter was originally composed as an address to the 13th international seminar of the committee on family research of the International Sociological Association in 1973, the subject being the domestic group cycle: this address is in course of publication (in French, 'Le cycle familial et le processus de socialisation caracteristiques du schéma occidental considéré dans le temps', in the proceedings of that seminar). The piece has been considerably revised and expanded since that time after discussions with Professor Hajnal who was in Cambridge in the year 1974—5, but the concentration on the life cycle and socialization has been retained. I should also like to record my thanks to John Hajnal and to the many scholars now working in various countries on European family structure, East and West, who have directed their attention to some of the suggestions made in *Household and family in past time* (Laslett and Wall (eds.) 1972). They include Emmanuel Todd, now of Paris but late of Trinity College, Cambridge; J.-L. Flandrin, of Paris, from whose book *Familles, parenté, maison, sexualité dans la société ancienne* (Paris, 1976) I have borrowed unsparingly, including results cited by him from the work of others, published and in progress; Aldo Piazzini, of the University of Florence, whose dissertation of 1974/5 has been similarly treated; P. M. M. Klep, F. Daelemans and J. J. M. Berendsen of the Netherlands; Heldur Palli, of Tallinn in Estonia; Rudolf Andorka and Gyorgy Granazstoi of Budapest; Joel Halpern of the University of Massachusetts; Andrejs Plakans of Iowa State University; Peter Czap of Amherst College; and F. J. Carney of Trinity College, Dublin. Lutz Berkner's criticisms have been particularly illuminating.

that there may have been a particular set of characteristics present in the Western familial setting at all periods for which we have information up to the point of original industrialization (whatever that may mean, or whenever it may be taken to have occurred). Now that historical sociology is starting to make its presence felt, we have to consider cultures and institutions not simply as they now are, or appear to us to be, but as they would have been if overall transformation had not intervened.

This is particularly the case in issues of socialization, of personality and character formation. It is only in this way that Westernness or any other cultural attribute can have a historical presence at all, since this requires that it must be seen to reproduce itself over time, in each succeeding generation. From my point of view, therefore, the scene of primary socialization, which is the familial group surrounding the infant in its earliest years, is the focus of attention. The period in the life of the individual which interests us here is when parents and their entirely dependent children are perpetually in company, a condition in which interaction between human personalities is at its most intense, and the human grouping at its solidest.

The general thesis will be that the distinguishing feature of the family in the Western tradition, in so far as it is discernible to the sociological historian over the last two or three centuries at least, has been the simultaneous presence during the period of primary socialization of the four following separable but interdependent characteristics:

1. The shape and membership of the familial group. In the West this has been confined for the most part to the parents and children themselves, what is called the nuclear family form or simple family household.

2. The age of the mother during the time of child-bearing. In the West this was generally relatively rather late, both in the life experience of the mother and also in the period of fecundity.

3. The age gap between spouses. In the West the number of years separating husband and wife has always been relatively few, with a relatively high proportion of wives older than their husbands, and marriage tending towards the companionate.

4. The presence as fully recognized members in a significant proportion of households of persons not belonging to the immediate family or even to the kin. These were the servants, and their salience in the West marks a peculiarity in the individual life cycle of those who went out to service as well as a characteristic of the domestic group.

The possible importance for the formation of the personality of each of these features of the Western familial form will be discussed here, though necessarily in a preliminary way and with only a few pieces of supporting evidence. Before proceeding, however, it is important that three points be set out about the characteristics which have been named and about the relationships between them.

First, that it is the *pattern*, the *combination* itself, which is being suggested as defining Westernness in familial terms. No claim is being made that simple family households were to be found exclusively in Western Europe in pre-industrial times, or that no other cultural area has been marked historically by late marriage or by the presence of servants. It can certainly be claimed that the simple family household is to be found in very many parts of the world other than Europe or Western Europe, and that it has existed for very long periods of time. 'It is simply untrue as far as we can yet tell', the phrase in *Household and family in past time* runs, 'that there was ever a time or place when the complex family was the universal background to the ordinary lives of ordinary people.'[2] There have been communities in the West where marriage was late and yet servants were few, or where many households were complex in structure although the age gap between spouses was narrow. There are known instances in the history of Western-type societies of early marriage predominating for a number of years, if never marriage as early as in countries such as India or in parts of what used to be called the Balkans. It is certain that among Great Russian serfs marriage was very early for both sexes but that wives could sometimes be a year or two older than husbands. Our hypothesis, in fact, is inclusive and weak, rather than exclusive and strong, maintaining that the four features which together describe Westernness in the familial group during the stage of primary socialization were interdependent to some degree, but never entirely so.

This is a situation only too familiar to the social scientist, and it raises the second of the points about the pattern we are considering. To name these characteristics and to attach a description like 'Western' to them tends inevitably towards the proposition that a familial system

[2] Peter Laslett in Laslett and Wall (eds.) 1972: xi. Since this statement was published, several areas of Europe have been investigated where complex family living was evidently much more widespread than in any area examined by the contributors to that volume, and the statement quoted has been questioned. Only one region of Europe as usually defined has, however, so far yielded a proportion of extended and multiple households which indubitably attains the required 'universal background', and that has been a number of serf settlements in Great Russia in the late eighteenth and early nineteenth centuries being examined by Peter Czap, though several regions have been shown to approach this situation, the Baltic states particularly. It was anticipated in 1972 that Russia might provide examples of a family pattern diametrically opposed to the European (ibid.: xi), but Professor Czap tells me that interspersed amongst these communities of serfs were occasional communities of craftsmen where the simple family form predominated even here. Great Russia is the area of which Moscow is the centre, stretching from Leningrad in the west to the river Volga in the east.

possessing each of them to the highest degree is to be thought of as quintessentially Western.

The disadvantages of such a habit of mind are well known, and this is not the place to enter into a discussion of Weberian ideal types and of their role in social theory. Immediately such a polarity is proposed, the question arises as to whether there is an antithetical ideal type, an 'Eastern' familial category, where all mothers were young when their children were born, and much younger than their husbands, with whom they frequently lived in multiple family households having no servants. The possible existence of extremes of such a kind in its turn suggests a continuum between them, even a gradation; thus some communities could be judged more 'Western' than others, on some criterion into which all four of our characteristics would enter.

The name itself might even bring to the minds of some people a division drawn out on a map, running perhaps along a line down the Baltic and passing through the Central European countries, where all to the left of the familial frontier was Western in type and all to the right was something else, perhaps Eastern. There are discouraging echoes here of religious and linguistic hatreds and rivalries.

It is surely scarcely necessary to insist that a literal division of areas of the world or of historic Europe itself is not here in question. The geographical implications of the typology look like being complex and puzzling, related to ethnic distribution and historical development in ways which will take a great deal of unravelling. What happened in fact was that when we began to examine familial composition in the past and to reflect on the family and the life cycle as it had been within the area of our own country, we discovered that the family group during the quarter of a millennium open to observation did tend to exhibit this set of related characteristics. This appears to have been consistently the case in England, certainly in respect of three of the four elements making up the pattern, with little variation over time and region up the point of industrialization and even up to the early twentieth century.

When we went on to look at northern France and other North-western European countries the same pattern appeared, though with significantly less homogeneity and much greater variance. Elsewhere, however, in the Baltic countries for example, or in parts of Hungary, even to some extent in southern France and central Italy, particularly in Serbia and above all in Great Russia, this pattern could scarcely be detected at all. There were indeed signs of other familial systems altogether.

Here it would be wise to confess how little is yet known of these matters over most of the area of our continent. Unfortunately what has been recovered so far can scarcely be called historical in the sense that we have adopted here, that is to say to provide a continuous overview of the situation for any country, other than for England over a century or two. Whereas a little is beginning to be discovered at isolated points in time about Scotland and Ireland, about Iceland, the Low Countries, Scandinavia, Germany, Switzerland, Austria and Italy, we know nothing whatever yet about Spain or Portugal. The position as to evidence is relatively good, at these low standards, for the United States and for Japan, even for Hungary, Russia and Serbia.

In principle there is little doubt that the knowledge we have for England could be replicated, indeed in most cases vastly extended, for any other European area. But it has to be recognized that it is a piece of hypothetical inference which is at issue in this essay, intuitive guesswork suggested by a striking contrast between a small body of evidence for one country showing pronounced homogeneity, and a number of scattered pieces of information from outside that country which point in a very different direction. One of the objects of publishing this hypothesis at all is to elicit the historical information which would show it to be wrong, partially or entirely. There seems no better way to proceed as these studies now stand.

The position, therefore, in respect of the second of our points, as to ideal types, is as follows. The typology is intended primarily as an aid to classification and only by implication as a guide to what may be expected to be true of a particular European community when all that is known is geographical location. It may make it possible to decide whether one society is more 'Western' in character than another, on the criterion suggested. But it emphatically does not follow that every community outside Western or North-western Europe and its daughter societies will show 'non-Western' characteristics, or that there will turn out to be a distinct familial frontier between the two tendencies.

It is more likely to appear that in historic times, beyond the borders of the Anglo-Saxon, Nordic region, which for these purposes may include northern France and parts of Germany as well as the Low Countries,[3] there was a considerable area of intermingled communities. In some, entirely 'Western' familial patterns seem to have existed in villages next door to others where the pattern was less pronounced, and where elements of other systems obtruded. Indeed, at this very time interesting evidence is beginning to come in from what may turn out to be a large intermediary area, stretching from Latvia and Estonia in the North, including Poland, the Czech lands, north-eastern Austria and

---

[3] It is significant that Hajnal, in his article of 1965, is disposed to think of the 'Europe' in his phrase 'European marriage patterns' as excluding Southern as well as Eastern Europe, and to this Southern area Languedoc may have to be added.

transdanubian Hungary, south as far at least as Florence, though not including the island of Corsica, for example, or even the Po valley.

In individual places in this large and ragged region simple family households predominated, accompanied by others of the characteristics we have listed. They can be found as early as the sixteenth century. But in others as late as the eighteenth and early nineteenth centuries, 'non-Western' familial characteristics (as here defined) were even more pronounced than those which have been found in the small group of Serbian and Japanese communities known to us at the same time, though never as extreme as in Great Russia. This seems to have been true for southern France in the Languedoc (as opposed to the area of the *langue d'oil*).

In villages of transdanubian Hungary given over not to the traditional Catholic faith nor to that of the Orthodox Eastern Church, but to Calvinism, non-Western characteristics were particularly prominent in the early nineteenth century. It is possible that, in parts of this region at least, one familial model predominated at one time but a different model at another time, and that the 'Western' was not always the later. Something like this is being hinted at by Hungarian scholars for their own country (see Andorka 1975). It may be true for Tuscany between the fourteenth and eighteenth centuries also.

Since Calvinism has been often thought of as the harbinger of rationalism, modernism, the capitalist way of life, the facts from the Danube lands serve to show how complicated yet fascinating the familial historical geography of Europe turns out to be. They may also confirm another claim made in 1972, that the very 'extremes of familial organization, from the simplest to the most complex, may once have existed within the confines of the European Continent itself' (Laslett and Wall (eds.) 1972: xi). But Calvinism is a belief, not an arrangement of individuals within the domestic group, and this brings us to our third point about the Western socialization pattern.

The disposition of the knot of persons co-residing with a child under five years old can always be recovered from a good listing of inhabitants surviving from the past, one which specifies ages and divides one familial group from another. But persons present within the household make up only a proportion of the influences from kin and from others close to the child. There is the affective quality of family life to be taken into account, as well as the impact of beliefs, customs, norms about child rearing and desirable behaviour for the young. Neither these, nor the geographical propinquity of kin folk other than the immediate family, nor the extent to which they would visit the household in question can be inferred from our evidence; we are only just beginning to develop measures of what we call kinship density for past communities.[4] Nor can we yet make confident judgements as to the relative importance of neighbourliness and kin connection in the traditional Western village, where so large a part of the population lived during the era before industrialization.

As for the effect of ideology on the developing child, we are in a quandary familiar to everyone who has become interested in the history of personality and of the subjectivity, or psycho-history, as it is now being called. There is certainly no lack of materials of the kind, although the child appears in the written remains of the past far, far less frequently than would be expected when it is remembered how youthful all societies were before our own day.[5]

Books were written in Europe about childhood from late medieval times, a few books that is to say, which tend to repeat scriptural and classical authority and to repeat each other. References to childhood occur in other books, too, and the investigation of these writings presents no problem of understanding to the investigator provided he is enough of a scholar to master the originals in their original language, and enough of a historian to recognize the meanings in their contexts of the statements which he reads. To these treatises written by certain members of the literate minority for the literate minority can be added the letters, diaries and other private documents of this same elite, which expands the store of information quite considerably. There are also verbal statements made on all occasions when official recording by others than the speakers was a necessity, statements made for all legal purposes and for some political ones. Here we meet for the first time the entirely un-educated mass of the societies of the past, for ordinary unlettered persons appeared in court, too, especially if they had any property. They were sometimes caught up in political occasions which gave rise to records, and they often, even the propertyless, had to explain themselves when they were being tried for crimes.

But it is well known how intractable the analysis of any body of docu-ments of this kind can be, so untidy is it, so variable and contradictory in its dogmas and doctrines, so capricious in what it preserves and what it must leave out. Most deceptive of all is the tendency of literary com-mentators and disputants to make confident assertions on subjects which they know little about, or which they could not in fact have known any-thing about, since the requisite information did not exist.

[4] Emmanuel Todd has worked on this set of problems at the Cambridge Group for the History of Population and Social Structure, and some measures of what he calls 'primary kinship density' are becoming available (see n. 46 to chapter 2 below). But we are some way from answering the important questions.

[5] See Laslett, *The world we have lost*, 2nd ed. (1971): 108–12 and references.

To infer from such evidence what the whole content of the attitude to children was amongst the elite minority would itself be an uncertain task, still more so to make a reliable decision on how far this attitude represented what all, or nearly all, persons experienced as children or acted upon as parents. And to attempt to go further and reconstruct on this basis the childhood experience and the child-rearing practice of a whole society, from the kings and the queens and the nobles with their great bodies of advisors and servants, down to the farmers, craftsmen, peasants and labourers in their little houses, cottages and shacks, would be formidable indeed.

Proverbial sayings, folk law, folk literature in general and the pictorial representations which have come down to us do portray children, poor children as well as rich ones, but these are often vague as to dating and not always intended as realistic. Pictures, like stories, are usually uncertain as to the area to which they may be taken to apply, and all the materials which we have to use share a common disability. They lack any indication as to whether they were likely to reflect the usual or the unusual, what was ordinarily done or what should have been done but ordinarily was not.[6]

We can therefore be more confident of finding out about the numerical structure of the households of French peasants, shall we say, as they were in the year 1700 or thereabouts and as they would have differed from area to area of that country, than we can be of determining the attitudes of French peasants to French children at any time or in any place so far back in the past as the eighteenth century. And this underlines our dilemma still more heavily.

[6] The historical pursuit known as *histoire des mentalités* has recently come into prominence for the purposes of recovering and interpreting such material. It has arisen largely under the influence of the French scholar Philippe Ariés, whose original work of 1960 (translated into English as *Centuries of childhood*) was dedicated to this particular subject, but has spread to include very much wider areas of social life. More recently Lloyd deMause has established a periodical for Ariés' original purpose, and a collective work, *The history of childhood* edited by him (New York, 1975; London, 1976), has been issued which incorporates the early results of this sustained activity. Valuable as these budgets of scattered information may be, when so little else is available, they are being put together, it would seem, with very little awareness of the difficulties which have had to be recorded above, and suffer from an evident anxiety to derive from the recalcitrant and miscellaneous mass of facts, half-facts and non-facts (misreports, misrepresentations) a connected and dramatic historical story about childhood and the ways in which it has changed over time. This is done with little or no discussion on the part of the editor of the fact that literature itself is subject to fashion and change.

An excellent example of the realistic, yet imaginative, use of such documents as wills, property settlements and so on, which illustrates what can be done, is Diane Hughes, 'Domestic ideals and social behaviour: evidence from medieval Genoa', in Charles E. Rosenberg (ed.), *The family in history* (Philadelphia, 1975): 115–43.

TABLE 1.1. *Proportions of extended and multiple family households and mean household size*

Country	Community	County/region	Date	No. of house-holds	Mean household size	Extended (%)	Multiple (%)	Total (%)
International sample:								
Colonial America	Bristol	Rhode Island	1689	72	5.85	3	0	3
England	Ealing	Middlesex	1599	85	4.75	6	2	8
France	Longuenesse	Pas-de-Calais	1778	66	5.05	14	3	17
Germany	Löffingen[a]	Württemberg	1687	121	5.77	[5]	[5]	[10]
Ireland	Household sample: Cavan, Meath, King's, Fermanagh, Galway counties		1821 (census)	2,810	5.29	17	5	22
Italy	Rome (parish of 12 Apostles)		1621	521	3.60	8	3	11
	Toffiel		1629	132	4.50	17	9	26
	Colomo	Parma	1782	66	4.16	9	11	20
Japan	Nishinomiya[b]		1713	132	4.95	27	21	48
				(87)		(25)	(14)	(39)
Japan	Yokouchi	Suwa County	1676	27	7.0	0	52	52
Japan	Yokouchi	Suwa County	1746	76	5.5	21	28	49
Japan	Yokouchi	Suwa County	1823	98	5.1	28	28	56
Japan	Yokouchi	Suwa County	1846	107	4.4	14	24	39
Poland	Lesnica	Silesia	1720	311	5.4	5	0	5
Scotland	Aross-in-Mull	Western Isles	1779	211	5.25	11	3	14
Serbia	Belgrade		1733–4	273	4.95	15	14	29

English sample:

Ardleigh	Essex	1796	210	5.48	10	2	12
Ardleigh	Essex	1851	366	4.48	14	0	14
Bilston	Staffordshire	1695	192	5.19	11	1	12
Bilston	Staffordshire	1851	329	5.14	15	5	20
Bilston	Staffordshire	1861	264	4.30	12	1	13
Chilvers Coton	Warwickshire	1686	177	4.41	8	1	9
Chilvers Coton	Warwickshire	1851	570	4.95	13	3	16
Clayworth	Notts.	1676	98	4.09	8	0	9
Clayworth	Notts.	1688	91	4.43	7	1	8
Clayworth	Notts.	1851	128	4.21	17	4	21
Colyton	Devon	1851	342	4.94	16	2	18
Colyton	Devon	1861	449	4.48	14	3	17
Corfe Castle	Dorset	1790	272	4.84	8	1	9
Corfe Castle	Dorset	1851	513	4.72	14	1	15
Corfe Castle	Dorset	1861	297	4.31	14	1	15
Ealing	Middlesex	1599	85	4.75	6	2	8
Ealing	Middlesex	1851	248	4.86	12	1	13
Ealing	Middlesex	1861	209	4.50	19	2	21
Puddletown^c	Dorset	1724–5	154	3.97	8	1	9
Puddletown	Dorset	1851	264	4.91	11	1	12
Puddletown	Dorset	1861	257	4.77	14	1	15
Puddletown	Dorset	1871	271	4.89	18	2	20
Puddletown	Dorset	1881	248	4.46	16	1	17

^a Figures approximate.
^b Alternative figures, leaving out adoptions.
^c Not quite complete.
Figures in italics are taken from samples.

21

Family life and illicit love in earlier generations

For it is undoubtedly quite possible that elements in the attitudes and beliefs of parents, siblings, relatives, clerics, influential personalities were more important in the formation of the personality of the child than the presence, or absence, of grandfathers, or aunts, or servants. Perhaps the impact of such a circumstance as the father's being 10 or 15 years older than the mother was trivial in comparison. In discussing the familial characteristics which have been laid down above with experts in child rearing and socialization in our own time, I have been struck by the comment that not all of these things are usually enquired into when a child is visited in the parental home, because other circum-

TABLE 1.2. *England and continental Europe: household composition and generational depth*

			Household composition (%)		
			Solitary householders	No family households	Simple family households
England					
Sample 1,[a] 30 reliably recorded communities: 1622–1821			8.5 (±1.6)	3.6 (±1.2)	72.1 (±2.7)
Sample 2,[a] 35 less reliably recorded communities: 1599–1854			8.7 (±1.7)	3.2 (±1.1)	71.9 (±2.3)
Master sample, 61 communities: 1599–1821					
Continent of Europe					
Belgium, Lisswege	pop. 796	in 1739	1.9	1.3	85.3
France, Longuenesse	333	1778	10	6	76
Hallines	241	1773	6	4	81
Montplaisant	388	1644	11	2	44
Trebozen	351	1773	5	2	55
Rognonas	117	1697	8	4	50
Germany, Löffingen	697	1687	0.8	0.8	82.4
Grossenmeer	882	1795	3.6	2.4	72.4
Vehrenbach	177	1705	5	5	80
Italy (Parma), Colorno	308	1782	8	0	73
(Tuscany), Pratolino[b]	346	1721	1	3	34
Chianti		1790	7	4	31
Fiesole	305	1790	6	1	40
Poland, Lesnica	1037	1720	1.0	1.0	92.3
Hungary, Kassa	304[c]	1549	8	3	78
Sziget	1163	1551	11.0	2.3	80.7
Alsónyék	685	1792	28	0	43
Kölked	643	1816	0	0	47
Serbia, Belgrade	1350	1733	304	2.8	54.5
Estonia, Vändra[d]	976	1683	2	1	45
Latvia, Daudzewas[e]	924	1797	0	0	24.5
Russia (Great Russia), Mishino[f]	1173	1814	0.8	0	7.0

[a] The two English samples, worked out by R. A. Laslett, are in course of publication. Interval estimates at 0.05.

[b] Workings of Emmanuel Todd.

[c] One quarter of the town now called Kosice, in Czechoslovakia. These figures, and those for Sziget (where recordings are regarded as a little suspect) are workings of Gyorgy Granazstoi.

stances have been judged to be more influential in the development of the child.

There is, however, a particular reason why the characteristics we are discussing must be given weight when the formation of personality is in question in the pre-industrial era. At that time societies, all societies, were arranged in families and households for almost all social and economic purposes, and the shape of the co-resident domestic group was accordingly of far greater consequence than it has been since. This third set of considerations does, however, make it advisable to qualify our original statements about the uniqueness of the Western pattern of socialization in the following way. Of these circumstances which are open to examination in past societies, at least at present, a particular

Extended family households	Multiple family households	Inde-terminate	Generational depth (%)		
			One generation	Two generations	Three generations or more
10.9	4.1	0.9			
11.9	4.1	0.3			
			25.1 (±1.83)	69.2 (±1.66)	5.7 (±1.43)
10.3	1.3	0	13.9	83.3	2.9
14	3	0	17	76	8
8	2	0	13	77	9
24	21	0	26	55	19
29	9	0	—	—	—
12	18	4	—	—	—
4.8	4.8	6.4	—	—	—
15.8	6.0	0	12.6	70.1	17.3
6	0	5	—	—	—
9	11	0	—	—	—
14	44	0	—	—	—
18	39	1	—	—	—
6	45	2	—	—	—
5.5	0.3	0	—	—	—
10	1	0	11	86	3
44	1.6	0	13.4	84.3	2.3
15	39	0	7	62	31
18	36	0	5	63	32
14.1	17.6	7.4	23	66	9
11	41	0	5	69	26
11.3	64.1	0	1.8	54.7	43.3
11.7	72.6	7.8	2.3	32.8	64.9

[d] Analysed by *houseful* (see Laslett and Wall (eds.) 1972: 36–9) and based on Palli 1974.
[e] 'Wirth' groups only; workings of Andrejs Plakans.
[f] Serf community on the Mishino estate, Riazan province; workings of Peter Czap.

combination seems to characterize the West. Once this is said, we are at least free of the error of mistaking the part for the whole.

Let us turn from the exposition and qualification of our general hypothesis and begin to provide something in the way of evidential substance to the contrast we have suggested as distinguishing the Western from other patterns of socialization. The tables published in 1972 in *Household and family in past time* contain in themselves a fair proportion of what is so far known in this still very immature field. In table 1.1, for example, will be found a conspectus of the evidence gathered by the year 1972 as to complication of households in the past, mainly from the five areas with which the original work was concerned, but including some from other countries (two items from Italy and one from Ireland have been added). The nation best represented in the table is that of the English, and it will be seen that these figures in themselves make out a preliminary case for the proposition that households in that country became more complex rather than less so in the course of the change between the sixteenth to the eighteenth century on the one hand and the nineteenth on the other, the era usually known as that of the Great Industrial Revolution.

We can now, in 1976, add the figures of tables 1.2 and 1.3 to this collection of evidence. The English material has been extended to cover over 60 settlements, and we can compare it in somewhat more revealing ways with 20 or more settlements elsewhere in Europe. This gives us the opportunity to observe a continental contrast, if not on a very convincing scale.

No detailed explanation of any of these sets of data is in order at the present time. The recovery and investigation of materials adequate for judgement on the cartography of European family composition would demand a great deal of collaborative work by many scholars in many countries, and considerable development in the techniques of analysis now in use would be necessary for appropriate handling of the evidence.

All we can do with the preliminary figures is to stress the following features: the extent to which the simple family household prevails in England, the Low Countries and northern France; the pronounced uniformity of English materials relative to Continental; the very remarkable contrast between northern France, where the simple family household seems to predominate as conspicuously as in England, and southern France, where complex households are almost as common as nuclear households; the rather confused and irregular situation which is revealed in other areas, in Italy for example. Germany and German-speaking lands may turn out to be variegated in respect of household composition in all sorts of ways; as has already been pointed out, this situation seems to have been present at very early dates. The fact that Kassa and Sziget

TABLE 1.3. *Northern France and southern France contrasted in household composition*

	Total households	Solitary householders (%)	No family households (%)	Simple family households (%)	Extended family households (%)	Multiple family households (%)	Indeterminate (%)
North							
Pas-de-Calais, Longuenesse	75 in 1778	1	6	76	14	3	0
Hallines	54 1773	1	6	81	8	2	0
Nord, villages autour de Valenciennes	333 1693	1.5	1.8	85.8	10.6	0.3	—
Valenciennes ville	2129 1693	12.9	3.1	75.7	8.1	0.2	—
Normandie, Rouen (1 parish)	1201 1793	39.0	3.8	54.9	2.4	0	—
Vexin, Brueil-en-Vexin	68 1625	7.3	1.5	83.8	7.3	0	—
Yvelines, Treil/Seine	541 1817	17.9	1.1	76.9	4.1	0	—
Median	—	7	4	77	{— 8 —}		—
South							
Dordogne, Montplaisant	63 1644	11	2	51	16	21	—
Aveyron, Mostuejouls	94 1690	3	2	51	{— 43 —}		—
Laguiole	214 1691	7	3	56	{— 32 —}		—
Provence, Rognonas	22 1697	8	4	50	12	18	4
Mirabeau	120 1745	6.7	0.8	50.8	19.2	22.5	—
Hautes-Pyrénées, Bulan	53 1793	4	0.8	55	32	9	—
Median	—	[7]	[2]	51	{— 41 —}		—

Note: Apart from those for places appearing in table 1.2, workings are those on which the results printed by Flandrin (1976: 241–2) are based. I should myself like to acknowledge the work of MM. Bardet, Lions, Lachiver and Flandrin and of Antoinette Chamoux.

TABLE 1.4. *Marital status by age and sex*

	Marital status	15-19	20-24	25-29	30-34	35-39	40-44	45-49	50-59	60-69	70+
						Male					
English standard	Single	100	82.8	54.5	23.7	13.4	8.8	8.4	6.9	9.4	5.3
(Ealing, 1599;	Married	0	16.3	44.6	73.5	81.8	88.0	89.3	82.0	70.2	60.5
Chilvers Coton, 1684;	Widowed	0	0.8	0.9	2.9	4.7	3.2	2.3	11.0	20.4	34.2
Lichfield, 1696;	Total	100	99.9	100	100.1	99.9	100	100	99.9	100	100
Stoke-on-Trent, 1706;											
Corfe Castle, 1790;											
Ardleigh, 1796)											
Pop. 7837											
English	Single	100	100	77	38	62	29	50	12	20	0
Ealing, 1599	Married	0	0	23	62	37	71	50	80	66	0
Pop. 427	Widowed	0	0	0	0	0	0	0	8	14	100
	Total	100	100	100	100	99	100	100	100	100	100
French	Single	100	100	90	89	31	25	26	22	0	33
Longuenesse, 1778	Married	0	0	10	11	69	75	73	56	75	33
Pop. 333	Widowed	0	0	0	0	0	0	0	22	25	33
	Total	100	100	100	100	100	100	99	100	100	99
Serbian	Single	100	67	32	15	17	3	7	7	5	10
Belgrade, 1733−4	Married	0	33	68	85	83	93	93	90	83	70
Pop. 1357	Widowed	0	0	0	0	0	3	0	3	11	20
	Total	100	100	100	100	100	99	100	100	99	100
Japanese	Single	100	100	86	71	21	0	0	0	0	0
Nishinomiya, 1713	Married	0	0	14	18	74	95	91	97	85	46
Pop. 653	Widowed	0	0	0	12	5	5	9	3	15	54
	Total	100	100	100	101	100	100	100	100	100	100

Sources as in previous tables, but see note 8.

show forth the nuclear arrangement in so pronounced a way in the middle of the sixteenth century, whereas Alsónyék and Kölked in the same region in the late eighteenth and early nineteenth centuries were marked by high levels of complication in their household arrangements, may be regarded as the most surprising feature of the evidence.

The considerable demographic differences which must have existed between dates and between places represented in the two tables will have to be allowed for when a systematic analysis of these issues is undertaken. But the columns recording multigenerationality in table 1.2 are an indication that fertility, mortality, nuptiality and expectation of life cannot have been the only determinants. It was clearly not these things by themselves which prevented the people of Lisswege or of Hallines, of the English places, or even of Belgrade from having those elder people in the household which would have given rise to greater generational depth. It must also have been a choice against such arrangements, a choice which had important consequences on the situation of the aged to which we shall have to return. The truly extraordinary figure

	Female									Age gap between spouses
15-19	20-24	25-29	30-34	35-39	40-44	45-49	50-59	60-69	70+	
98.5	81.0	48.1	26.6	16.6	7.1	8.6	4.9	6.2	5.3	
1.5	17.9	49.8	70.9	75.7	72.0	76.2	67.4	48.2	60.5	
0	1.0	2.1	2.4	7.7	20.9	15.2	27.7	45.5	34.1	
100	99.9	100	99.9	100	100	100	100	99.9	99.9	
100	84	57	36	14	0	12	0	12	0	Mean — 3.50
0	15	43	64	64	62	38	86	75	50	Median — 3.25
0	0	0	0	21	38	50	14	13	50	Proportion of wives — 21%
100	99	100	100	99	100	100	100	100	100	older than husbands — $n = 62$
100	100	73	64	36	10	0	20	0	0	Mean — 2.35
0	0	18	29	64	85	100	60	75	12	Median — 1.50
0	0	9	7	0	5	0	20	25	88	Proportion of wives — 27%
100	100	100	100	100	100	100	100	100	100	older than husbands — $n = 48$
23	3	2	4	0	5	0	0	0	14	Mean — 10.82
77	92	95	87	73	81	60	25	8	14	Median — 10.18
0	5	3	9	27	14	40	75	92	72	Proportion of wives — 0.5%
100	100	100	100	100	100	100	100	100	99	older than husbands — $n = 192$
100	72	17	13	0	0	0	0	0	0	Mean — 10.36
0	28	83	87	92	76	83	50	31	0	Median — 9.10
0	0	0	0	8	24	17	50	69	100	Proportion of wives — 1.9%
100	100	100	100	100	100	100	100	100	100	older than husbands — $n = 105$

from the Russian serf settlements makes this plain and demonstrates the astonishing range of generational depth in pre-industrial Europe as measured in proportions of households with three or more generations, from a level at 5% or less in the European West or Far West in England and the Low Countries, to a level at 60% or more in the European Far East in Great Russia.[7]

Table 1.4 (see table 1.5 of Laslett and Wall (eds.) 1972) contains figures for proportions married in various age groups, age gaps between spouses, and numbers of wives older than their husbands. They are based on an

---

[7] The figures for Mishino show no less than 7% of four generational households. Microsimulation studies now in course of composition and publication on the relation of demography to family arrangements indicate convincingly that household structure was in general fairly robust to demographic variation. The overriding issue as to how far the form of the household was an independent, 'causal', variable, being part of the cultural complex of the settlement or area concerned, and how far the shape of households was in turn determined by such things as conventions of inheritance or land-holding, will also be considered there.

English standard sample (summarizing the results from six places before 1800),[8] an individual English settlement (Ealing), a northern French community (Longuenesse) and two 'non-Western' communities.

The differences we have discussed are clearly apparent. Less than a fifth of the women in the English sample were married in the age group 20—24, and none of the French women at Longuenesse, but in Belgrade over three-quarters were married between 15 and 19 and virtually all between 20 and 24. The sharpest contrast comes at ages between 25 and 29, where under a fifth of the French women and under a half of the English had husbands, or had had them, but four-fifths of the Japanese and all of the Serbs. It will be seen that proportions married amongst males differed accordingly, taking into account the varying age differences between spouses.

Gaps in age between husbands and wives have not been calculated for the English sample, but it is obvious from the figures for individual communities that the Western places were quite dissimilar from the others in this respect. We can supplement the table with similar evidence from elsewhere in the Western area. In three of the counties of Iceland in the year 1729, for example, 13.7% of women aged 20—24 were married and 45.8% of those aged 25—29; in twelve deaneries of Norway in 1769 10.6% of women aged 20—24 were ever married, and 66.6% of those aged 24—32.

These details are close to those for England, and the other statistics are similar, too. In the 5,800 marriages extant in Iceland as a whole in 1703, husbands were on average 2.9 years older than wives, but in 1,914 of those marriages, almost exactly a third, wives were older than husbands; in Norway in 1769, 35% of 7,000 wives were in this position.[9] The figures of table 1.4, therefore, are not unrepresentative of the Western familial pattern we are trying to distinguish, though we shall see

---

[8] This sample is highly unsatisfactory, not only because the number of places is so small, but because the largest of them, Lichfield, has peculiarities in its age composition which may distort the proportions. Age listings are extremely rare in English archives, and this fact makes it out of the question to consider whether failure to marry was a feature of English and 'Western' populations in the past. Hajnal (1965) suggests that this was a part of the pattern we are considering, and our documentary disadvantages are therefore a serious matter.

[9] In all the statistics on age differences between spouses, all marriages, not simply first marriages, are included. The Icelandic figures for 1703 are from *Manntali þ 1703* (Reykjavík, Statistical Bureau of Iceland, 1960), and for 1729 from Hans Oluf Hansen, *Manntal 1729: population census 1729 in three counties* (Reykjavík, Statistical Bureau of Iceland, 1975; figures quoted here from a preliminary mimeograph version of 1971). The Norwegian figures are based on table 8 and other tables in Michael Drake, *Population and society in Norway, 1735—1865* (1969), which discusses age relations between spouses at varying social levels in some detail.

in chapter 6 that in certain places at certain times the commonest age at marriage could occasionally fall below 20 as it happens to have done in Stratford-upon-Avon during Shakespeare's youth. The two sets of statistics from 'non-Western' communities cannot be said to represent any region effectively, but they make a vivid contrast with those we have quoted from England, northern France and Scandinavia.

Table 1.5 sets out resident relatives so as to make possible the same blank contrast between the 'West' and other areas. The differences here reciprocate those in household composition brought out in tables 1.1 and 1.2, and there is an impressive range of percentages — 3% to 58% — of households with relatives. It is also notable that the highest figure does not belong to an area outside what is traditionally thought of as Europe, but to the well-known settlement at Chianti in Tuscany near to Florence in the year 1790, an area of particularly high and specifically European cultural achievement. This displays once again the irregular character of these statistics outside the North-west region.

A clear division can be seen in the figures, however, between the English collection of statistics, those from the Low Countries and northern France on the one hand, and the rest of the recovered evidence on the other hand, with Grossenmeer in Germany in something of an intermediate position. There has as yet been little analysis of numbers and types of kin in Scandinavia, but we know that in the countryside around the Dutch cities of Leyden and Gouda in 1622 they made up less than 6% of the population, and they never reached the English level in West Brabant or in northern Holland in the seventeenth and eighteenth centuries. In the university city of Leyden itself in 1581 resident relatives made up 4.5% of the population and were present in 13.3% of the households.[10]

In table 1.6 will be found a selection of statistics on servants, proportions in the population and proportions of households which contained them. The distinction between our chosen area and the rest of Europe and elsewhere is not as clear with respect to this characteristic, and the available facts make up rather a complex picture which cannot be analysed in detail here, any more than can comparative household composition. Changeability from place to place is greater in both servant variables in the English 'master sample' than it is in household com-

[10] For the Dutch figures see P. M. M. Klep, 'Het huishouden in Westelijk Noord-Brabant: struktuur en ontwikkeling 1750—1849', *A.A.G. Bijdragen* 18 (1973), tables 21, 38; F. Daelemans, 'Leiden 1581: een socio-demografisch onderzock, ibid. 19 (1975), table 9; and J. J. M. Berendsen, 'De omvang en samenstelling van de huishoudingen op het platteland rond Leiden in 1622 en het platteland rond Gouda in 1622 en 1680', mimeograph (1971).

TABLE 1.5. *Resident relatives other than spouses and children: numbers, types and proportions*

Type of kin; head's (and/ or wife's)	English standard, 44 communities, 1574—1821	English Ealing, Middlesex, 1599 Pop. 427	Dutch West Brabant, 1800 Pop. 7688	French Longuenesse, Pas-de-Calais, 1778 Pop. 333	German Grossenmeer, Oldenburg, 1795 Pop. 892
Father	—	1	$2(22)^b$	0	4
Mother	—	1	$4(8)^b$	3	25
Sister	—	4	$(35)^c$	6	8
Brother	—	0	$(40)^c$	3	9
Nephew	—	3	—	1	0
Niece	—	1	—	0	0
Son-in-law	—	0	—	2	3
Daughter-in-law	—	1	—	2	1
Grandchild	—	0	15	2	17
Other kin	—	0	62^d	3	3
Total	—	11	188	22	70
% in population	$3.4\% \pm 0.3\%$	2.6%	2.4%	6.6%	7.9%
% households with relatives	$11.7\% \pm 0.8\%$	13.0%	[*c.* 10%]	19.7%	28.4%

[a] Analysed in housefuls (see table 1.2, note *d*).
[b] Fathers/mothers-in-law.
[c] Brothers/sisters-in-law.
[d] Includes nephews, nieces, sons/daughters-in-law.

position.[11] The resemblance between England, northern France, the Low Countries and Scandinavia is less apparent, and there is more overlap with some of the 'non-Western' settlements, even with Belgrade. Nevertheless, John Hajnal's suggestion (made verbally in 1975) that

[11] This is illustrated by the following figures:

	% of servants in the population ($n = 63$)	% of households with servants ($n = 63$)	% of simple family households ($n = 30$)
Coefficient of variation $\left(\dfrac{\text{standard deviation}}{\text{mean}}\right)$	58%	54%	11%
Range	1.3% — 34.8%	3.7% — 88.4%	55.0% — 82.1%

There are differences in servants between urban and rural areas (differences in numbers, sex ratios etc.) which cannot be discussed here. In England anyway such differences are on the whole rather slight, and the contrast between individual villages is more marked than between country places and urban places.

Serbian Belgrade,[a] 1733–4 Pop. 1357	Estonian Vändra,[a] 1683 Pop. 976	Hungarian Alsónyék, 1792 Pop. 685	Japanese Nishinomiya, 1713 Pop. 653	Italian Chianti, Tuscany, 1790 Pop. 491	American Colonial Bristol, Rhode Island, 1689 Pop. 421
2	3	9	5	0	0
35	11	13	31	4	0
21	7	7	18	4	0
34	18	5	24	20	0
13	12	7	5	21	0
12	14	9	6	23	0
7	9	8	5	1	0
9	21	31	4	23	0
5	45	60	36	56	4
28	13	16	19	29	0
166	153	165	153	181	4
12.3%	15.7%	24.1%	23.4%	36.8%	1.0%
27.0%	51.7%	52.5%	53.0%	58.0%	3.0%

Notes and references to original figures will be found in Laslett and Wall (eds.) 1972, p. 81; for West Brabant, in Klep, 1973; for Vändra, in Palli, 1974; for Chianti, in Piazzini, 1974/5.

most Western communities can be expected to have 10% or more of servants in the population seems to hold in general, and although places elsewhere sometimes have as high a proportion – or even higher in the case of Estonia – there are a number of considerations which make the contrast rather more convincing than might appear from table 1.6. Two of these will have to be discussed in a preliminary way.

The first is the fact that it is very rare indeed to find a Western population, either in the country or in the town, with no servants at all, even though at particular places and at particular times the proportion could be very low. In other areas, however, servantless communities were commonplace, as for example in Japan at all times, or at Orasac in Serbia in 1863, and apparently also at Laguiole in southern France in 1691. Servants were virtually an unknown class of person in Russian serf villages.

The second and much more important consideration is to do with the nature of service, the age of the servants, and the part which going into service played in the careers of those who did it. The difference between service in the West and service elsewhere is seen in the indications in table 1.6 that marriage was exceedingly rare, though not in fact entirely unknown, among English, French, Scandinavian and Dutch servants,

TABLE 1.6. *Servants: numbers and proportions*

	Number of servants	Sex ratio of servants	Proportion of servants in population (%)	Proportion of households with servants (%)	Presence of currently married servants
England					
Standard sample (63 places, 1574–1821)	4,600	107	13.4 ± 1.9	28.5 ± 4.4	
Ealing, 1599 (pop. 427)	109	166	25.5	34	
Goodnestone, 1676 (pop. 280)	51	—	18.2	31	
Crosby Ravensworth, 1787 (pop. 276)	25	150	9.1	30	
France					
North, Longuenesse, 1778 (pop. 333)	66	145	12.6	19.7	
Rouen, 1770s (pop. 60,000)	—	[105]	8.2	—	
Tours, 1770s	—	[100]	11.6	—	
South, Montplaisant, 1644 (pop. 363)	21	133	5.8	19.3	
Rognonas, 1697 (pop. 117)	8	All male	7	31	
Provence, 1770s (pop. 702,000)	—	[137]	5.7	—	
Lyon, 1770s (pop. 19,500)	—	[80]	9.7	—	
Riom, 1770s (pop. 19,000)	—	[115]	8.2	—	
Low Countries					
Holland-Noorderqwartier, 1622–1795	—	—	5.9	17.6	
Overijssel, 1748	—	—	11.9	33.1	
Veluwe, 1749	—	—	14.0	32.0	
West Brabant, 1750	—	—	14.9	36.1	

Scandinavia					
Norway, Hedemarken, 1801 (pop. 9,246)	921	51	9.9	—	
Denmark, Island of Moer, 1645 (pop. 5,500)	672	126	12	—	
Iceland 1729 (pop. 8,077[a])	1,387	62	17.2	—	
Germany					
Grossenmeer, 1795 (pop. 882)	94	67	10.7	30.5	
Estonia					
Vändra, 1683 (pop. 976)	120[a]	84	12.3	44.7	√
Hungary					
Kassa, 1549 (pop. 503)	107	39	21.4	38	
Alsónyék, 1792 (pop. 685)	27[a]	286	3.9	20	√ √
Sárpilis, 1804 (pop. 534)	30[a]	150	5.6	15	
Serbia					
Belgrade, 1733–4 (pop. 1,537)	140	637	10.3	29.6	√
Japan					
Nishinomiya, 1713 (pop. 653)	26	420	4.0	13.3	
Yokouchi, 1671 (pop. 169)	6	—	3	18	

[a]There were 10 couples marked as married at Vändra: with the children the total is 239; 1 married couple at Alsónyék with 1 child (28); and 5 at Sárpilis together with 2 widows having 8 children all together (158).
Sources: as for previous tables with communications from John Hajnal and Rudolf Andorka.

33

but was fairly common elsewhere, especially in Estonia. Western servants in fact were, to a very large extent, young, unmarried persons —
indeed, sexually mature persons waiting to be married, for four-fifths
of male servants and two-thirds of female servants were under the prevalent age of marriage. Service in England and the West was a stage
in the life cycle for large numbers of people. 'Life-cycle servants' is the
distinctive title we shall use for them in the chapters of this book, where
servants and service will continually recur.

These facts about servants in the West, which do seem to distinguish
them from servants elsewhere, though quite how far cannot yet be told,
mean that a good part of all children could be servants before marriage.
On the Danish island of Moen in 1645, 3% of children aged 5—9 and
22% of those aged 10—14, and 48% of the unmarried aged 15—19 and
52% of those aged 20—24 were in service. Well over half, and perhaps up
to two-thirds or more, of young people could therefore expect to go into
service on this island. The following medians for proportions of the
population in service in various age groups can be suggested for England
(table 1.7).

TABLE 1.7.   *Percentages of age groups in service, England: six
pre-industrial settlements* (medians)

Age	Male (%)	Female (%)
0—9	1	1
10—14	5	4
15—19	35	27
20—24	30	40
25—29	15	15
30—34	7	10
35—39	4	5
40—44	2	2
over 45	2	2

The difference in the pattern between males and females is certainly
interesting. Though women married younger than men, it would seem
that more of them were in service at the marrying ages in England. Girls
apparently went out to service rather older, but boys may have left
service a little younger, and spent some of their time-to-marrying back
at home, or even as single householders. It is important that only a
minority of all children were, at any one age, in service, though a
majority of them may have been in this situation at some time in their
lives. Moreover, there were servants at all ages. You could be a nubile

unmarried all your adult life in the West, or become a servant again if you were widowed.

We have insufficient information as yet to say how far the pattern we are describing was distinctive. There are indications, for example, that Japanese servants, though far fewer in number, could also be young and unmarried, as they were at Nishinomiya in 1713. But Japanese servants cannot at all appropriately be called nubile unmarrieds as a class, and the evidence seems to point to the fact that their social-structural role was fundamentally different. In the village of Yokouchi they were usually old people, sometimes married people and always few, in the scores of successive lists of inhabitants which survive for that settlement from the late seventeenth to the early nineteenth century. Servants, then, cannot be called a perduring feature of Japanese social structure. They died out as a class (using 'class' here in the purely numerical sense) in Yokouchi quite early, and Akira Hayami has traced their virtual disappearance in a whole county, a centuries-long process which was complete before ever Japan was industrialized (see Hayami in Laslett and Wall (eds.) 1972: table 1.12 and p. 18).

In England, however, servants were the largest single occupational group, until within living memory, that is up to the early 1900s. They may have changed their social-structural position by that time in Europe, but they made up 7.3% of all household members in Baden in 1885, 6.6% in Austria in 1890, 7.7% even in Polish Silesia as late as 1921. Life-cycle servants may be the least amenable to analysis of the familial characteristics of the West, and the presence of servants (perhaps of a different kind) elsewhere in the world can be said to underline what I have called the weak and inclusive nature of the hypothesis we are considering. But enough has been said to show that servants as here defined must have been a crucial element in the pattern we are laying out.

Having now, it is hoped, established a general presumption in favour of the hypothesis which is being expounded, we may turn to the four characteristics one by one and discuss them with the socialization stage of the life cycle of the individual and with the family cycle in mind. We shall be able to marshal a certain amount of further numerical evidence, more particularly directed towards that subject. We begin with characteristic number one: the shape of the household in the West and its predominantly nuclear character from a long way back in time.

From our point of view what matters most is the situation in the households whose membership was affecting children in the first stage of the life cycle, in the West and elsewhere. A conspectus of some of the available evidence on this issue is given in table 1.8, where the years

TABLE 1.8. *Children undergoing socialization (aged 0–5) in various past communities in England, France, Serbia and Japan, by structure of household*

Living in	Ealing England 1599	Lichfield England 1696	Stoke-on-Trent England 1701	Longuenesse France 1778	Belgrade Serbia 1733	Yokouchi Japan 1671	Nishinomiya Japan 1713
Simple family households	33 67%	312 94%	189 90%	27 79%	101 66%	88 33%	13 28%
Extended family households	4 8%	11 3.4%	14 6.6%	7 21%	16 14%	0	12 26%
Multiple family households	2 4%	5 1.6%	4 1.9%	0	27 15%	15 63%	21 46%
Otherwise	10 20%	4 1.2%	3 1.4%	0	8 5%	1 4%	0
Living in company with servants	10 20%	102 32%	33 16%	5 15%	28 18%	0	5 11%

Note: These must be taken as approximate figures, especially for Belgrade. The difficulties with the data for that community, and a description of three of the others, will be found in Laslett and Wall (eds.) 1972 : 50 – 1. In assessing the figures for Japan, it must be borne in mind that children in the first and second year are omitted, and that adoption was extensively practised : 42% of all children in complex households were affected by this, but since the very young were rarely adopted, the relationship taken account of in the figures is always to that of the biological parent.

from birth to age five are taken to be those of primary socialization.[12] There are conspicuous contrasts in this set of figures, especially between the English county and cathedral city of Lichfield in 1696 — no industrial centre this, although situated not far from Birmingham — and the small, entirely rural settlement of Yokouchi in Japan in 1671. In Lichfield nearly all the little children were in nuclear families, but in Yokouchi nearly two-thirds were in complex family groups, each containing at least two conjugal family units. Even in Yokouchi every third child was in a simple family household, and that category was everywhere substantial. Figures from the Baltic states or Great Russia would no doubt show virtually every child being brought up in a complex family, and most of them as being grandchild as well as child in relation to one or other member of the domestic group.

Since previous historical discussion of the influences on socialization has tended to be in terms of the composition of the family group, it is tempting to leave the topic here with two dogmatic generalizations and go on to our other two distinguishing characteristics.

One such statement would be that the strongest single effect on the child from the presence of other personalities has always been that of parents and siblings. The effect of the presence of other persons, kin folk or not, has been incomparably weaker, not only in terms of the strength of the bond, but in numerical terms as well. The 'West', then, in historic times has simply been that cultural area where this generalization is at its most powerful. The second of our dogmatic statements would be even more specifically historical. The most important of all the effects on the family group of the process of modernization has undoubtedly been the physical removal from the household of the father and other earners for all of every working day. The perpetual presence of the father, the paterfamilias, the household head, must have had an enormous effect on the pre-industrial family and household. It follows that the influence of the shape of the family on the formation of the personality of the child must have been greater in the past than it is today. It follows further that this influence must have been strongest of all in the West, where the predominance of the nuclear family was most pronounced, with children alone in the company of their parents.

[12] If the very earliest years are taken, say 0–2, the result is little changed. At Belgrade, for example, 45 or 71% of the babies were in simple family households, 8 or 14% in extended family households and 15 or 24% in multiple family households. In Stoke-on-Trent 93% of those aged 0–2 were in simple family households, 5.1% in extended family households and 1.1% in multiple family households. The proportions could be somewhat higher in England, nevertheless. In Cardington in 1787 (an incomplete listing, unfortunately) 11% of children aged 0–3 were in extended family households and 9% in multiple; of the age group 0–5, 8% and 5%.

There are, however, one or two comments which should be added here to these two dogmatic claims. We may begin with the limitations of our evidence in indicating the true extent of the prevalence, or clear predominance, of simple family households during the lifetimes of individuals. When a familial system is being judged from lists of inhabitants alone, as is the case in the tables we have presented, it has to be remembered that these lists are almost always isolated at points in time rather than being members of sets of chronological series. Only such successive listings would make possible the actual tracing of individual households through a complete family cycle, or through a series of them.

A household has a higher probability of containing the parents or a parent of the spouses at the stage of family formation than it has in later years, when these parents are likely to be dead, and this probability is higher again at the stage when offspring are themselves getting married. It follows that the proportion of simple family households at any one time, in any one list of inhabitants, is not a direct measure of the propensity for any household in that community to be extended or multiple at some point in its domestic cycle.

The figures in our tables, then, are not of themselves sufficient indicators of the presence or absence of such traditions as that of the stem family amongst the populations to which they refer. They are, of course, quite adequate to dispose of the view that there was no difference at all between rules of family formation in the West and elsewhere, and, as we have seen, it appears that the contrasts recorded cannot be explained by demographic vicissitudes. The criterion used in table 1.8, proportion of children in infancy in various familial situations, is perhaps a more useful indicator than that of household composition when socialization is at issue.

As must be expected, the weak and inclusive nature of the relationship between the characteristics we are examining gives rise to intermediate and indeterminate familial forms and situations. The stem family might be taken as an instance. This tradition of household formation seems often to have accompanied impartible inheritance amongst European peasant landholders, and to have encouraged the presence of multiple family households at particular periods during the family cycle. But it is certainly compatible with late marriage for most women, if not always for the bride of the designated heir, and might well actually encourage the institution of service. It is impossible to decide — indeed it scarcely makes sense to try to do so — whether the stem family as usually conceived is itself to be described as 'Western'. When present in a French- or German-speaking community it seems to have affected the life cycles of a minority rather than a majority of the village population and was so flexible in its provisions even amongst them that it must certainly be thought of as compatible with the constellation of characteristics we have combined under that heading. An extreme and rigid form of these arrangements, on the other hand, affecting the socialization of nearly all children in every succeeding generation, would be classified as 'non-Western' in its tendency.

In some parts of Europe, particularly in the German-speaking lands and in Sweden, too, there seems to have been a traditional sentiment about 'das ganze Haus', the large, multigenerational, kin-enfolding, servant-employing household. It would seem best to leave the relationship of this element to the pattern with which we are concerned undecided for the present. Research in progress should make it clear how frequently 'das ganze Haus' did in fact consist in complex, communal, family living, amongst large proportions of the population, and how often it illustrated not so much the form of families themselves as the residential conventions which grouped individual households together in the huge *housefuls* which seem to have occupied the great galleried peasant houses, still to be admired in the village streets of Alsace or Württemberg or Switzerland.

The second of our characteristics, age at marriage for women, or, rather, the ages between which a wife would have her children, has obvious connections with household composition. Only if she married early enough would her parents have been able to share the household with her and only if her children were born when she herself was young enough would she in her turn be able to share a household with those children after they had married. Some notion of the contrast between the 'West' and other regions can be gained from the figures marshalled in table 1.4 above, both in this respect and in respect of the relative ages of husbands and wives. The relationship of age gap between spouses on the one hand and household composition on the other is not so obvious, but we may nevertheless consider the two together.

Age at marriage and age gap between spouses, of course, can be much more accurately known for the past than such things as household composition. Where they are not contained in official statistics, that is, before the mid nineteenth century for the West and before the early twentieth century for most of the rest of the world, these facts can be derived with great reliability for individual settlements by subjecting registers of baptisms, marriages and burials to the process of family reconstitution. In such a context as the present one, therefore, it is sufficient to point to the work already done by historical demographers by means of family reconstitution on the ecclesiastical registers of France, Italy, England, Japan and even the colonial United States in order to underwrite the claim that Western marriage was late for women, a claim already established for statistical times by Hajnal in 1965. It is accepted that no country in the West has ever had mean age at first marriage for women as low as 20 years, or at least for no sustained period of time, whatever may have happened in Warwickshire in Shakespeare's youth. In the seven available English reconstitutions (for Colyton and Hartland in Devon, Banbury in Oxfordshire, Alcester in Warwickshire, Gainsborough in Lincolnshire, Aldenham in Hertfordshire and Hawkshead in the Lake District) the figures are as follows (unweighted means of years of age): 1550–99, 24.9; 1600–49, 25.9; 1650–99, 27.0; 1700–49, 27.2; 1750–99, 25.5; 1800–49, 24.5.

Historical demography, however, has yet to gain a firm hold in any non-'Western' country other than Japan, and in any case the opportunities for carrying out family reconstitution are severely restricted. This is so even in countries like England where ecclesiastical registration of vital events was passable and where much of its documentation has survived. It is doubtful whether this process will ever provide ages at marriage for many of the areas already mentioned here as having a family regime differing from the West, at least for any century earlier than the nineteenth.

Moreover, our present interest is not simply in the results of historical demography as such, for we want to know more than the fact of a woman's having children early or late in her childbearing period. Our concern is with the children who survive and live under her care within the family provided by her husband and herself. The only evidence for these facts comes, once more, from the analysis of listings of inhabitants, and evidence of this kind for an English and a Japanese community is set out in table 1.9. As the note to that table indicates, these statistics are the least reliable of those which are being presented in this essay. It is difficult to estimate the effect which the faulty data may have had on the figures of this table. There seems little doubt, however, that the most striking contrast between Stoke-on-Trent and Nishinomiya which comes out here is also the most likely to be reliable: that is, the difference in age between fathers and mothers. What is known of the omissions, moreover, would seem to imply that the other contrasts are less marked in the table than they were in reality. The failure to include children less than two years old at Nishinomiya, a feature which is common to all Japanese material of this kind, presumably means that a fair number of young parents are not taken into account in our statistics for that settlement, though such parents are represented in the figures for Stoke-on-Trent. Japanese mothers, then, may well have been even younger in relation to their children and to English mothers than these figures imply. The same may have been true, though to a lesser degree, of Japanese fathers as well, though the indications are that in spite of the much greater super-

TABLE 1.9. *Relative ages of mothers, fathers and their children: Stoke-on-Trent and Nishinomiya*

		Stoke-on-Trent, Staffs., England, 1701	Nishinomiya, Japan, 1713
Mothers and fathers		$n = 248$	$n = 114$
Number of years by which ages of fathers exceed ages of mothers	Mean	2.5	9.5
	Median	1.6	10.5
	range	−16 to +20	−4 to +28
Proportion of mothers older than fathers		29%	2.6%
Mothers and their children		$n = 740$	$n = 261$
Ages of mothers at births of their children	Mean	30.4	27.0
	Median	30.7	26.7
	Interquartile range	27.6 to 38.9	23.9 to 34.1
Proportion of children	25 years or less younger than their mothers	21%	39%
	30 years or more younger than their mothers	50%	34%
Fathers and their children		$n = 635$	$n = 239$
Ages of fathers at births of their children	Mean	35.4	36.3
	Median	35.4	37.0
Proportion of children	25 years or less younger than their fathers	15%	3.4%
	30 years or more younger than their fathers	59%	83%

Note: Figures obtained by differencing ages given in the two listings; widows and widowers included if accompanied by children. Children of under two years absent from the Nishinomiya listing. No attempt has been made to allow for this omission, nor for distortions due to second and later marriages, nor for the effect of children having left the parental home.

iority in age over their wives and their children which they enjoyed, they were not significantly older than their English counterparts.

The picture suggested by the facts from Stoke and from Nishinomiya can be filled in to some extent by pieces of approximate evidence from elsewhere in the West and outside. In the two counties which can be studied in the Icelandic Census of 1729, for example, it appears that the mean age of the mothers of resident children was about 32.6 years, and that under 10% of children were twenty-five years or less younger than their mothers. At Kölked, the Hungarian village already cited, however, mean age of mothers was some 25.6 years, and over 40% of children had been born when their mothers were aged 25 years and younger. In this village, not as many as one mother in ten was as old as the father, whereas in Iceland 22% of the mothers were in that position or older.

The substantial proportion of female spouses older than male spouses, ranging from one-fifth to one-quarter, I believe must establish itself as the most consistent indicator of 'Westernness' in familial matters. It has been found in every instance examined. If something like a necessary indicator of 'Westernness', this characteristic cannot, however, be called a sufficient one. For it must not be overlooked that Russian serfs seem sometimes to have had wives older than themselves, although in every other way their family life was different from the Western pattern.

The inference which has already been drawn from these facts, that Western marriage has always tended to be companionate, comparatively companionate, that is to say, is a hypothetical venture. Only the attitudinal or ideological evidence we need so much to discover could vindicate the claim. Nevertheless, something must follow for the socialization of children from such an unexpected characteristic of long-established European familial institutions.[13] Most important, perhaps, from very many points of view is that Western marriage conventions, along with the nuclear family under the responsible, individual, independent control of a mature couple, may have made possible flexible and effective control of population.

In the West, then, children seem always to have been born of mature women with an average age in the late 20s or the early 30s. Elsewhere they have tended to be produced by women three or four years younger, in the middle or early 20s, some of them even in their teens. One-tenth of all children resident at Kölked in 1819 and at Yokouchi in 1671 had teenage mothers, but not one in a hundred of those in Ealing in 1599 or Stoke-on-Trent in 1701. The experts on the psychology of child rearing will have to judge what difference maturity in the mother makes to the child, and also to judge how the child is affected by the mother's being

[13] A series of works on marriage, which include evidence on attitudes of husband to wife and wife to husband, began to appear in the mid 1970s, especially from such writers as Martine Segalen and Jean-Louis Flandrin in France. I have not been able to take account of this evidence here. The figures from Iceland and Hungary are subject to the disadvantage of ignorance of the languages. It must be remembered in judging the above statements that age at marriage in the West, and no doubt elsewhere, *varied* over time, and is indeed one of the most interesting of social-structural variables. It is the *relatively* late age and the *relatively* brief age gap between spouses which we are claiming to be general.

closer in years to the bread-winner and family head, quite often older and more experienced than he was.

In other regions the young mother must surely have felt her inferiority of age. If authoritarianism and patriarchalism rest (for any cultural complex) on superior years, then it is clear where we must seek for predisposing circumstances.

So much for the first three of our set of characteristics. The fourth of them is slightly more complicated as a proposition, since it affects more than the first stage of the family cycle and of the life cycle. For if a boy or a girl became a servant at some age between 12 and 22, he underwent the experience of service at the stage of secondary socialization. Whilst he was doing so, he was, presumably, having an effect on the infant children of his master and mistress. How many young people found themselves in that position and at what period in their lives can be judged from the contents of table 1.10.

The figures of this table along with those of tables 1.6 and 1.7 prompt us to make the following summary statements. In the West something like one-fifth (20%) of all children were, during their earliest, impressionable years, members of domestic groups which contained servants. Of the other four-fifths, something like a half (40% of all children) — though the proportion was very variable — themselves became servants in their late teens or early 20s. At most one in five, then, of all young people escaped the experience of living with servants or of living as servants. Once again it is for the child psychologists and family sociologists to judge of the effect of such circumstances on the formation of personality. It seems to me of considerable consequence that in so high a proportion of early childhoods, including virtually all of those experienced by members of the elite, strangers should have figured in the family, strangers nearly always from outside the social class of the parents and below it.[14] These imported personalities, imported for their youth and their vigour, were two or three times more in number than resident kin. Although the general theory of the socialization process implies that less should be expected to follow from the experience of a young man or woman of going out to service during the period of secondary socialization, I believe that this must have had tangible con-

[14] Laslett in Laslett and Wall (eds.) 1972: table 4.16 (p. 154) shows that 84% of all gentry households had servants in traditional England. The literature about the role of servants in higher-class households, and their relationship to the children, is extensive in earlier centuries, and is beginning to be so amongst the scholars of our own day. It must be remembered, however, that only a minority (not yet determined) of all servants were in gentry households, and that most persons in conditions of service were not household helps, but farm hands, apprentices, dairy workers and so on; males slightly exceeded females (see ibid. table 4.13).

TABLE 1.10. *Proportions of various ages in service and proportions ever married, in England, Serbia and Japan*

Age groups	Ealing, England, 1599 In service (%)	Married or widowed (%)	Lichfield, England, 1696 In service (%)	Married or widowed (%)	Stoke-on-Trent, England, 1701 In service (%)	Married or widowed (%)	Ardleigh, England, 1796 In service (%)	Married or widowed (%)	Belgrade, Serbia, 1733/34 In service (%)	Married or widowed (%)	Nishinomiya, Japan, 1713 In service (%)	Married or widowed (%)
Males												
0–9	0	0	1	0	0	0	0	0	0	0	0	0
10–14	15	0	4	0	3	0	3	0	22	0	0	0
15–19	72	0	47	0	10	0	48	0	47	0	24	0
20–24	78	0	24	18	16	11	38	16	24	33	19	0
25–29	47	29	5	25	20	52	11	52	17	68	8	14
30–34	28	47	1	73	5	73	5	73	13	85	6	26
35–39	43	43	1	76	2	93	4	83	8	83	0	79
40–44	29	71	0	89	0	94	0	79	3	96	0	100
45 +	9	89	0	82	1	85	7	80	7	92	0	100
Females												
0–9	3	0	0	0	0	0	0	0	1	0	0	0
10–14	7	0	1	0	3	0	5	0	9	0	4	0
15–19	47	0	18	1	30	0	27	0	6	77	8	0
20–24	58	15	42	8	28	17	20	33	0	92	3	28
25–29	36	50	23	38	10	63	9	56	1	97	0	83
30–34	27	63	12	59	7	72	0	89	0	98	0	87
35–39	14	86	4	74	7	73	0	94	1	96	0	100
40–44	0	100	0	78	2	85	3	91	0	100	0	100
45 +	5	92	0	76	2	78	6	75	2	95	0	100

sequences, too. In the old world, in the West anyway, the form of sub-ordination, political and economic as well as personal, was overtly familial. We touched upon the implications of this for political language and imagery in the Introduction.

There are many other ways of looking at the institution of life-cycle service, and we shall return to the subject repeatedly in this book. Although we shall insist that servants are not properly to be described as a class, the practice of the poorer families offering up their children to the richer families at the very time when those children were at the height of their productive powers must certainly be called exploitation of one set of persons by another set. The figures we have looked at demonstrate that this exploitation could be on a considerable scale in Western countries.

Not all, or not quite all, servants were of a lower social level than the heads of the households in which they worked, and not everything which they did was for the benefit of their masters and mistresses alone. Nor, perhaps, was the practice of exchanging adolescents between house-holds entirely confined to servants: some parents, in the opinion of some social historians of the West, sent out their children to other households as boarders or as lodgers for training or 'educational' purposes. Accord-ing to an impressive recent account of the social structure of a mid-Victorian Canadian city, where the numbers of servants were still considerable, and the number of young persons, especially young males, living as boarders was very large as well, this practice continued until incipient factory industrialization began the process which finally obli-terated life-cycle service altogether.

We know much less about the history of boarding and lodging than we know about the history of servants. There are grounds for supposing, however, that the practice was sometimes quite common, in the town if not in the countryside. In Leyden in 1581, 4% of the population were lodgers, and their numbers were four or five times bigger in central London in the 1690s. But it is not very likely that many of the people who lived in this way in Western countries in traditional times were in the same position as servants undergoing secondary socialization. Indeed, many of them were grouped in their own families

The evidence we have does not seem to indicate that individuals who lodged were usually of an age when they were seeking spouses for them-selves. In this they were unlike servants, and the courtship aspect of service must be taken as of great significance in traditional European social, emotional and sexual life. Circulating, as we shall see in our next chapter that they did, from household to household and from village to village, servants were in perpetual contact with their potential partners. Yet marriage was ordinarily forbidden until the opportunity came for both of them to pool their savings, their skill and their experience, and set up households for themselves. It is possible to see in this process a good deal of the imaginative life and literary imagery about courtship which we have inherited from the traditional social order on our continent.[15]

With the transformation of the institution of service in Western countries during the nineteenth century to a purely domestic matter, and with its complete disappearance in the middle years of the twentieth century, the familial pattern we are limning out in this essay lost its singularity. Meanwhile marriage ages, marriage relationships, familial relationships as a whole changed as well. We began by insisting that our subject was essentially historical, a subject in historical sociology, because we had to recover what had largely disappeared, but that it was of signal importance to the study of society because it had existed for so long. We cannot linger on the topic of how and why the Western familial pattern finally gave way before industrial transformation, though when we come to consider such things as illegitimacy, orphanage and especially aging, some of the features of the change should make themselves apparent. But we must spare a sentence or two for the question of how old the pattern was. Can it yet be said when 'the West' began to diverge from the rest of Europe and the rest of the world in its familial outlook and behaviour?

In his original essay of 1965 John Hajnal was disposed to place the initiation of the European marriage patterns in the sixteenth century. Appropriate enough, it might be said, since this was the time when the modern history of Europe is always supposed to have started, the time when the Renaissance and Reformation thrust medieval institutions into the past, and when the discovery and conquest of the Americas began the period of Western world supremacy. The advance of our information in the last twelve years has confirmed this claim in a very important respect. In England, anyway, nothing has been discovered which would cast doubt on the European marriage pattern's already being virtually universal in the seventeenth and eighteenth centuries.

Our earliest well-founded and accurate ages at first marriage for women are, as has been seen, comfortably above those which Hajnal quotes for the non-Western pattern in the early twentieth century, and

[15]   See Laslett 1976, and for Canada, see Katz 1975, esp. pp. 256—71. Macfarlane (1970) is quoted in support of Katz's view of Western secondary socialization, of which he sees boarding in Hamilton as a continuation. High-status households in that city had more boarders than low-status households, which is certainly very different from what we find in traditional English cities, towns and villages, and which may distinguish the New World from the Old.

it should be noticed that this is true for the last half of the sixteenth century, too.

No sign here, then, of an approximation with the Continent—if indeed that is the approximation we should be looking for—in late Renaissance times, and the few pieces of relevant evidence which we have go to show that this was true of household composition in the mid sixteenth century, too. In the little seaside town of Poole in Dorset in 1574, and in the depressed city of Coventry in the 1520s, simple family households were heavily predominant, and servants were as conspicuous as they were throughout the seventeenth and eighteenth centuries, and as they were so disconcertingly in Kassa in 1549. In England, therefore, we can scarcely look upon the familial pattern as being more pronounced as we go forwards in time and less pronounced as we go backwards. For all that we can see, it was the same in the 1550s as it was in the 1820s.

Concerted research on the evidence which has been used to suggest that before the sixteenth century marriage in England was non-European is now in progress at the Cambridge Group for the History of Population and Social Structure. It is the particular interest of Richard Michael Smith, whose data on the position of the aged in medieval English households will be cited in chapter 5 below. The more closely he has looked into the documents surviving from the English Poll Tax of 1377, which convinced John Hajnal and the authorities on whom he had to rely that numbers married in that nationwide survey were of an order too high to be reconcilable with the European marriage pattern, the more sceptical he has become. It begins to appear that it may not be correct to say that in England in 1377 'those married amongst the over 15 must have been over 70% ... [whereas] on the European marriage pattern the percentage who were married in a country as a whole was below 55 and usually below 50 in the nineteenth century' (Hajnal 1965: 119, a tentative statement assuming unbiassed data). Moreover, Dr Smith has found documents for the Poll Tax which reveal the presence of servants in the households of these English persons counted in 1377 on a scale which, if it becomes possible to estimate it firmly, might well be similar to that which characterized England two or three hundred years later.[16]

This investigation of medieval familial and other practices is not confined to age at first marriage for women, nor to the existence of life-cycle servants, nor is it confined to the fourteenth century, which is after

[16] Some of these servants are given as married, however. Although it is not quite certain whether the vocabulary used consistently indicates life-cycle servants, this should warn us against exaggerating the similarity between the medieval English household and that of early modern England. We shall have to consider references to married 'servants' in England in our next chapter. Dr Smith believes, however, that life-cycle service was present on an appreciable scale in English medieval villages.

all not so very distant in what might be called social-structural time from the sixteenth or seventeenth century. Evidence of a different character bearing on more features of the society is being surveyed for the thirteenth century, and once again it seems that it might be difficult to describe the position in the English household, in English marriage habits, in English domestic arrangements generally as being of a character markedly different seven hundred years ago from what we have sketched out for early modern times. The further we go back, so it appears at the moment, the more elusive the origins of the interrelated characteristics of the Western family. As of the present state of our knowledge we cannot say when 'the West' diverged from the other parts of Europe.

At that tantalizing point in the progress of this new field of social historical exploration, we must leave the familial pattern of the West and its perdurance over time. When the Russian file, as we may be permitted to call it, comes fully into the analysis; when it is possible to compare not individual settlements but dozens of places with the scores we have already mustered for England over the years from the 1550s to the 1800s; when the medieval English evidence has been brought into order and its robustness to comparison has been tested, then and not before shall we be in a position to talk with greater exactness and conviction, for and against the thesis of this essay. It is a particular disadvantage to the case we have presented that it has been so often necessary to make our numerical comparisons with places in Japan in Tokugawa times, a cultural region so alien to the European West that it is difficult to see when we are comparing like with like. It should not be very long before we can do better than this, but we shall only be able to approach a decision on the many points at issue when historical sociology, and especially the historical demographic component of it, has been established at many sites in the relevant parts of the world.

In the remainder of this book 'the West' will be absent from the centre of the stage. Nevertheless, many of the subjects we have touched upon will come up again: family composition, age at marriage for women, age relation of spouses, servants and the socialization of children. They will concern us most closely when we come at the end to consider the interesting and exceptional case of household and family amongst the slaves of the American South. The topics of succeeding chapters, moreover, have an evident relationship with the pattern we have run our fingers over.

Late and moveable marriage for women means a relatively long, but variable, interval between the time of sexual maturity and the beginnings of reproductive life. Measures of illegitimacy are of critical interest in a system which postpones sexual gratification and leaves so large a part of vigorous youth without socially allowable ways of engendering children. The composition of households and their generational depth is of the first importance to the welfare and companionship of the old. The hypothesis that the West, until industrialization, had a unique familial pattern of its own is fundamental to the present work. So also are the potential consequences of that newly discovered possibility for the social, political, economic and even the industrial life of the world as a world.

2. Clayworth and Cogenhoe

NOTE: The original study bearing this title was published jointly with John Harrison as one of the *Historical essays, 1600-1750, presented to David Ogg,* edited by H. E. Bell and R. L. Ollard in 1963. Sections I and II of the text below reproduce for the most part what then appeared, but with considerable correction and extension. Some of the documentary details then published have been omitted to ease the footnotes in this version: the researcher wishing to recover all the materials should consult the first printing of this piece.

An attempt has been made here, particularly in the footnotes, to draw attention to the work which has subsequently been done on the topics raised in that first exercise in the historical analysis of familial and social structure, and to present some of the results where they serve to provide a context for Clayworth and its characteristics. Though the comparison with Cogenhoe was part of the original study, the comparison with turnover at Hallines and Longuenesse, in north-west France, which forms section III of the present text, appeared independently in French in *Annales de Démographie Historique* (1968) as 'Le brassage de la population en France et en Angleterre au XVIIe et au XVIIIe siècles', translated by Jacques Dupâquier, and is printed here in a shortened and revised form for the first time in English. Section IV, the tabular analysis, replaces the numerical addendum attached to the essay of 1963. The tables were worked out between 1964 and 1967 as part of the hand analysis of the collection of well over a hundred listings of the inhabitants of English pre-industrial communities then being carried out by the Cambridge Group for the History of Population and Social Structure: they form part of a standard series. These two sets of figures are the first to be printed in full from that large body of numerical evidence, though extensive use has been made of it in other publications of the Cambridge Group.

In the course of the research which we did together for the first version John Harrison carried out the detailed study of the Clayworth documents and prepared the original figures for that village. His analysis of the evidence on what happened between 1676 and 1688 was carried out after our publication of 1963, and has been used extensively in this revision. I would like to express my heartfelt gratitude to him, though the responsibility for the text is entirely my own.

I myself discovered the documents at Cogenhoe (pronounced 'Cooknoe') and did the original analysis. This was subsequently extended by Susan Stewart and by others; the results are included in Section IV. Mr Harrison also attempted to reconstitute the families of Clayworth from the parish registers, but the quality of the registers proved insufficient. This was the first trial undertaken at Cambridge of the method of reconstitution developed by Louis Henry, and it yielded much important information in spite of our inability to work out demographic rates for the relevant years.

I. Clayworth in 1676 and 1688

William Sampson, rector of Clayworth, began keeping his Register on 27 March 1676, and his entries continued until 8 March 1701. He had held the benefice of this Nottinghamshire parish, five miles to the north of East Retford, since the year 1672 and had resided there since November 1675. For exactly a quarter of a century, therefore, from the beginning of one year in the Old Style, until the end of the twenty-fifth year after that, this shrewd, intelligent clergyman recorded everything of importance which happened to the little community under his spiritual care.

The rector's book, Clayworth, Nottinghamshire, as this document has come to be called, was published in full in the year 1910.[1] It is a record well known to historians of the county and quoted by ecclesiastical, social and economic historians of Stuart England. Here was a man who well understood why it should be that barley from the clay soils should fetch a better price than barley from the sand soils which lay side by side in the seven great fields of Clayworth, fields here and there already enclosed. Sampson was an improver and an encloser himself, quite aware of the importance of drainage in those parts of the village which were waterlogged all year or liable to flood in winter. He husbanded his rectory glebe with notable skill and economy —an implacable, not to say aggressive, champion of the rights of the Church, financial and social, as well as religious, but also a faithful and painstaking shepherd of souls.

Sparrows of the Spirit is the extraordinary title of the only book which

[1] Transcribed and edited by Harry Gill and Everard L. Guilford: Henry B. Saxton, Nottingham, publisher. In the early 1960s the original was still in the safe in Clayworth Church, and comparison showed the transcription to be fair. Together with the registers of the parish, this document is now in the Nottinghamshire Record Office. Much is owed to the late Rev. Cyril Blomefield, then rector of Clayworth, for the study of the materials from his village.

has tried to make Sampson a figure of popular interest.[2] A strange misnomer this, even if satirically meant, for a man who could record, without sign of emotion or regret, that George Richardson, blacksmith's apprentice of some years' standing in the village, was hanged at Tyburn in March 1695 for stealing two horses out of the rectory stable. In 1679, at the very rails of the altar, and in sight of nearly fifty of their neighbours, Sampson withheld the communion cup on Palm Sunday from Ralph Meers and Anne Fenton, 'upon a common fame that they lived and lodged together, not being married'. Both of them had been servants in the largest house in Clayworth until a little time before, and within a few months they themselves were householders.

In 1682 Ralph Meers, now describing himself as labourer, was one of the churchwardens of the parish. Nevertheless, we know that his first child was conceived several months before his marriage. This is one of the few pre-nuptial pregnancies we can trace at Clayworth.[3] The improvement of the minds and the manners of his people was the evident object of Sampson's pastorate. When he died he left the means to the village to set up a regular school, the necessity and importance of which had been felt for many years. In *The Towne-Booke of Claworth* are still to be seen the proud, clumsy signatures of the poor boys of the village who had learnt to write from Sampson's benefaction.[4]

Sampson begins the actual text of his *Rector's book* by setting out twelve reasons for the necessity of such a record which he evidently thought of as in some sense belonging with the registration of baptisms, marriages and burials. Apart from these events, the document should contain the names of office-holders in the village, everything to do with tithe and with parish funds, details of the weather, the price of crops, and 'all differences and controversies of note' which affected the

[2] *Sparrows of the Spirit* is a paperback by F. West (London, 1961). The Rector's book contains annual accounts of the income of the church land, rising satisfactorily over the years. See W. A. Tate, 'The Clayworth manorial map', *Transactions of the Thoroton Society* (1940), for the intermediate, enclosed mixed with unenclosed, fields of the village as it was in Sampson's time, and for a reproduction of a manorial map of the year 1749. His farming activities can be usefully compared with those of Ralph Josselin, vicar of Earl's Colne, Essex, from 1641 to 1683, excellently described in Macfarlane 1970 (see esp. pp. 33–80) from Josselin's own diary. Sampson differed from this Puritan clerical improver in that, as far as can be seen from the *Rector's book*, he never acquired land of his own.

[3] From this first reference to such behaviour in England, the study of prenuptial pregnancy has been developed by P. E. H. Hair and others in an interesting and revealing fashion. See Hair 1966 and 1970; Laslett 1965 (1971 ed.: 147–9); and p. 128 below.

[4] 'The Towne-Booke of Claworth containing the Names and accompts of all Parish Officers Beginning in the Year of our Lord 1674' preserves the details of Sampson's benefaction. It was particularly designed for the teaching of poor children, who sometimes signed the book if they won one of the prizes. This volume is now likewise in the Nottinghamshire Record Office.

Church. The ninth of his reasons is the one which interests us most. The record ought to set out, he claims, 'All the names of the Inhabitants of the Parish by a yearly Poll, and out of them to be noted the Communicants at every Sacrament.'

It cannot be said that the *Rector's book* does contain such yearly lists of the villagers, any more than it does an entirely complete series of high and low prices of their produce, valuable as the price recordings are. The rector may have been persuaded that it would be a good thing to have an up-to-date list of his parishioners, because in that very month of April 1676 when he began to write his record he received from the Archbishop of York the questionnaire for a religious census, generally called the Compton census. This enquiry, and Sampson's response, recalls an ancient and it seems a somewhat ineffective tradition of the Christian Church of the West, codified and made stronger by the Council of Trent for the Church of Rome. The historian of English parish registers, J. S. Burn, has this to say about it: 'Among the general canons set forth in some old Rituals is a direction for four books to be kept by the clergyman in every parish; one for baptisms, another for marriages, a third for burials, and a fourth, the *Liber Status Animarum*.' In this fourth book, Burn continues in the original Latin: 'singulas familias suae parochiae, cum omnibus qui in ea vivunt, diligenter conscribat, annotabitque qui ad Communionem apti, qui ad scholam catechisticam aut Confirmationem'[5] — 'he must carefully inscribe [in this book — the *Liber status animarum*] each family in his parish, with everyone living in it, and take note of those fit for Communion, and those fit for catechistical instruction or for Confirmation'. If every beneficed priest of the English Church had in fact kept all these four registers — indeed if even some of them (a very small proportion would have sufficed) had kept a *Liber status animarum* to hand down to us — then the task of the historian of social structure would be transformed. We should have the chance of reconstructing the population of our country as it was during all those generations which went by before the official census began in the early nineteenth century, of doing it swiftly, accurately and completely.

But the first chastening lesson learnt by the beginner in the historical study of the social structure of England, and of most of Christian Europe, is that such a body of evidence scarcely exists. This is in spite of what might be expected on the analogy of the parish registers of baptisms,

[5] *History of the parish registers in England* (1st ed. 1829, 2nd ed. 1862): 212. I have not been able to find these 'old rituals' in English ecclesiastical history, and it would seem that Burn may have had a Continental source in mind, and perhaps the ordinances of the Council of Trent itself. Earlier in his book (p. 11) Burn refers to these four registers' being enjoined by the Roman ritual printed in 1617. For the relevant regulations of the diocese of St Omer, see p. 76 below.

marriages and burials, which were instituted in most if not all of the Western European countries in the sixteenth or seventeenth century, which have survived in considerable quantities and which can be exploited by the demographic historian.

No document headed *Liber status animarum* has yet come to light in England, but in this, as in much else to do with numerical recordings, we seem to have been unfortunate. In France such documents are certainly known, and we make use of two series of them later in this study. They may in the end turn out to survive in some numbers in that country.[6] Few, apparently, bear the title specified, though it is now confirmed that some such lists do survive for Austria. In Italy, or at least in Tuscany, series of repeated spiritual censuses were carried out, and have survived. Sweden, Finland and the rest of Scandinavia possess spiritual censuses of a similar character on an impressive scale, though mostly for the eighteenth century and later. Outside the West, but still within Catholic Europe, Polish series of *Libri status animarum* look as if they will turn out to be plentiful and promising.[7]

It is reasonable to hope that other Christian countries, perhaps even in the area which fell within the sway of the Eastern Orthodox Church, may have retained such archives, to the benefit of the historical sociologist.[8] Nevertheless, it seems certain that the study of social groups, and especially of domestic groups, will never have as its source in these listings a body of evidence anything like as complete or as revealing as are the parish registers for demographic history. In England the situation is likely to remain as it now is, tantalizing but unpromising.

Sampson's record-keeping resolution, then, quickly leads the historian of the family and of social structure generally a long way away from his English and Anglican parish of Clayworth in 1676. On 9 April of that year the rector announced a 'brief' to his congregation, an appeal that is, enjoined to be read by every parish priest in aid of a charitable purpose, in this case relief and repair at Northampton after a disastrous fire.[9] Not content on this occasion with taking up coins in church, the

[6] Emmanuel Todd goes so far as to claim that over 1,000 lists of inhabitants probably survive for France before 1790, almost all of them yet to be located, though Flandrin 1976 shows that they are beginning to be exploited.

[7] For Tuscany, see S. Shifini d'Andrea, 'Exploitation des listes nominatives à Fiesole', *Population* 26: 573–80; for Austria, Michael Mitterauer, 'Zur Familienstruktur in ländlichen Gebieten Österreichs im 17. Jahrhundert', *Beiträge zur Bevölkerungs- und Sozialgeschichte Österreichs*, ed. H. Helcmanovski (Vienna, 1973); and for Poland, Boleslaw Kumor, 'Ksiegi status animarum w diecezjach polskich', in *Przesztošč Demograficzna Polski*, 1 (1967) and 7 (1975) (an actual example).

[8] The listing of the Orthodox Christian inhabitants of Belgrade 1733/34 used in chapter 6 below certainly looks like a *Liber status animarum*: for a social-structural analysis of the list, see Laslett and Wall (eds.) 1972: ch. 15.

[9] *Rector's book*, p. 14.

rector 'went with the Churchwardens from house to house to collect it'. The entry continues thus: 'Whilst they were collecting this brief, I took occasion to enquire at the same time the names of all my parishioners which were these that follow Nominatim et (ad evitandam invidiam) alphabetice.' Then follows the list,[10] household by household, in alphabetical order — it was typical of Sampson to do all he could to avoid invidiousness between neighbours — and within the household according to function. The head of household had his calling registered, and widowers and widows were so described. Wives, children, servants, kinsfolk, mothers-in-law, apprentices, journeymen, all were specified, with only a detail missing here and there.

With this elaborate list in his hand, Sampson gave his answers to the questions put by his archbishop. There were 401 persons living in Clayworth in April 1676, and 236 of them were mature enough to communicate, that is, had attained the age of sixteen. No fewer than 200 of the 236 actually took the sacrament during the Easter festival in that year: there was no popish recusant or protestant dissenter in the village.[11] Much has recently been said, and often with justice, about the failure of the Christian Church to reach all of the people in England, even before economic transformation began, and of the positive dechristianization of France in the eighteenth century. But evidently in such a place as this, where a faithful, energetic, able steward of souls gave up his whole life to the pastoral vocation, the traditional faith could be all-encompassing even in England in Restoration times.[12]

The persisting power of the Anglican Church over the inhabitants of this rural parish is another lucky circumstance for the sociological and demographic historian. For with neither Roman Catholics nor dissenters to worry about we can be the more confident that pretty well every inhabitant had his child baptized by the rector, was married in church and buried in the churchyard, so that the totals of baptisms, marriages and burials entered yearly in the *Rector's book* can be relied upon. Even then Sampson tells us of two persons who apparently escaped registration at birth, one a child baptized privately who died before his name was entered and another an adult seeking baptism who had been brought up a dissenter. Some of his parishioners may have gone elsewhere for these purposes, of course, and there are signs in the evidence that this

[10] Ibid. pp. 14–18.

[11] Ibid. pp. 18–19. Sampson actually reported to York 'under 400' as the population, but examination shows that seven names were overlooked at first, including the parson's own household. They were added later, presumably after he had sent his answers. Easter communicants rose to the notable figure of 212 in 1677, but they went down in the 1680s and 90s; during the last five years of Sampson's ministry the number was steady at 125.

[12] See Laslett 1965 (1971 ed. 75–6), and for France (where the eighteenth century is said to have been a century of 'dechristianization'), e.g. Bouchard 1972.

was so. But we can hope that they were counterbalanced by exactly similar persons coming in to the village, and these details must not be allowed to draw attention away from the outstanding importance of this list of all the men, women and children alive in the village of Clayworth in the month of April 1676. At the present time it must undoubtedly be regarded as one of the best and best-authenticated early censuses of an English community. The purpose of the Clayworth census is known: the collection for Northampton, which was quite unlikely to lead to evasion. It was drawn up by men who knew the parish intimately, by the church-wardens, in fact, who happened that year to be two of the most substantial men in the village, Thomas Dickonson and Christopher Johnson, gentlemen. It was compiled neither by sitting at a desk and counting heads, nor by attempting to assemble the people, nor by asking them to report themselves, all of which ways of taking a census are likely to lead to omission, but by house-to-house enquiry, the most reliable method. Above all it was written down at the time and on the spot, except, it seems, for one afterthought, by an exact and experienced man, precise in business of this sort. Until he came to live at Clayworth, William Sampson had been President of Pembroke College, Cambridge, in charge of accounts and estates. In 1693 he was actually elected into the mastership, but he declined to serve.

Though of peasant stock from the neighbouring village of South Leverton, he was the brother of an eminent dissenting minister turned medical doctor and related by marriage to Nehemiah Grew, F.R.S., the botanist.[13] The rector of Clayworth undoubtedly belonged with the high intelligentsia of that great age of scientific and social enquiry, and it would be tempting to see in his statistical interest in his parishioners something of the attitude which was giving birth to demography in the work of Graunt, Petty and King.[14]

But this can only be presumption. What is quite certain is that in the document which he left behind him from the year 1676 he gives to the historical sociologist something like certain ground, as certain as is ever likely to be found in Stuart England. What is even more remarkable is the fact that exactly twelve years later he wrote out the names of his parishioners all over again. We can be confident of who was living at Clayworth for two separate years, 1676 and 1688, and therefore we can compare the community over time.

[13] See *Dictionary of National Biography* as corrected by E. S. de Beer, in the *Bulletin of the Institute of Historical Research* (1943, pub. 1947), pp. 47–8.

[14] On these authors in relation to the early English scientific movement, see Laslett, Introduction to a reprint of works by Graunt and King, together with one of King's manuscripts containing amongst other things workings for his famous *Scheme* of English social structure in 1688 (1973).

Unfortunately we cannot be quite so confident that on this second occasion the numbering was as accurate as it was on the first. All Sampson tells us about it under the year 1688 is: 'About May-Day I took the names of the Inhabitants of this my parish of Clayworth, and placing them according to the Order of Houses and Families, down the North side of the Town, and up the South-Side, and lastly those of Wyeston.'[15]

The purpose of this second numeration, then, is known by assumption only, that it was to satisfy the interest of the rector in having a precise list of his parishioners; we have to assume also that he himself did the compiling, and take the hint provided in the passage just quoted that it was by house-to-house survey. But Sampson himself wrote out the document, and by 1688 he is so securely established as a reliable recorder, and he so clearly knows his parish like the back of his hand, that there must be a very strong presumption in favour of the quality of this list being as high as that of 1676. It is even more detailed in its descriptions of the households and their members, down to the particulars of the number of times individuals had been married.

It has to be added, alas, that on neither occasion did he think to record the ages of his people. Nevertheless it has been found possible to analyse the household and family life of the village, together with the structure of the community, in sixteen different ways from these two documents alone.

It is difficult to exaggerate the value of lists of inhabitants to the sociological historian. Even the bare copying out of names can tell him a great deal, if he treats the evidence imaginatively; a mere string of household heads yields something, especially if the number in each household is given.[16] The results for Clayworth in 1676 and Clayworth in 1688 are set out in the tabular analysis to be found in the fourth and final section of this chapter. The outstanding feature of these tables, of course, apart from the consistent presence of information which is so often either lacking or irregularly stated in so many similar English exercises, is that they portray the same society twice, with half a generation between the two delineations.

Sampson himself could hardly have anticipated that such an elaborate exercise would be carried out by posterity on his recordings. But he was aware of some of the points of social interest in the listing of 1688, and remarks on the number of previous spouses who were reported to him in that year. Remarriage had been particularly common amongst

---

[15] The list follows on pp. 84–7 of the *Rector's book*. Wiseton is a second settlement in the parish of Clayworth, an independent manor.

[16] The principles used in analysing such lists, and the documentary criteria, are set out in Laslett 1966. These principles have since been extended in some points and modified in others; some of them have proved too exacting to be followed.

the inhabitants of the hamlet of Wiseton. When we reconstruct from the information he gives us the marital state, as it might be called, of the whole of this English community in the year of the Glorious Revolution the result is astonishing. No fewer than 26 — 39% — of the 67 couples then living in the village included one partner or more who had been previously married, and two of the widowed had had more than one spouse, which makes 28. Of these marriages 13 were second marriages, 3 were third marriages, 4 were fourth marriages and 1 a fifth marriage; the number is not given for the 7 others. We have discovered from other sources that up to one-third of all marriages in Stuart England were second or later marriages for at least one of the partners, but this is the only opportunity we have found for examining the effect of this on a village society, perhaps the only one we shall ever have.[17]

The marital history of the men and women of Clayworth can be illustrated by the varied experience of John Brason, who in 1676 was a servant and of course a bachelor. He married in that year, and his wife died in 1681. He married for a second time five months later and lost this wife in 1683, shortly after her child was born. We do not know when he married his third wife, but we do know that by 1688, when he cannot have been much more than forty years old, he was established as the village butcher and living with his fourth wife. In this final year he had no child of his own; the only one in his family was a son of his wife's by a former husband, one of the orphans of his parish. Because they are so exceptionally well described, the orphans of Clayworth in 1676 and in 1688 form an important part of the evidence on which our study of orphanage in traditional England is based, as will be seen in chapter 4.

Perhaps it may seem a little arbitrary to have begun our consideration of the significance for social structure of this extremely rare double census by picking out such an unexpected set of figures as those on remarriage. Amongst the more ordinary items of information, Sampson tells us that there were eight empty houses in the village in 1688, which is interesting from several points of view, particularly that of the living space of the people and its effect on the constitution of the household. There was evidently no pressure on accommodation, and the households in this village were a little undersized, especially in 1676, as compared with what has become known of households elsewhere in England in the seventeenth and eighteenth centuries. They were smallish both in

[17] See Laslett 1965 (1971 ed.: 103 and note on 289). It is not uncommon in listings of inhabitants for the fact of remarriage to be mentioned, but in 1975 we had so far discovered no other where the actual number of the current marriage is recorded for each candidate. Baker 1973: 37 gives a partial analysis for Cardington, Bedfordshire, in 1782, also revealing surprisingly large numbers of remarriages.

their average size and in their range: no really big domestic group was present in either year, and the occasional outsized household we have found to be typical of England in traditional times is lacking in Clayworth. Nevertheless, there are places now known to us where households were on a more modest scale. In this matter, as in almost every other which the sociological historian can now discuss with some confidence, Clayworth seems to have been a very ordinary village.[18]

It can easily be shown from Clayworth and from all the other evidence that a considerable part of the population at that time was not living in small households at all, but in large ones, in groups consisting of six persons and above. In general over half the population was in this position, and in Clayworth this figure was nearly 35% in 1676, 45% in 1688. It can be shown also that there were very few persons living outside families, living alone, that is to say, or in institutions. This is a point which is raised by an interesting difference between Clayworth in 1676 and Clayworth in 1688.

In 1676 all households at Clayworth were also families, though six of them consisted of solitary persons, two widows, two widowers, and two spinsters. By the later date something which might possibly be called an institution of the only type which was then at all common had come into existence for the poor and solitary: they could now live 'in the common-Houses on Alms', and nine of them were doing so.[19] A Joan Bacon and her daughter Anne were amongst them.

Now in 1676 Francis Bacon, cooper (or barrel-maker), his wife Joan, and their children Nicholas, Anne and Francis had been an independent

---

[18] See tables 2.8 and 2.9 of section IV below. Comparison between the figures for the distribution of households by size and those for 45 English communities at varying dates between 1650 and 1749 shows that in both 1676 and 1688 there was at Clayworth a shortfall of households sized six and above and an excess of those sized one to three. For subsequent work on household size, and for its limitations as an indicator of social behaviour, see Laslett 1972a. When this essay was first written (1961–2), figures of household sizes were very scarce, and in the original text it was erroneously stated that in the seventeenth century mean household size was smaller in English communities than it subsequently became in the eighteenth and nineteenth centuries. In fact it seems to have been constant at about 4.75 persons per household over the whole period (see Laslett 1972b).

[19] *Rector's book*, 86. No mention of the foundation of the common-houses, whatever they were, is found in the Towne-Booke or in the *Rector's book*, which shows that Sampson's recordings should not be accepted as exhaustive. These houses contained three widows, all of whom had been wives of householders with children in 1676, and two of whom still had children with them; a married couple, also ex-householders, and a spinster, not present in 1676. All are disregarded by Sampson in his totals for families, and omitted here in calculations of the size and characteristics of households. In the general sample of 100 English pre-industrial communities, very few people indeed are shown as living in institutions, but the data are hardly impressive.

household. So indeed was the family of Nicholas Bacon, cooper, the son, in 1688: himself, his wife Elizabeth whom he had married in 1686 after his father died, and two children by her former husband. Apparently Nicholas, the son, had turned out his mother, Joan, and his sister, Anne, when he became head of the household, not willing or not able to give them shelter or sustenance. There they were, two years after his marriage, paupers in the parish institution for the poor.[20]

This example serves to illustrate some of the principles which governed social and domestic relations, the principle that households did not ordinarily contain more generations than two, that living with in-laws or relatives was on the whole not to be expected and that orphans were normally the only persons who often found themselves living with relations. Most important is the rule that it was quite unusual to find two married couples within the same family group. These somewhat unexpected features of family life in traditional England can be clearly seen in the figures of tables 2.12, 2.20 and 2.21 below, where few resident relatives are recorded, and many households are marked as simple in structure and shallow in generation depth. There was one complicated living group in 1688 headed by Elizabeth Wright, widow, dwelling in the hamlet of Wiseton with her sister, her son and another son who was married and had his wife and two children with him: this is the only household in either year which has to be classed as 'multiple' by the criteria used in our table 2.21, and it included a servant as well. It is not uninteresting that the head of this household was evidently an elderly widow, as we shall see when we come to consider the position of the aged in chapter 5.

No household at all at Clayworth in either year contained two married couples, either a married son or daughter living with parents, or married brothers or sisters living together, or a married couple living in service with another married couple. Far and away the most usual household, 50—60% in both years, was the household we are now accustomed to — man, wife and children — but with the interesting addition in one household out of three of resident servants. Of those not headed by a married couple, most had widows in charge and a sprinkling had widowers. This brought up the total of what are now usually called 'nuclear families' to about 80% — perhaps a little high, for the average in traditional England was nearer 72%. Only 8 out of the combined total of 189 households were headed by unmarried people, and 2, or

[20] For a few further facts about the Bacons and their relatives, see Laslett 1965 (1971 ed.: 98—9). Baker 1973 also reports instances of close relatives of established householders living in the village work-house at Cardington in 1782. For the significance of this evidence on the fate of the old in relation to their families, see chapter 5 below.

at most 3, had persons in them who could possibly be described as lodgers.[21]

These details may seem wearisome: they certainly cannot be said to belong to traditional historical enquiry. But the precise study of the situation at Clayworth in these two years and comparison with what can be more inexactly known from the other communities we can now examine makes it possible to put forward a general thesis about the structure of English society in Stuart times, and in earlier times as well. It suggests that the nuclear independent family, that is, man, wife and children living apart from relatives, was the accepted familial unit. It suggests, therefore, that the more generally accepted impression that the independent nuclear family (now given the name *simple family household*) came into existence with industrialization is not in fact justifiable for England.[22] Households of one or two unmarried persons living on their own, childless households, are nevertheless very much more common in our country now than they were then. The one really telling difference between the family in Stuart England and the family which we know in our own time is, as we have already hinted, that servants were then counted as belonging to it.

Servants, in the language of that day, the language we shall use here, covered men and women, boys and girls, working for their livings at every agricultural, commercial and industrial task, as well as the personal domestics which our own parents or grandparents once employed. Apprentices, journeymen (when living with their masters, as often they did), 'hinds', 'maidens' or 'maids' are some of the titles they were given, though the word 'servant' was the most often used, and was pretty well universal for the girls and the women. This description must be sharply distinguished from that of 'labourer' or 'agricultural labourer'.

There was often little difference in the work which a labourer and a male servant performed, though a labourer would usually have greater experience and often a specific skill, like hedge-cutting or 'plashing': it is in their roles as persons that they are to be contrasted with each other. Service, living and working with a master and mistress, was a stage in the life cycle through which something like a tenth or more of the whole population of traditional England was passing at any one time, the stage between leaving home and getting married. This was true of both sexes. Labourer was one of the occupations which men took up after marriage, for humble people by far the commonest; the women, of course, had only

---

[21] Compare tables 1.1, 1.2 and 1.5 above. It is possible that Clayworth had fewer lodgers than was usual.

[22] These original statements of 1963 were confirmed and elaborated in Laslett and Wall (eds.) 1972.

a single occupation open to them, to be wives. A labourer could not live with his master, even if he frequently occupied a cottage on his property, and he was not usually referred to as a servant.[23] There is therefore a crucial difference from the point of view of the family between servant and labourer, but it is quite common, nevertheless, even in the writing of historians who are very well informed on social distinctions and descriptions, to find such expressions as 'labourers who lived in'.

In 1676 there were 67 servants at Clayworth, in 1688 there were 65: first 16.7% and then 15.8% of the whole population.[24] But this must have been a forbidding village for servants, for their meagre wages were liable to tithe. A farthing in the shilling was due to the Church — about a fiftieth — and a servant usually only earned between 50 shillings (£2.50) and 100 shillings (£5) in a whole year.

The custom was dying when Sampson came, but he was not the man to let it drop. He frightened the servants so much that by 1679 he received £1.17s.5d (£1.87) from this source, out of a total receipt of nearly £250. Isabel or Elizabeth Bett died in 1677, and Thomas Bett, her son, a servant, came and paid 'fully for his wages at one farthing in the shilling. The occasion of his mother's death brought him to an honest mind.' But the rector had to proceed against the others in the spiritual courts, and even then he was told 'that all I could do was to excommunicate them, which was only their not going to Church etc.' So he actually took the case to the Exchequer Court in London; it became the bitterest 'controversy of note' recorded in his book. Not until the gentlemen in the vil-

---

[23] A married person could become a servant, provided spouse and children were left behind and residence was taken up with the master. Occasionally married couples, perhaps of higher status by birth and even sometimes related to the family, are found in gentle households, and it is possible to suspect that older, officially celibate, servants did have 'wives' or 'husbands' with whom cohabitation of some kind was going forward: one such case is observable in Clayworth itself. Moreover, the word 'servant' and the concept of service had other uses, and could sometimes denote married labourers and others in a context which ensured that they would not be confused with those to whom we have given the title 'life-cycle servants' in chapter 1. The expression 'out-servant' seems to have been intended for such persons, but unfortunately some expressions are ambiguous, such as 'servants in husbandry'. It is not clear, moreover, whether what we would call a day servant, who waited on one household during the day but slept at home, would have had the personal title 'servant' (sometimes given to such individuals in the nineteenth-century census returns) or indeed whether they existed at all in traditional times.
There has been a difference of view on these points. For an interpretation dissenting from the one favoured here, see C. B. Macpherson, *The political theory of possessive individualism* (Oxford, 1962), and especially his *Democratic theory* (Oxford, 1972), ch. 12, 'Servants and labourers in seventeenth-century England'. For other expositions of the present interpretation, see Laslett 1964, 1973 (esp. Introduction, n. 3), and Kussmaul-Cooper 1975.

[24] See tables 2.13 and 2.14, and compare tables 1.6 and 1.7 in the preceding chapter.

lage, fearful that they would find themselves unable to get servants, combined against the embattled rector did he give up this part of his tithe in return for other concessions.[25]

Servants were young people: at least they must be reckoned amongst those not old enough and lucky enough to find an opening to allow them to marry and become householders. But children, children not old enough to be described as sons or daughters, were the most numerous of the young. We have seen that 165 out of 401 people in Clayworth in 1676 were, in the opinion of their parish priest, too young to communicate, that is, under the age of 16. 'Children' were indeed a considerable proportion of the whole Clayworth community, as is shown in table 2.11. There were 154 in 1676, or 38.4% of the whole population, and 162 in 1688, or 39.3%. In 1676 73 out of the 98 households at Clayworth had children so described, and in 1688 76 out of 91, that is, three-quarters and more. The average number of children in those households which contained them was 2.11 and 2.13, though in both years a quarter of all children lived in sibling groups, as the psychologists say, of over three.[26]

This is almost as far as we can go in the pursuit of the historical study of the structure of society from the evidence provided in these successive listings. But nothing has been so far said about the distribution of land and wealth, or about the division by occupation, of these 400 people: how there were 21 freeholders at Clayworth in 1688, though 6 of them, the rector says, possessed less than £40 a year; how there were about 20 to 25 husbandmen, about the same number of labourers, 3 or 4 gentlemen, 3 or 4 weavers, 1 or 2 shepherds, blacksmiths and wrights; a butcher, a tailor, a cooper, a thacker (thatcher), a bricklayer, sometimes a shoemaker, a cutler, a spinner, a badger (corn-dealer), and still more callings amongst the heads of households — an astonishing variety, com-

[25] *Rector's book, passim,* esp. pp. 59–62. This is a rare record of servants acting as a body in self-defence. It implies, among other interesting things, that about £90 a year was spent on servants' wages in the village in the 1670s, some £1 3s per head per year. This is too low, even for young maidservants, but it seems that quite a high proportion of the wages paid were in fact tithed.

[26] These figures (see table 2.11) have been sharply revised, mostly upwards, from those published in 1963, when the definition of 'children' had not been finally decided. This definition, it must be noted, is irrespective of age, and the proportion of children is no direct measure of young persons, since it excludes servants. The 'English standard' (see Laslett 1972b: 148) for the proportion of children in the population is 42.6%, of households with children 74.6%, and of mean size of sibling group (or child group) 2.73. Clayworth, then, had slightly fewer children than might be expected, but distributed them fairly evenly between households. In general, it might be added, pre-industrial England, and perhaps pre-industrial Europe as a whole (with something like 40% of the population aged 0–19), probably had fewer dependent children in the population than the underdeveloped societies of our own day, just as they had more old people; see chapter 5 below.

mercial and industrial as well as agricultural, in one single village. In tables 2.16 and 2.17 it will be seen that the size and the structure of these households varied with the occupations they pursued and with their standing in the community.

The 18 separate occupations listed in table 2.15 for the village in 1676, and the 24 for 1688, mark a highly distinctive and crucially important feature of English society during the final interlude before industrialization began. A dozen or so of the 27 callings in the two lists could be called non-agricultural — commercial, even manufacturing, manufacturing perhaps for more than a local market. Only the United Provinces are so far known to have had as many — perhaps even more — craftsmen in the rural villages at that time. Elsewhere, in Southern and Eastern Europe, for example, lists of occupations in the countryside were much more restricted, except, significantly, in the countryside of Japan. Handicrafts in that country, however, seem to have been the bye-employments of farmers and land workers, rather than full-time avocations.[27]

We know the birth rate, marriage rate and death rate in Clayworth between 1676 and 1688: this is one of the important advantages of having its exact population and also a reliable register of baptisms, marriages and burials. Since the number of inhabitants at the beginning was 401 and at the end 412 it seems reasonable (though we shall find ourselves being cautious about this) to assume a steady total over the years of some 400. The number of baptisms was 190, the number of burials 197 and the number of marriages 35 over the relevant period, 1 May 1676 to 30 April 1688, so that the birth (baptismal) rate can be reckoned at 39.8 per thousand, the marriage rate at 6.9 and the death (burial) rate at 40.6.

Now these are crude rates, so crude and so likely to mislead that demographers no longer use them very much, although this is still the ordinary way of expressing the liability of a community to produce children, to marry and to die. The numbers in this case are so small that considerable variation can be expected from year to year, and the figures as a whole over so short a period could be unrepresentative even of settled trends in Clayworth itself.

Nevertheless, it must be said that the birth rate at Clayworth was obviously very high indeed as compared with what it is now in England and Wales, and the death rate even higher; the marriage rate was much the same. The birth rate reached 35 over the whole country at the height

[27] Compare Laslett 1975, and for Holland, see the very interesting article of H. K. Roessingh ('Village and hamlet in . . . the Netherlands in the middle of the 18th century', *Acta Historiae Neerlandica IV* (1970): 105—29), and for Japan, T. C. Smith, 'Farm family by-employments in pre-industrial Japan', *Journal of Economic History* 29, 4 (1969): 687—715.

of Victorian fertility, but the death rate was in the 20s; nowadays they vary between 12 and 17.

Another striking feature of vital statistics in the village is that there were more deaths than births at the time which concerns us. Moreover, we now know that there were areas of England with surpluses of burials over births and that the whole country was experiencing a halt in population growth, possibly even some tendency for the population to fall, when parson Sampson was writing out his facts and figures so painstakingly in the 1670s, 80s and 90s.[28]

II. Turnover of population in Clayworth and Cogenhoe

One of the comments made by Sampson in his list of his parish for 1688 states 'that the parish is encreased since the number was taken before (twelve years agone, vizt. 1676) − 10 souls' (11 on our reckoning). The phrase *natural increase* was not used, but Sampson seems to have had it in his mind; clearly he was not aware that burials had exceeded baptisms over the twelve years. The slight rise in population (if genuine) must have come from a net influx into the community of some 18, and we might expect that with such birth and death rates turnover of persons in Clayworth would have been high. But nothing previously known about settled, rural, traditional populations prepares us for the turnover figure which can be worked out by comparing the names of those present in 1676 with the names of those present in 1688. John Harrison has shown that 255 of the persons recorded in 1688 were new: they had not been there in 1676. This is a turnover rate of no less than 61.9%.

If we put it the other way round, we find that only 157 of the 401 persons living in the community in 1676 were still to be found in it in 1688: 244 of them had disappeared, that is, 60.8%. Now only ninety-two of these 244 who disappeared are recorded in the parish register as dying,

---

[28] This has become clear from the analysis of some 400 or 500 records of baptisms, marriages and burials over the years from the mid sixteenth to the early nineteenth century now being undertaken. The results will be contained in a forthcoming publication of the Cambridge Group. The late Professor J. D. Chambers, the acknowledged authority on the history of population in the English Midlands was not so confident that the later decades of the seventeenth century were marked by stagnation in the area where Clayworth was situated (see Chambers 1972: 24, 29−31, referring to his own earlier work of 1957). In Laslett, *The world we have lost* (1971 ed.: 132−4), Sampson's prices and his demographic recordings are used to work out a crude price index for comparison with infant mortality between 1680 and 1703. Chambers (1972: 90−1) reproduces these figures, but asserts emphatically that the mortality record for the village is not to be explained by dearth, since food was plentiful in the area at the time, but by contagious disease which did great damage in the middle of the 1680s. The figures of the parish register and Sampson's references to sickness on the whole bear out this statement.

so that all or practically all of the rest must have moved away. The start-ling fact is that a settled, rural, perfectly ordinary Stuart community could change its composition by well over half, getting on in fact for two-thirds, in a dozen years. So surprising is it that we do not yet know quite what to make of it.

The uniqueness of the Clayworth record leaves us without adequate means of appreciating its significance. No doubt as studies of this sort become established, comparable documents will be discovered, and work will be done on the question of how much turnover we might ex-pect to find under given conditions.[29] We are fortunate that the recogni-tion of the possibility of so much change of this kind has led almost at once to the recovery of a record which does do something to provide a context for the Clayworth evidence. Acting on a hint from Burn's *History of parish registers*[30] we found that the earliest of the register-books still preserved in the parish chest in the church of Cogenhoe, a village a few miles on the Bedford side of Northampton, contained no less than six listings of the inhabitants, family by family, and name by name, dating from the decade 1618—28, and less useful earlier listings, too. They were made by Christopher Spicer, rector of Cogenhoe during those years.[31]

One of the notable features of this extraordinary series of recordings is the variation in the totals of persons and households. This is evident from the full range of figures set out in table 2.1 below. Perhaps the pop-ulation of Clayworth went up and down in the same way, which would make our vital rates less convincing. At Cogenhoe, with an average of 5.2 baptisms, 2.0 marriages and 2.7 burials a year from 1611 to 1635, the registered crude birth (baptismal) rate was something between 26.0 and 35.0 per thousand, the crude marriage rate 10.0 to 13.3, and the crude death (burial) rate 13.5 to 18.0. Birth and death rates, then, were lower than at Clayworth, the death rate so much lower that it looks as if there may have been under-registration. But —and here is the critical

[29] No further set of documents of the same standard of accuracy had been found for England by 1977, and the analysis of Clayworth, along with Cogenhoe, has not been ex-actly replicated for any other community in our country — see section III below.

[30] 1862 ed.: 212, mentioning the Cogenhoe register immediately after describing the *Liber status animarum* as 'the one best answering the description', though the year of the list (*sic*) is given as 1640, and no list for that date is to be seen in the document.

[31] A documentary description of this record is of some importance to the exact study of turnover at Cogenhoe and is published in full in the original version; see Laslett 1963: 175—6. The original document is now in the Northamptonshire Record Office at Delapré Abbey. Unfortunately we have as yet been unable to find out anything further as to why or on what occasions Christopher Spicer compiled these listings. Susan Stewart did a great deal of painstaking work on these materials, and analysed the listings for Cogenhoe on the lines used in section IV for Clayworth. So much inference was found to be neces-sary, however, and so many of the cells in the tables were left empty because the figures were tiny that we have thought it best not to publish these analyses.

point of comparison with Clayworth — the turnover of population was of the same order in both villages. Of the 180 persons named at Cogenhoe in 1628, some 94 had appeared since 1618. The turnover at Clayworth in the twelve years from 1676 to 1688 was about 62%; at Cogenhoe in the ten years from 1618 to 1628 it was about 52%.

Rough as these Cogenhoe figures have to be — and even the interval of ten years could be up to six months out either way — they make one thing immediately obvious: the turnover of population we have discussed for Clayworth may not have been unusual for seventeenth-century England. Indeed, the comparison suggests that Clayworth was the less mobile of the two, and the evidence which we have surveyed since the village was first analysed in 1962 all points in this direction: that the people of Clayworth were somewhat more likely to stay put than English people generally in that era. These facts should surely persuade us to look very carefully at our assumptions about the settled immobility of persons in pre-industrial times. For this reason, and because after ten years and more the documents for these two parishes remain without companion anywhere else in our country in spite of a determined and continuing search, every recoverable detail of turnover at both places has been established as accurately as possible. The figures are set out in the final tables of section IV, numbered 2.22–2.24. The remainder of our discussion of turnover is necessarily for the most part a commentary on this set of figures.

We may observe to begin with that it might be easy to exaggerate the importance of the rate of *structural* change which these figures imply. A 60% turnover of persons in twelve years is after all only 5% of the whole population in a year, and we should probably overlook the replacement of one person in twenty every year in an organization which we belonged to, just as Sampson did at Clayworth. Most of the people moving, moreover, may not have moved very far, not in or out of Sampson's area of acquaintance. If we had recovered evidence from groups of neighbouring villages and not from single villages, much less turnover might have shown up.[32] A part of the turnover could perhaps have been due to

[32] The registers of neighbouring parishes are unfortunately too badly kept and preserved to throw much light on where these people moving in and out of Clayworth and Cogenhoe came from and went to. But some idea of the likely distance can be gained from the study of Cardington in 1782, where the origins and destinations of immigrants and emigrants are recorded. Nearly a half of heads of families and their wives resident in Cardington but not born there came from within 5 miles, and a quarter from over 15 miles away; of those born of Cardington families who had left for service and marriage elsewhere, 39% were living within 5 miles and 35% over 15 miles away (figures derived from Schofield 1970). Similar but less complete evidence from other English communities examined by Wall and others confirms the very local character of the movement, which is the same for marriage partners.

seasonal movement of persons in search of work, and so should not count as change of settlement.

Some of these considerations may finally make this turnover of persons seem less startling than it does on its first discovery. It seems doubtful, however, whether in these particular cases seasonal employment explains very much. The considerable variation in the demand for labour over the year in agriculture was undoubtedly one of the governing influences on the lives of our ancestors, and on the structure of their society. The number of people needed to work the land may have been three or four times as many in late summer as in midwinter, or even more. Important as this is, it cannot affect the Clayworth counts because each of them was taken well before harvest-time. Even in mid-August at Cogenhoe it is difficult to discern any sign of a temporary influx of labour. The migration we are examining seems to be of a different character.[33]

We may distinguish five different components of turnover of population: biological causes, birth and death; marriage; the movements of whole households or families; the entry and exit of servants; and individual migration of other types of person. In tables 2.22–2.24 these five classes have been roughly adhered to, but some arbitrary decisions have had to be made. This is because we cannot always tell whether or not individuals appeared and disappeared for one of our five reasons, or whether they did so on quite other grounds, including mere whim. A class of 'unaccounted for' has had to be left for some of the disappearing. We must recognize, then, as we go through them, that our categories are rather uncertain in composition, particularly the last, and that this affects all numerical discussion.

First, change due to birth and death. The figures in the table show that it was easily the most important element in turnover in both these communities, accounting for something like two-fifths of the whole. When known deaths, in the form of burials registered by Sampson, and known births, registered baptisms, are subtracted from the numbers of disappearing and appearing names, turnover proportions fall from 60.8% exits to 37.9% and from 61.8% entries to 39.6% at Clayworth. At Cogenhoe the change is from 53.5% exits to 44.9% and from 52.2% entries to 36.1%. It is clear that in some of the individual yearly or two-yearly periods there, deaths, and especially births, could count quite noticeably as a component of change.

Births and deaths are not movements of persons. If our study was of

[33] No research known to me has yet been done on seasonal migration in England. It undoubtedly existed in the West Riding of Yorkshire in the 1640s. The dozen paragraphs which succeed at this point in the text are an insertion of 1975, incorporating work done on all the relevant archives since the original was composed. Some of the figures are corrections of what was first published, but most are novel.

migration alone, of the transfer of people from place to place, they would be irrelevant, and they have indeed been disregarded in later studies of this kind.[34] But our interest here is in the composition of the community, and in its continuity or discontinuity over time. Many funerals are of considerable importance to the structure of a local society, and some baptisms affect it, too.

It will be seen from the tables that 38 out of the 92 persons present in Clayworth in 1676 but dead by 1688 were household heads; in Cogenhoe the proportion between 1618 and 1628 was 8 out of 16. Now these deaths change the village. The status of household head was a qualification for holding office in the secular and ecclesiastical order of the locality, and in its social order, too. Even widowed women heading households were of weight, although they were usually excluded from official positions. Their deaths, as well as those of male householders, meant the passage of property, the breakup or the remodelling of households, changes in the membership of the directive group.

We can see these processes going forward in our two communities, and death cannot be left out of the analysis of turnover. Births were usually of much less significance, though events like the long-delayed arrival of an heir, or the development of a childless family into a large bevy of young siblings and their parents, do modify a community and the experience of its members. There are births and deaths, of course, of negligible import for the composition of a society, even if they deeply affect mothers and fathers, brothers and sisters; these are the baptisms and funerals of babies and of young children, which formed so large a part of fertility and mortality under the old order. The rector of Clayworth recorded, for example, the baptism on 9 March 1687 of Anne Maples, daughter of John Maples, husbandman, 'in the midst of her mother's funeral', for John's wife was buried on the same day. He married again within a year, but little Anne Maples died when she was fourteen months old. She appears in the parish register as buried on 3 May 1688, two days after Sampson's second listing in his *Rector's book*, where her name is clearly set down.

Her death does not enter into the reckoning of infantile mortality, which takes account only of those dying during the first twelve months of life. Nevertheless, infantile mortality was very heavy in Clayworth between 1676 and 1688, at about 300 per thousand children born, high even for a pre-industrial community at an unfavourable time. Most of these infants were present in the village neither in 1676 nor in 1688 and so do not figure on Sampson's lists: they appeared and disappeared all within a day or two, a week or two or a month or two at various times

---

[34] As for example by Blayo (see n. 43 below) and by Todd (see section III).

during the twelve years. Older people were also present in the village after 1676 and died there before 1688, and these deaths explain why the number of funerals in the parish register during the twelve years is more than twice the number of persons named in the listing of 1676 who had been buried by 1688. Although we are concerned with social continuity we have to confine ourselves for the most part at Clayworth to the beginning and the end; we lack the evidence to comment on what went on during the intervening years, in respect of biological change or of change of any other kind. We should be in a somewhat better position with Cogenhoe — and our tables do give figures at points intervening between 1618 and 1628 — if only the data there were not so coarse. But Emmanuel Todd has established that even a yearly census misses a great deal of change of the brief, intervening type. Though these considerations affect the biological component of turnover most obviously, they must be borne in mind when we turn to component two, marriage.

The conspicuous fact about the movement of persons in and out of these two villages as marriage partners is how very small a part it played in total turnover or in total migration. Considering that much historical study of migration has made use of marriage figures as representing such movement as a whole, this fact is of some general importance both demographically and sociologically. The proportion of inward movement due to marriage is much more realistic than the proportion of outward movement, because those who left the village to marry passed out of the record. Table 2.22 shows that only some 7% of appearances in Clayworth are known to have been due to marriage. In this village the 18 people who married in brought no less than 16 children with them, children of their former unions. The movement of these individuals must also be counted as due to marriage, and perhaps the movement of one or two servants, too; but if we look exclusively at marriage partners as such, we find that their arrival made up only 11.0% of all inward movement, that is, of arrivals less those baptized. The proportion is even lower at Cogenhoe, probably under 5% of known immigration.

Not all of the weddings of immigrants appear in the registers of the two villages, nor did all the weddings in those churches represent additions to the populations. This is because some people chose spouses from within Clayworth or Cogenhoe, and because marriages usually took place in the parish of the bride when she lived elsewhere. However, the introduction of new wives into village society can be recovered by observing their presence in that role in later lists of inhabitants. It is difficult to see how any immigrating marriage partners can have escaped us, therefore, and the small portion of change arising from this process must be regarded as the most reliable inference as to turnover from our documents.

Surprising as this may be, the part played in turnover by the third of our components, the circulation of whole families or households,[35] is perhaps more surprising. The tables show that movement of persons in this way, when the head of the household decided to take up or relinquish a holding in land, or a job, or a practice as a craftsman, made up over 20% of all the appearances in Clayworth, rather less of the disappearances. If baptisms and burials are disregarded, the proportions are about 35% in each case. We can reckon, then, that movement of whole families or households made up a good third of all movement of persons, so that change of residence after marriage had a palpably greater effect on the society of this village than movement at marriage. It will be noticed, indeed, that the actual turnover in family units in Clayworth during the twelve years — the larger part of which must have been due to migration rather than to births and deaths — was actually higher than the turnover of the population as a whole if fertility and mortality are disregarded. The same is true of household turnover at Cogenhoe.

The interpretation of turnover figures is confusing and demanding, and we shall have to satisfy ourselves with a salient fact or two. Between 1618 and 1620, as will be seen, 5 of the 33 households moved out of the village of Cogenhoe, taking some 34 persons with them, and reducing the population by 18%, since they were not replaced at the time. This must have meant a considerable change in the social structure, for the household at the manor was one of those which vanished, leaving the place unoccupied apparently for the five following years. In the 1623 list, however, the manor was inhabited again; a big family with servants had come in from outside. These people were themselves replaced by 1628: three different families in the great house within a decade, a change-about which hardly accords with the reputation of English landed families for continuity in their ancestral seats.

The perambulation from settlement to settlement of such large familial groups recalls what has been discovered in eighteenth-century Tuscany, where extended and even multiple families of humble sharecroppers moved about in a similar way.[36] But the circulation of smaller

[35] At Clayworth this is reckoned in families (conjugal family units as defined in Laslett 1972a), and in Cogenhoe, where servants can be seen to accompany the families of their masters as they arrive or depart, in households. This distinction is of importance in only a few cases because in most, conjugal family unit and household were identical.

[36] See Todd 1974. Corsini, in his study of 1974, *Pour connaître la population de la Toscane aux XVIIᵉ, XVIIIᵉ et XIXᵉ siècles* (University of Florence, Statistics Department), finds that sharecroppers in this area resided for very varying periods in the same parish, from a median as low as four years at Chianti to a median as high as fourteen at Fiesole in the eighteenth century (p. 32, table 8). The parish in Tuscany was a much larger area than that of Clayworth or Cogenhoe and contained numbers of settlements: movement of households from residence to residence in the same parish could be quite marked (see his table 7). Comparable estimates for family residence periods are not available from English evidence.

households, of modest husbandmen and labourers, seems to have just outweighed that of the big ones at Cogenhoe, and to have made up most of the movement of this type at Clayworth. Here the fragmentary nature of the information on both places and the want of other English cases for comparison begin to exasperate the observer. We can see that Clayworth households were less mobile than those at Cogenhoe; we can guess that a reason was that the manor house in the second village was let at lease. But we do not know which was the more typical, and we perhaps shall never know how frequently responsible householders wended their way across the English countryside, with their furniture piled up on the ox carts or let down into the river barges, and their personal possessions strapped to their backs, walking, as many of them must have had to do, with their children trotting along beside them.

We do know, however, that they were outnumbered as travellers by servants moving from job to job, and that the fourth of our components of turnover comprised the most mobile members of the village population. Even if these individuals do not always seem to have accounted for as much turnover as the classes we have so far considered, servants shifted more often than anyone else.

Quite a substantial part of this section of the population could, in fact, be replaced within a single year, and after a decade scarcely a servant name was the same. Anne Bingham was the solitary servant in Clayworth in 1688 who had been there in 1676, and she had changed her place. The other 66 had either ceased to be servants, or left the village, or both. Only Elizabeth Stocking of the 26 servants at Cogenhoe in 1628 had been amongst the 28 present there in 1618: even she had been out of the village in 1621 and had changed households between 1624 and 1628. Our information about servants and their movements appears to be fairly complete in five selected years for this tiny settlement; and individual changes of servants have been painstakingly worked out household by household from these difficult documents by Susan Stewart.

These close details make it plain that servants must not be regarded as permanent members of the households where they worked, even if some of them stayed so long that they became the family retainers of literature and sentiment. Towards the end of summer every year, master and mistress, manservant and maidservant, all had to decide whether to go on with the engagement for a further twelve months. Officially, indeed, a quarter's notice was required, that is at midsummer, but this regulation seems not to have meant a great deal. In half the cases, or perhaps rather less, the servant would stay for the succeeding year, and in the others he or she would leave. Most of these would seek another place, and the purpose of the statute fairs or mops which came on at Michaelmas-time was to provide a public market for the purpose. In the

North the day was November 11th, St Martin's Day or Martinmas, and the autumn was certainly a time of general turnaround amongst the community of employers and employed all over the country.[37]

The fragmentary but revealing documents from Cogenhoe can be used to establish something in the way of an estimate of how long servants stayed. Taking the proportion leaving at the end of each year to be a half, it can be estimated that the average length of service in this village was nearly three years, perhaps about two and three-quarters. This figure is misleading in some ways, because it is evident that whereas most servants moved often, probably every year, some servants moved seldom, and the longer they stayed the longer they were likely to stay. Servants in London seem to have stayed longer than those we analyse here, and length of stay may have been quite variable from place to place.

These particulars are enough to establish the fact that the entrances and exits of servants to and from households were not all moves from parish to parish. Nevertheless, changes within the community were few in comparison with exchanges involving other communities. Mrs Stewart has shown that 90% of the known shifts of place by the servants of Cogenhoe, 150 out of the total of 165 she has been able to recover for these few years, went across the boundary of the parish. Sometimes a servant would return to Cogenhoe after a year or two of absence, presumably in a household in another village. Sometimes he or she would go home for a time to his or her own family in the locality. But such movement could not have been to a village very far away, for, as we have said, transition was local and ties to home appear to have been strong. It seems to have been mostly the younger boys and girls who moved between their homes and their situations in the village; older servants could go far.[38]

---

[37] Ann Kussmaul-Cooper finds that the autumnal move was very widespread indeed, even for servants who arrived at other times, and that it was rare for engagements to last for less than one or a complete number of full years; the function of the annual fairs or statutes was more complex than on-the-spot engagements of persons previously unknown. Her study is based on a series of revealing documents, some of them from these fairs, and takes the study of mobility and its rationale further than is attempted here. Of the 101 servant names appearing on the Cogenhoe lists between 1615 and 1628, 74 are found on one only, 22 on two, 4 on three and 1, Elizabeth Stocking, on five. If all the lists had been physically complete, and if we had them for the intervening years, many more names would be known for the thirteen-year interlude, and many more servant moves. Only 3 of the 101 names also appear in the Cogenhoe parish register between 1615 and 1628, 2 as marrying, 1 as being buried.

[38] See Schofield 1970, for movement over long distances, particularly to London. He finds that if servants went there, they sometimes came back to the area of their birth, if not to the actual village, when they married; this was particularly true of the women.

The appearances, disappearances and reappearances of servants in Cogenhoe, going on as they did year after year throughout the brief interval during which we know the households in the village really well, remind us again that the change which can be seen to have occurred after a decade or so gives us no conception of what went on in between. There remain, moreover, changeovers in names about which we know nothing other than that the names appeared or disappeared: this is the fifth and final component in turnover. Much of the movement seems to have been of children leaving home for a while and coming back, perhaps more than once in the period we can observe. Some persons in this class were probably dependent relatives, some wandering paupers, some singletons of solitary habits. We should not expect to be able to get to know why every individual change of place occurred so long ago in a situation so strange to us, nor to distinguish classes of turnover exactly one from another. But it is this residual category of apparently arbitrary change of abode by individual people which contrasts most sharply per-haps with our expectations of a settled, agrarian, familial society, with only elementary means of communication, highly localized market relations and above all a profound attachment to a particular place.[39]

We must not ourselves end by exaggerating this phenomenon of turn-over in the population of our two villages. We could if we wished go on to show that in spite of sudden change of the kind we have described, and of the more gradual change which came about through the succes-sion of son to father, kinsman to kinsman, the impression of permanence given by the households which composed a Stuart community is easy to understand. It may be, as our table shows, that a half of the heads of households had changed after twelve years at Clayworth, and after ten years at Cogenhoe. Nevertheless, most of their successors presided over units of persons which were recognizably the same. Although so many whole households came and went, and although these households were sometimes so large and important at Cogenhoe, it is still true that over three-quarters of them did survive, even in that small settlement, appar-ently so vulnerable to shifts of residence by its substantial people. There they were after ten years of coming and going, with a membership often extensively revised, but still the same households, inhabiting the same buildings, working the same fields.

In Clayworth, and in most other places as well, landholders were usually more static than at Cogenhoe, especially the yeomen, the free-holders, the husbandmen in a bigger way of farming. In trying to work out how the tendency to move differed from status to status and calling to calling, what impresses the observer is continuity in the number of

---

[39] At this point the text of 1963 resumes; see n. 33 above.

husbandmen and the number of labourers, and continuity in the list of craftsmen and shopkeepers to be found in the village. When one man got old, or went to the bad and gave up or died, he was replaced, so that there tended always to be a cooper at Clayworth, or two or three tailors, a butcher, and a blacksmith. In spite of the new faces and the vanished personalities, those who returned to the village after an absence can have had no doubt that it was the same place, the same ongoing society. The system, that familial, patriarchal system which dominated and gave structure to pre-industrial society, had succeeded in maintaining permanence in the face of the shortness of life, the fluctuations of prosperity, the falling in of leases, the wayward habits of young folk in service and the fickleness of their employers.

The faithful servant who loved and was loved, who stayed in the household as part of the family year in, year out, for the whole of a working life, is not entirely a sentimental fiction and can sometimes be observed outside the pages of the imaginative writers of the time. On one of the flagstones in the remote little parish church of Nynehead in Somerset is cut the following inscription:

> 'Here lyeth the body of Eleanor Pike, spinster, who departed this life April 8th 1722, aged 72, having lived a true and faithful servant above 50 years with Edw. and Jepp Clarke of Chipley Esq. to whose memory this stone was placed by Mrs. Anne Sanford, widow, one of the daughters of the said Edw. Clarke Esq.   May 18 1722'

This is the only memorial to a servant from an employer which I have seen in an English church, and leafing through Sampson's *Rector's book* it is obvious how exceptional it was for a mere servant to be buried inside the sacred building rather than in the churchyard. Eleanor Pike must have had the respect of the Clarkes and the Sanfords, a respect due to her both because she was who she was and because she had been in her place for so long.

The institutions of the old world should be looked upon in this way, as expedients to provide permanence in an environment which was all too impermanent and insecure. The respect due to the old and experienced, the reverence for the Church and its immense, impersonal antiquity, the spontaneous feeling that it was the family which gave a meaning to life because the family could and must endure, all these things helped to reconcile our ancestors to relentless, remorseless mortality, and mischance. But they need not deceive the historian into supposing that the fixed and the ancient were the only reality; an unchanging, unchangeable social structure may well be essential to a swiftly changing population.

III. A comparison with eighteenth-century France

In the year 1641 the Bishop of St Omer issued a particularly stringent set of directions to all the clergy in his diocese about the preparation each Easter of a *Liber status animarum* in every parish. This ordinance was published again in 1727,[40] but it does not seem to have given rise to any large number of surviving sets of such documents for the villages in this region of north-western France, which stretches inland from Calais and Boulogne to Arras.

At the very end of the *ancien régime*, however, between the years 1761 and 1790, two conscientious *curés de village* did carry out the orders to the letter, one of them annually for a span of sixteen years in the parish of Hallines and the other on thirteen successive annual occasions in the parish of Longuenesse. They must have resembled our two English parsons, William Sampson and Christopher Spicer, of the preceding century, faithful parochial clergy in that rather different world of clerical celibacy and the Roman rite. The rural society in which they worked, we now believe, was organized in a very similar way to the English, so much so that Longuenesse has been described as more English than an English village, at least in its family structure.

There were differences, however, in the way the two French parsons went about their work of recording. First there is the alien language which they used — or so it must appear to the English reader. The gentleman, the yeoman, the innkeeper, the labourer and the blacksmith are scarcely recognizable in the *seigneur*, the *laboureur*, the *cabaratuer*, the *journalier* and the *maréchal ferrant* of Hallines and Longuenesse. The second contrast is in the much superior tradition of registering the facts about persons which distinguished this part of France not only from our own country but from many other French regions, too.

The bishop's book of 1727 gave an example to show how men and women, households and families should be written down: every individual and every unit should be numbered, ages had to be supplied — a capital difference, this, from the listings we have been discussing — relationship to head of household specified for each person, and so on. At Hallines in the 1760s and 1770s most of this was carried out regularly once a year and brought into being a repetitive record of greater utility in studying turnover of population than any that we have found in the English language. There were defects, unfortunately, in the Hallines documents, relationships or ages omitted, especially for servants, or household spaces left blank. But in Longuenesse the job was done

---

[40] See *Rituale ecclesiae Audomarensis, una cum necessariis instructionibus, ab Francisco de Valvelle de Tourbes, Episcopi Audomarensis*, St Omer, 1727; copy in the Archives Départementales at Arras.

Eastertide after Eastertide in the 1770s and 1780s with a zeal unmatched in any record of this kind that I have so far seen. He was still at it in 1790, this perfectionist priest, when the Revolution overtook the Diocese of St Omer and the Church of France, and swept the ecclesiastical documents of the parishes of Hallines and of Longuenesse into the possession of the French State. There they remain, now in care of the archive office of the *département* of the Pas-de-Calais at Arras, along with a set of materials of other kinds relating to the parishes which can only fill the English visitor with admiration and with envy.[41]

Longuenesse is a few miles south-west of the town of St Omer, and Hallines a little further away in the same direction. They are not exactly neighbouring villages, therefore, but must have been very similar in their surroundings and in their economy. The list of population totals over the years of the listings for both these parishes and for Clayworth and Cogenhoe at the times in question (table 2.1) shows that they were all of the same order of size, with Clayworth a little larger than Longuenesse and Hallines a little larger than Cogenhoe.[42] Nothing in the considerable body of information about the French parishes seems to indicate that they were different from other French communities in that region in the later eighteenth century, any more than the two English ones can be shown to be exceptional for our country a century and more earlier.

There is a pronounced tendency for the population to grow over the period concerned at Longuenesse, and to decline at Hallines, whereas no such thing seems to be in evidence for the English parishes. As for fluctuation from year to year, which is likely to be associated with turnover in population, this was not dissimilar at Cogenhoe and in the two French parishes, which may imply that change of this kind was indeed of the same order in the two countries. This effect was nevertheless sig-

[41] All sets of registers exist for these two parishes, and are of uniformly high quality; the families of Hallines have been reconstituted by Louis Henry and his associates at the Institut National d'Etudes Démographiques in Paris as part of the national sample of reconstitutions. M. Henry drew attention to the existence of the listings for Hallines, and M. Bougard, the archivist at Arras, announced the Longuenesse documents in 1964 (see P. Bougard and M. Reinhard, *Les sources de l'histoire démographique du Pas-de-Calais*, Paris). Tabular analysis along the lines pursued in section IV below for Clayworth was carried out by Valerie Smith on the Longuenesse listings of 1778 and 1790, and some tables were worked for Hallines as well; see a few of the results in ch. 1 above as well as in Laslett and Wall (eds.) 1972: 75–85. Mrs Smith was also responsible for most of the figures published here on the French listings.
[42] Longuenesse resembles Clayworth in being a multiple parish, but instead of two settlements it has three (Longuenesse itself, Ste Croix and Wisques). Todd in his analysis combines the first two and distinguishes them from the third, but we have regarded the population as a whole, just as in the case of Clayworth and Wiseton.

TABLE 2.1. *Population totals over time*

Clayworth 1676–88

Year	Population	Households	Mean size
1676 (April)	401	98	4.09
1688 (May)	412[b]	91	4.43

Cogenhoe 1616–28

Year	Population	Households	Mean size
1616	187	—	—
1618	185	33	5.61
1620 (30 May)	150	30	5.00
1621 (29 June)	154	31	4.97
1623	174	34	5.11
1624 (15 Aug.)	176	33	5.33
1628	180	33	5.45
Mean population	172		
Variance	184		
Standard deviation	13.56		
Coefficient of variation	7.89%		

Longuenesse 1778–90[a]

Year	Population	Households	Mean size
1778	333	66	5.04
1779	341	67	5.09
1780	349	67	5.21
1781	357	—	—
1782	357	—	—
1783	364	—	—
1784	359	64	5.61
1785	375	72	5.21
1786	378	—	—
1787	379	72	5.26
1788	375	73	5.14
1789	[380]	—	—
1790	386	75	5.15
Mean population	363		
Variance	130		
Standard deviation	11.39		
Coefficient of variation	3.14%		

Hallines 1761–76

Year	Population	Households	Mean size
1761	271	52	5.21
1762	237	53	4.47
1763	272	57	4.77
1764	255	54	4.72
1765	258	56	4.61
1766	254	51	4.98
1767	236	51	4.63
1768	242	51	4.75
1769	239	50	4.78
1770	238	51	4.67
1771	243	52	4.67
1772	236	53	4.45
1773	241	54	4.46
1774	247	56	4.41
1775	241	56	4.30
1776	228	52	4.38
Mean population	246		
Variance	104		
Standard deviation	10.20		
Coefficient of variation	4.14%		

[a] All lists made at Easter. [b] Total in households 403; 9 in 'common houses'.

nificantly larger at Cogenhoe and may not simply be an effect of its small size, which hints at greater movement in the English communities. Moreover, the series of figures as a whole suggests a general statement about pre-industrial populations like these. None of the measures recorded — total population, numbers of households, mean household size — should be taken to be an unvarying constant even over short periods of time.

The obvious way of comparing turnover between the two pairs of parishes, and of finding out whether it was of the same order in all four, is to look at the figures for Hallines and Longuenesse in exactly the same way as was done for Clayworth and Cogenhoe. A crude comparison of this kind is set out in Table 2.2, with the addition of figures for 'annual average' exit-with-emigration proportions and entrance-with-immigration proportions for each parish.[43] By exit we mean disappearance for all reasons, including death, and by emigration disappearance due to outward movement only; similarly with entrance and immigration.

TABLE 2.2.   *Crude turnover proportions by period and by year*

	Exit and emigration proportions (%)		Entrance and immigration proportions (%)	
	Whole period	Annual average	Whole period	Annual average
Clayworth 1676–88	Exit proportion 60.8	5.1	Entrance proportion 63.6	5.3
	Emigration proportion 40.1	3.3	Immigration proportion 39.3	3.3
Cogenhoe 1618–28	Exit proportion 52.0	5.2	Entrance proportion 53.0	5.3
	Emigration proportion 49.5	4.9	Immigration proportion 36.1	3.6
Hallines 1761–73	Exit proportion 45.2	3.8	Entrance proportion 51.3	4.3
	Emigration proportion 33.2	2.8	Immigration proportion 23.2	1.9
Longuenesse 1778–90	Exit proportion 45.1	3.8	Entrance proportion 36.3	3.0
	Emigration proportion 10.1	0.8	Immigration proportion 29.6	2.5

[43] The 'annual average' figure is simply the total change over the whole period (twelve complete years for all except Cogenhoe, where it is ten) divided by the number of years in the period. It does not represent the actual change in any one year. An effective and interesting method of analysing mobility (rather than turnover) using repetitive listings more frequent than those of Clayworth and with more reliable detail than those of Cogenhoe has been worked out by Yves Blayo (1970).

These figures show that overall turnover in our English villages in the seventeenth century was of the same order as that in the two French villages in the eighteenth century but make it clear that there was greater change in Northamptonshire and Nottinghamshire under the Stuarts than there was across the Channel under the later Bourbons. When the emigration and immigration figures alone are compared, much sharper contrasts between the French villages and the English villages show up, and the English levels are higher on all counts, especially those at Cogenhoe. Particularly interesting is the fact that the emigration proportion at Longuenesse could fall as low as 10% in the twelve years, which is only a quarter of that at Clayworth and a fifth of that at Cogenhoe. This is evidently an implication of the rise of population in Longuenesse over the twelve years: the village seems to have grown to a large extent because it retained its potential emigrants. At Hallines, on the other hand, the situation seems almost entirely reversed, with immigration the lowest of the four, and emigration nearly up to English levels.

We know so little, of course, about the range of variation in such things as these that it is not easy to judge the importance of the differences recorded in the table. It would seem reasonable to suppose that there was something in the employment situation and in the general workings of society in the French villages to account for their turnover levels being lower than those in England, but it has to be said that their fertility and mortality rates were also lower. People being born and dying can stimulate movement as well as change the constitution of the population. Death rates in both French parishes were 20–21 per thousand, markedly below the English death rates, and though the birth rate at Longuenesse at 37 per thousand approached that at Clayworth, that at Hallines was only about 20 per thousand.

Little would be gained by pressing our comparison of turnover in such crude terms very far, since the fine detail available for Hallines and Longuenesse makes possible more searching analysis, and shows up the ways in which our calculations for Clayworth and Cogenhoe, the only calculations open to us, may be misleading. Nevertheless, it is instructive to range the figures for one of the French parishes under some of the headings used in section IV in our turnover tables for English parishes. When this is done for Hallines, the results are as in table 2.3, the figures in brackets being those for Clayworth, 1676–88.

All particulars taken together seem to me to suggest that the reason why total turnover was decidedly higher in Clayworth than at Hallines cannot have been to any great extent due to higher rates of fertility or mortality: indeed, fewer arrivals at Clayworth are known to have been due to births than at Hallines. The important influences seem to have

TABLE 2.3. *Hallines and Clayworth: turnover for twelve years compared*

Hallines			(Clayworth proportion)
1761 pop. 271			
1773 241			
Number and proportion of names persisting	132		49% of original population (39%)
Number and proportion of names disappearing	139		51% of original population (61%)
Of which 139,	49	or	28% known to have died (38%)
	15	or	11% known to have left in 3 migrating households (18%)
	9	or	6% known to have left as marriage partners (2%)
	13	or	9% known to have left as servants (22%)
	53	or	38% unaccounted for or otherwise reckoned (20%)
Number and proportion of names appearing	109		45% of final population (62%)
Of which 109,	53	or	49% born (36%)
	33	or	30% arrived in 8 migrating households (23%)
	7	or	6% arrived as marriage partners (7%)
	8	or	7% arrived as servants (23%)
	8	or	7% unaccounted for or otherwise reckoned (11%)

Of heads of households in 1761, 23 or 45% persisted in 1773 (50%), and of the 29 disappearing 24 or 83% died (75%), and 3 or 12% (16%) migrated. Of heads of households in 1773, 31 or 53% had appeared since 1761 (45%), and of these 31, 15 or 54% had been present in 1761 (55%), though not as heads.

been in the circulation of whole households, and above all in the replacement rate of servants. In comparison with an entrance and exit proportion for whole households (i.e. proportion of all households which arrived or departed) over the twelve years of some 36% for Clayworth, the exit proportion for whole households at Hallines was about 6%, and the entrance proportion about 15%: at Longuenesse the exit proportion for households was about 15% and the entrance proportion about 19%. As for servants, it is a fact that there were many fewer at Hallines than in the other three parishes (5.5% and 3.5% at the two ends of the period),[44] and we shall see that in both French parishes they apparently stayed rather longer than they did in England. We may notice once more that even at the French levels of population change, marriage makes up only a small proportion of turnover.

We can make use of the much more accurate evidence from Longuenesse to illustrate in a preliminary way how much greater the sum of yearly changes in population turns out to be than the overall change which is reckoned when an initial year is compared with a final year and no account is taken of the intervening movement. Table 2.4 distinguishes the immigration rate from the entrance rate and the emigration rate from the exit rate. The percentage figures here (called rates) are proportions of people in the actual population of the parish at the count made at the beginning of the year concerned who moved, were born, married or died.

TABLE 2.4.   *Longuenesse 1778–90*

	Exit rate	Emigration rate	Entrance rate	Immigration rate
1778–79	4.2	3.9	6.2	4.7
1779–80	5.0	4.1	6.8	3.4
1780–81	4.3	4.3	4.8	4.2
1781–82	8.1	7.3	7.8	6.4
1782–83	5.6	4.8	8.2	4.9
1783–84	7.2	5.2	5.3	4.4
1784–85	6.1	4.4	10.4	7.4
1785–86	6.2	3.8	6.5	4.4
1786–87	8.2	7.6	7.1	4.7
1787–88	8.0	6.5	8.5	6.1
1788–89	3.2	1.9	5.2	3.9
1789–90	9.5	9.2	10.1	6.7

[44] Servants are a bit of a difficulty at Hallines, because they are rarely marked as such, and never for the year 1773. Nevertheless, the low level of servants in the village seems to be genuine.

If the overall exit proportion during the twelve years had been the sum of the 12 annual exit rates it would have amounted to over 75% of the initial population rather than 36%, and the entrance proportion to 87% instead of 45%. These figures demonstrate in full an effect which is visible for Cogenhoe in the broken and irregular figures of the table in section IV. They are a further and detailed illustration of the distinction between actual movement of persons and turnover of persons, a difference whose significance we can pursue no further in this context.[45]

A count of all the names appearing in the lists for the parish of Longuenesse between 1778 and 1790 comes to 620, which is three times the 206 names which persisted throughout the period. In a further exercise (table 2.5) devoted this time to the movement of persons and excluding births and deaths, the precise numbers coming and going for each year are given, distinguishing between servants and other persons.

The picture, then, of this French parish and of the English parishes which it seems to resemble so closely is of a community with a majority of settled persons, who change only because of births and deaths, and a minority of moving persons, who change so frequently that after a dozen years or so they come to several times the number of those who stayed put. Well over half of the transients were servants. Even more of the

TABLE 2.5. *Longuenesse, 1778–90 : emigrants and immigrants*

	Emigrants		Immigrants	
	Total	Of which servants	Total	Of which servants
1778–79	13	11	15	11
1779–80	15	8	12	10
1780–81	15	8	15	6
1781–82	26	11	23	15
1782–83	18	13	18	10
1783–84	19	12	16	8
1784–85	16	7	28	14
1785–86	14	9	17	10
1786–87	29	17	16	13
1787–88	25	15	23	15
1788–89	7	6	15	9
1789–90	35	17	26	13
Total	232	134 or 58%	224	134 or 60%

[45] See Todd 1975. Important as the distinction between migration and turnover is, it will be seen that the two proportions are quite close to one another at Longuenesse for most annual entries and exits, and once even identical.

emigration was due to servants than the Longuenesse particulars imply, because some of the leavers must have been on their way to enter service for the first time in households outside the village. The more we examine movements amongst populations of this character the more important does the part played by servants seem to become, although the example of Hallines, which cannot be analysed as closely as Longuenesse but where servants were certainly fewer, warns us not to exaggerate their role.

It is much more difficult to decide how long each individual actually remained in the parish even when as much has been recorded as at Longuenesse. This is because we have no way of telling how long the people there at the beginning of the recorded interlude had actually been in the place, or how long those there at the end would remain. We can, however, count the numbers of lists in which each name appears. When this is done for the Longuenesse documents, it turns out that 19% of the inhabitants were present on one list only, 6% on two lists, 7% on three lists, 6% on four, and so on. All the proportions come to 5% or less for those appearing from five times to twelve times. But it rises to 34%, 206 of the 620 names which are contained in the whole number recorded in the thirteen documents for 1778–1790, in the case of those who were present for the whole time during which the community can be examined.

If you came to a parish like this in the late eighteenth century, therefore, and perhaps to a seventeenth-century English parish as well, you were rather more likely to stay one year than other periods of time, though any interval up to five years was not improbable. If, on the other hand, you were born into the village you were very much more likely to stay there for the rest of your life than if you were an immigrant. We are now well aware that servants make up much of the migration, and the last of our tables in this section is the number of years for which each servant stayed at Longuenesse. We assume here, as we did at Cogenhoe, that each engagement lasted for a full year and the full year only, so

TABLE 2.6.   *Servants in Longuenesse, 1778–90: years of residence*

78 or 51% stayed for one year, that is, appeared in 1 list
22 or 14% stayed for two years, that is, appeared in 2 lists
13 or 8% stayed for three years, that is, appeared in 3 lists
9 or 6% stayed for four years, that is, appeared in 4 lists
6 or 4% stayed for five years, that is, appeared in 5 lists
15 or 10% stayed for from six to twelve years, that is, appeared in 6 to 12 lists
10 or 7% stayed for thirteen years or more, that is appeared in all 13 lists
153

that presence on only one list implies residence for twelve months.

Here we have the same effect as is hinted at in the fragmentary Cogenhoe figures, and which is confirmed by everything else we are getting to know about servants. A good proportion of them, perhaps usually a majority, here 78 out of 153, stayed for one year only. Not many, here just over a quarter, remained for more than three years, but a small minority for a much longer time. An 'average' (mean) stay at Longuenesse was well over three years allowing for some who had been there for several years in 1778 or who would stay for several years after 1790, however, and it seems clear that they shifted less often in France than in England, and so helped to ensure that the households there were slightly stabler, a little less given over to annual change in their personnel.

Servants were young people, as we saw in chapter 1, and since we have ages at Longuenesse we can demonstrate how far migration in the village was undertaken by the younger members of the community. Young married couples and their families shifted residence much more than the older ones, along with the young servants changing places and the young men and women going out to service and going out to be married. We could also show from the French materials that there may have been other reasons why population was marginally stabler there than at Clayworth and Cogenhoe. Children seem to have stayed in their parental households slightly longer in northern France at this time; they married late (men at 30 to 31, women at 28 to 29, which is about as high as age at first marriage ever went in the English pre-industrial populations that we know of, at least for men); they may even have been more willing than in England to wait for the death of their parents before marrying, or to live with them after their marriages. Perhaps they were ever so little more conscious of kinship, or in fact calculated their kin a little more carefully, even if they never approached that degree of subordination to kin and the kin network which the study of traditional societies outside Europe may have led us to expect. But we can go no further than to present some of the evidence from Hallines and Longuenesse so as to provide a context for Clayworth and Cogenhoe, a comparative case for the extraordinary instability of part of the population in these English villages which so surprised us when we first discovered its presence.

The study of age at migration and its relationship with servants, with family structure and with what we call primary kinship density, with the general shape of the economy, the structure of landownership and the exploitation of the soil, can all be undertaken in France, Italy and Sweden and in other countries where the evidence demanded survives in sufficient quantities.[46] As of the moment (1976) it appears that we may never know enough to carry out such exercises for English villages, and our truncated, frustrating pieces of information from Clayworth and Cogenhoe may remain most of what we shall ever know about turnover of population in settled, rural, traditional English society. But it is reassuring to be able to suppose that Clayworth and Cogenhoe can be taken as revealing to us some at least of the general features of Western society as a whole, its familial and community structure, its intriguing disposition to change the composition of a local population over time.[47]

[46] Primary kinship density covers relations within the conjugal family unit only (parent–child, child–child), and Emmanuel Todd has calculated measures for this in villages in the countries named for dates in the eighteenth century, along with profiles by age of migrating individuals and households. His findings seem likely to show that kinship domination in traditional Europe was less than anthropologists have posited for contemporary pre-industrial societies. The comparisons in turnover by age between Tuscany and Artois (Longuenesse) are published in his article of 1975, but not as yet the analysis of kinship. In Tuscany he finds that migration was not particularly confined to the young, since it involved whole households, often large and complex households.

[47] The study of turnover of population has become part of the study of migration as a whole since 1963, and use has been made of the figures originally published for Clayworth and Cogenhoe, now revised in this section and in section IV. An article by Wilfrid Prest, 'Stability and change in Old and New England: Clayworth and Dedham', in the *Journal of Interdisciplinary History*, 6, 3 (1976): 359–74, provides a useful guide to this literature. He also records the differences in the figures for Clayworth issued in tables 2.22–2.24 below from those originally printed in 1963. These differences are of little importance, with one exception. The proportions moving in and out of Clayworth as members of whole households are significantly greater in the new tables. Partly in consequence of this, the proportions 'unaccounted for' are less than they were announced to be in 1963; indeed, this category has disappeared in the case of arrivals. Mr Prest has seen the final revisions of these figures undertaken by Margaret Jones, late of the Cambridge Group, and whilst they agree in nearly every particular, there are slight differences in his numbers and ours arising from particular choices.

IV. Tabular analysis of the parish of Clayworth, 1676 and 1688

TABLE 2.7. *Clayworth: population by sex and marital status*

Marital status	April 1676; pop. 401						May 1688; pop. 412					
	Males		Females		Total		Males		Females		Total	
	No.	%	No.	%	No.	%	No.	%	No.	%	No.	%
Married	67	32.7	67	34.2	134	33.5	67	32.9	67	32.2	134	32.5
Widowed	7	3.4	24	12.2	31	7.7	8	3.7	21	10.1	29	7.0
Single	131	63.9	105	53.6	236	58.8	129	63.4	120	57.7	249	60.5
Total	205	100%	196	100%	401	100%	204	100%	208	100%	412	100%
			Sex ratio 105						Sex ratio 102			

TABLE 2.8. *Clayworth: distribution of households by size*

Size	April 1676; pop. 401				May 1688; pop. 412			
	Households		Persons		Households		Persons	
	No.	%	No.	%	No.	%	No.	%
1	6	6.1	6	1.5	4	4.4	4	1.0
2	10	10.2	20	5.0	12	13.2	24	6.0
3	31	31.7	93	23.2	20	22.0	60	14.9
4	16	16.3	64	16.0	20	22.0	80	19.8
5	16	16.3	80	20.0	11	12.1	55	13.6
6	7	7.2	42	10.5	7	7.7	42	10.4
7	3	3.0	21	5.2	5	5.5	35	8.7
8	7	7.2	56	13.9	6	6.6	48	11.9
9	1	1.0	9	2.2	5	5.5	45	11.2
10	1	1.0	10	2.5	1	1.0	10	2.5
Total	98	100%	401	100%	91	100%	403	100%
Persons in institutions			0				9	

TABLE 2.9. *Clayworth: measures of household size*

	April 1676; pop. 401	May 1688; pop. 412
Mean household size (MHS)	4.09	4.43
Variance	3.72	6.89
Mean experienced household size (M(E)HS)[a]	5.01	5.73
Range of household sizes	1–10	1–10
Median household size	4(4.21)	5(4.58)
Median experienced household size	5(5.11)	6(6.29)

[a] Average household size from the point of view of each *individual*; see Laslett 1972a:40.

87

TABLE 2.10.   *Clayworth: marital status of heads of households*

| Marital status | April 1676; pop. 401 | | May 1688; pop. 412 | |
| | Households | | Households | |
	No.	%	No.	%
Married couple	67	68	64	70
Widower[a]	7	7	8	9
Widow[a]	18	18	17	19
Single male	4	4	2	2
Single female	2	2	—	—
Unspecified male	—	—	—	—
Unspecified female	—	—	—	—
Total	98	99%	91	100%

[a]Including all cases where spouses were absent.

TABLE 2.11.   *Clayworth: distribution of children in groups*

| Size | April 1676; pop. 401 | | | | May 1688; pop. 412 | | | |
| | Groups | | Children | | Groups | | Children | |
	No.	%	No.	%	No.	%	No.	%
1	29	40	29	19	31	41	31	19
2	18	25	36	23	20	26	40	25
3	16	22	48	31	14	18	42	26
4	9	12	36	23	6	8	24	15
5	1	1	5	3	5	7	25	15
Total	73	100%	154	99%	76	100%	162	100%

Proportion of children in
  the population 38.4%
Proportion of households
  with children 74%
Mean size of groups of children 2.11

Proportion of children in
  the population 39.3%
Proportion of households
  with children 83%
Mean size of groups of children 2.13

'Children' here are all resident offspring, i.e. all unmarried children and stepchildren of household head.

TABLE 2.12. *Clayworth: resident kin other than spouses and children: numbers, types and proportions*

	April 1676; pop. 401						
	Kin of husband	Kin of wife	Kin of widower	Kin of widow	Kin of single head	Kin of other member of household	Total
Father	—	—	—	—	—	—	—
Mother	2	3	—	—	—	—	5
Brother	—	—	—	1	—	—	1
Sister	1	—	—	1	—	—	2
Nephew	1	—	—	—	—	—	1
Niece	—	1	—	—	—	—	1
Other kin	3		—	—	—	—	3
Daughter-in-law	—	—	—	—	—	—	—
Grandchild	—	—	1	—	—	—	1
Total	7	4	1	2	—	—	14

Proportion of kin in population 3.5%
Proportion of households with kin 12/98 = 12%

TABLE 2.12 *(continued)*

	May 1688; pop. 412						
	Kin of husband	Kin of wife	Kin of widower	Kin of widow	Kin of single head	Kin of other member of household	Total
Father	—	—	—	—	—	—	—
Mother	—	—	—	—	—	—	—
Brother	—	—	—	—	—	—	—
Sister	1	—	—	1	—	—	2
Nephew	1	—	—	—	1	—	2
Niece	—	—	—	—	—	—	—
Other kin	1		—	—	—	—	1
Daughter-in-law	—	—	1	1	—	—	2
Grandchild	—	—	1	4	—	—	5
	3	—	2	6	1	—	12

Proportion of kin in population 2.9%
Proportion of households with kin 8/91 = 9%

TABLE 2.13.   *Clayworth: servants: categories and proportions*

Category	April 1676; pop. 401				May 1688; pop. 412			
	Males		Females		Males		Females	
	No.	%	No.	%	No.	%	No.	%
Described as servants	35	81	24	100	29	88	32	100
Described as apprentices	5	12	—	—	3	9	—	—
Described as journeymen	3	7	—	—	1	3	—	—
Total	43	100%	24	100%	33	100%	32	100%

Sex ratio of servants 179
Proportion of servants in the
  population 67/401 = 16.7%

Sex ratio of servants 103
Proportion of servants in the
  population 65/412 = 15.8%

TABLE 2.14.   *Clayworth: servants: distribution in households*

Groups		April 1676; pop. 401		May 1688; pop. 412	
		Households		Households	
Size	Composition	No.	%	No.	%
1	1 male	7	23	4	15
	1 female	4	13	5	19
2	2 males	3	10	1	4
	1 male, 1 female	7	23	5	19
	2 females	—	—	1	4
3	3 males	—	—	—	—
	2 males, 1 female	5	17	4	15
	1 male, 2 females	—	—	2	8
	3 females	—	—	—	—
4	4 males	—	—	—	—
	3 males, 1 female	2	7	—	—
	2 males, 2 females	1	3	1	4
	1 male, 3 females	—	—	1	4
	4 females	—	—	—	—
5 +	5 and more	1	3	2	8
	Total	30	99%	26	100%

Proportion of households with servants, 1676 30/98 = 31%
Proportion of households with servants, 1688 26/91 = 29%

TABLE 2.15. Clayworth: occupations

April 1676; pop. 401

Occupation	Numbers	
	Householders	Others not householders
Bricklayer	1	—
Butcher	1	—
Cooper	1	—
Gentleman	4	—
Labourer	18	—
Parish clerk	1	—
Pindar	1	—
Rector	1	—
Sheppard	4	—
Shoemaker	1	—
Smith	3	—
Tailor	2	—
Thacker	1	—
Weaver	4	—
Wright	3	—
Husbandman [assumed from 1688 list]	12	—
Freeholder [assumed from 1688 list]	2	—
Husbandman freeholder [assumed from 1688 list]	2	—

Total householders of known occupation 62
Total householders 98
Proportion of householders of known occupation 63%
Householders of unknown occupation, of whom 18 were widows 36(37%)

May 1688; pop. 412

Occupation	Numbers	
	Householders	Others not householders
Badger	1	—
Bricklayer	1	—
Butcher	1	—
Cooper	1	—
Cutler	1	—
Gentleman	4	—
Horserider	1	—
Housewright	1	—
Labourer	22	—
Parish clerk and tayler	1	—
Petty-grocer	1	—
Pettyler	1	—
Plasher	1	—
Rector	1	—
Sheepherd	1	—
Shoemaker	1	—
Smith	2	—
Spinner	1	—
Swineherd	1	—
Tailor	2	—
Thacker	1	—
Weaver	3	—
Wheelwright	1	—
Husbandman [of whom 8 were freeholders]	23	—

Total householders of known occupation 74
Total householders 91
Proportion of householders of known occupation 81%
Householders of unknown occupation, all of whom were widows 17(20%)

TABLE 2.16.   *Clayworth: size of household by status of head*

April 1676; pop. 401

| Status category of head | Size of household | | | | | | | | | | Total | | |
	1	2	3	4	5	6	7	8	9	10	House-holds	Persons	Mean size
Gentleman	0	0	0	0	0	1	0	2	1	0	4	31	7.75
Clergy	0	0	0	1	0	0	0	0	0	0	1	4	4.0
Yeoman	0	0	0	0	1	1	1	1	0	0	4	26	6.5
Husbandman	0	1	4	2	2	1	0	1	0	1	12	56	4.6
Tradesman and craftsman	1	0	9	3	8	2	0	0	0	0	23	92	4.0
Labourer	0	4	7	4	2	1	0	0	0	0	18	61	3.3
Pauper	0	0	0	0	0	0	0	0	0	0	0	0	0
Other	0	0	0	0	0	0	0	0	0	0	0	0	0
Not stated	5	5	11	6	3	1	2	3	0	0	36[a]	131	3.6
Total	6	10	31	16	16	7	3	7	1	1	98	401	4.09

[a] 18 of these households headed by widows.

TABLE 2.16   (*continued*)

May 1688; pop. 412

| Status category of head | Size of household | | | | | | | | | | Total | | |
	1	2	3	4	5	6	7	8	9	10	House-holds	Persons	Mean size
Gentleman	0	0	0	0	1	0	0	0	2	1	4	33	8.7
Clergy	0	0	0	0	0	1	0	0	0	0	1	6	6.0
Yeoman	0	0	0	3	1	1	0	1	2	0	8	49	6.1
Husbandman	0	2	0	2	3	2	2	4	0	0	15	85	5.7
Tradesman and craftsman	1	3	6	6	1	1	2	0	1	0	21	83	3.9
Labourer	0	3	9	3	4	2	1	0	0	0	22	84	3.8
Pauper	0	0	0	0	0	0	0	0	0	0	0	0	0
Other	0	0	1	1	1	0	0	0	0	0	3	12	4.0
Not stated	3	4	4	5	0	0	0	1	0	0	17[b]	51	3.0
Total	4	12	20	20	11	7	5	6	5	1	91	403	4.43

[b] All headed by widows.

TABLE 2.17. *Clayworth: households with children, kin and servants, by status of head*

	April 1676; pop. 401							
	Households							
	With children				With kin		With servants	
Status category of head	Total	Number	Pro- portion (%)	Mean size of groups	Number	Pro- portion (%)	Number	Pro- portion (%)
Gentle- man	4	3	75	2.6	2	50	3	75
Clergy	1	0	0	0	0	0	1	100
Yeoman	4	3	75	2.3	1	25	4	100
Husband- man	12	10	83	2.2	1	8	12	41
Tradesman and craftsman	23	17	74	2.2	2	9	7	30
Labourer	18	12	67	1.7	5	28	1	6
Pauper	0	0	0	0	0	0	0	0
Other	0	0	0	0	0	0	0	0
Not stated	36 [a]	28	78	2.0	1	3	4	11

[a] 18 of these households headed by widows.

TABLE 2.17 *(continued)*

	May 1688; pop. 412							
	Households							
	With children				With kin		With servants	
Status category of head	Total	Number	Pro- portion (%)	Mean size of groups	Number	Pro- portion (%)	Number	Pro portion (%)
Gentle- man	4	4	100	2.2	1	25	4	100
Clergy	1	0	0	0	1	100	1	100
Yeoman	8	7	87	3.9	0	0	7	87
Husband- man	15	12	80	2.8	2	9	8	53
Tradesman and craftsman	21	16	76	2.1	0	0	5	24
Labourer	22	20	91	2.0	1	5	0	0
Pauper	0	0	0	0	0	0	0	0
Other	3	3	100	2.0	0	0	0	0
Not stated	17 [b]	14	82	1.6	3	18	3	6

[b] All headed by widows.

TABLE 2.18.   *Clayworth: surname analysis*

	April 1676; pop. 401	May 1688; pop. 412
No. of households per surname	1.3	1.2
% of servants sharing a surname with the head of the household	0	0
% of servants sharing a surname with other members of the community	32%	21%
% of heads who share a surname with a pauper	0	3%

% of individuals sharing a surname with *n* others				% of individuals sharing a surname with *n* others			
n	0−9	10−19	20−30	30 +			
%	84.6	15.4	0	0			

n	0−9	10−19	20−30	30 +
%	85.4	14.6	0	0

TABLE 2.20.   *Clayworth: households by generational depth*

Number of generations	Description of household	April 1676; pop. 401 Households		May 1688; pop. 412 Households	
		No.	%	No.	%
1	Containing only members of same generation as head	20	20	13	14
2	Containing offspring of head and/or members of offspring generation	72 } 75	77	74 } 74	81
	Containing parents of head and/or members of parent generation	3 }			
3	Containing offspring etc. of head and grandchildren of head and/or members of grandchildren generation	1		4	
	Containing grandchildren of head but without offspring etc. of head	— } 3	3	— } 4	4
	Containing offspring etc. of head and parents etc. of head	2		—	
	Any other three-generational combination	—		—	
	Total	98	100	91	99

TABLE 2.19. *Clayworth: widowed persons by household position*

| | April 1676; pop. 401 | | | | May 1688; pop. 412 | | | |
| | Widowers | | Widows | | Widowers | | Widows | |
Position	No.	Proportion (%)	No.	Proportion (%)	No.	Proportion (%)	No.	Proportion (%)
Solitary	2	29	2	8	1	12	3	14
Head of household which includes married son[a]	—	—	—	—	1	12	—	—
Head of household which includes married daughter[a]	1	14	—	—	—	—	1	5
Head of household which includes unmarried offspring[b]	4	57	15	62	6	75	12	57
Head of household containing only those not offspring	—	—	1	4	—	—	1	5
In household headed by son	—	—	2	8	—	—	—	—
In household headed by son-in-law	—	—	3	13	—	—	1	5
In household headed by other kin	—	—	1	4	—	—	3	14
In institution	—	—	—	—	—	—	3	14
Total	7	100	24	99	8	99	21	100

[a]Includes households having both married and unmarried offspring.
[b]Excludes households with married offspring.

95

TABLE 2.21. *Clayworth: households by structure*

Categories	Classes
1 Solitaries	(a) Widowed
	(b) Single/of unknown marital status
2 No family	(a) Co-resident siblings
	(b) Co-resident relatives of other kinds
	(c) Persons not evidently related
3 Simple family households	(a) Married couples, alone
	(b) Married couples, with children
	(c) Widowers with children
	(d) Widows with children
4 Extended family households	(a) Extended upwards
	(b) Extended downwards
	(1) Nephews and nieces
	(2) Grandchildren
	(3) Both (or other)
	(c) Extended laterally
	(1) Brothers
	(2) Sisters
	(3) Other 'kinsman'
	(d) Combinations of (a)–(c)
5 Multiple family households	(a) Secondary unit/s up
	(b) Secondary unit/s down
	(c) Units all on one level
	(d) Frérèches
	(e) Other multiple families (including types (a)–(d) having extensions)
6 Provisional categories	P(2, 3) simple
	P(4) extended
	P(5) multiple
7 Indeterminate	
	Totals
	Households with lodgers

April 1676; pop. 401				May 1688; pop. 412			
Without servants	With servants	Total	%	Without servants	With servants	Total	%
3	—	8	8	3	1	6	7
3	2			1	1		
—	1	1	1	—	—	1	1
—	—			—	1		
—	—			—	—		
6	3			4	3		
33	16	76	78	39	14	76	84
4	—			4	2		
10	4			9	1		
2	1			—	1		
—	1			1	—		
1	—	8	8	2	—	6	7
—	—			—	—		
—	—			—	—		
1	—			—	1		
1	1			1	—		
—	—			—	—		
—	—	—	—	—	—		
—	—	—	—	—	—		
—	—	—	—	—	—	1	1
—	—	—	—	—	—		
—	—	—	—	—	1		
—	—			—	—		
4	—	4	4	1	—	1	1
—	—			—	—		
—	1	1	1	—	—	—	—
78	30	98	100	65	26	91	101
—	—	—	—	—	—	2	2

Note: Cf. tables 1.1–3 of ch. 1, and see notes and references there for explanation of categories.

TABLE 2.22.   *Turnover table 1: turnover of persons*

Persons	Clayworth, 1676—88		Cogenhoe, 1618—28 (full period)	
Totals	1676	401 = A	1618	185 = A
	1688	412 = B	1628	180 = B
Persisting		157		86
Proportion of A		39.2%		46.5%
Proportion of B		38.1%		47.8%
Disappearing		244		99
Proportion of A		60.8%		53.5%
Of those disappearing				
Died		92 (37.7%)		16 (16.1%)
Married		6 (2.5%)		*c.* 5 (*c.* 5.1%)
Household members out-				
migrating		45 (18.4%)		*c.* 40 (*c.* 40.4%)
Servants		53 (21.7%)		18 (18.2%)
Unaccounted for		48 (19.7%)		*c.* 21 (*c.* 21.2%)
Appearing		255		94
Proportion of B		61.9%		52.2%
Of those appearing				
Born		92 (36.1%)		29 (31%)
Married		18 (7.1%)		*c.* 3 (*c.* 3%)
Household members in-				
migrating		58 (22.7%)		*c.* 4 (*c.* 15%)
Servants		60 (23.5%)		25 (27%)
Unaccounted for		0 0		*c.* 23 (*c.* 24%)
Children of marriage partners		16 (6.3%)		?
Lodgers, kin etc.		11 (4.3%)		?

Turnover categories: *Died* signifies recorded as buried in the village during the period. *Born* means registered as baptized. *Married*, under 'disappearing', means registered as married to a spouse not in the listings and leaving no further record; under 'appearing', means recorded as marrying an individual in the listings and present in final listing. *Servants* can all be treated as individuals in Clayworth, but in Cogenhoe some servants have had to be treated as members of migrating households.

Further details of Clayworth categories: Of the 157 names persisting from 1676 to 1688, 79 (50.3%) appear in the register as buried by the year 1714. Of the 45 out-migrating household members, 27 were members of 8 identifiable household groups moving out with their heads, 10 disappeared along with women whose husbands had died, and 8 disappeared as members of two other groups whose heads had died.

TABLE 2.23. *Turnover table 2: turnover of households and household heads*

Households	Clayworth 1676–88		Cogenhoe 1618–28 (full period)	
Totals	1676	98 = A	1618	33 = A
	1688	91 = B	1628	33 = B
Persisting		60		25
Proportion of A		61%		76%
Proportion of B		66%		76%
Disappearing		38		8
Proportion of A		39%		24%
Disappearing households moving out		10 (26%)		8 (100%)
Appearing		31		8
Proportion of B		34%		31%
Appearing households moving in		19 (61%)		4 (50%)
Household heads				
Persisting		49		17
Proportion of A		50%		52%
Proportion of B		54%		52%
Disappearing		49		16
Proportion of A		50%		49%
Of those disappearing				
Died		37 (75%)		8 (50%)
Heads of out-migrating households		8 (16%)		8 (50%)
Temporarily absent in final year		2 (4%)		0
Removed to institution		1 (2%)		0
Unaccounted for		1 (2%)		0
Appearing		42		16
Proportion of B		46%		49%
Of those appearing Present in first list but not head		23 (55%)		11 (69%)

Further details of Clayworth categories: Of the 23 household heads in 1688 who had been present in 1676, 11 were the widows of men heading households in 1676, 6 were the children of 1676 heads, 6 the servants of such heads. Of the 19 who had not been present in 1676, 10 bore surnames represented in the 1676 list.

Further details of Cogenhoe categories: Of the 11 household heads in 1628 who had been present in 1618, all had been members of the households which they formally headed. None of the 5 who had not been present in 1618 bore surnames represented in the 1618 list.

TABLE 2.24. Turnover table 3: Cogenhoe: turnover of persons and of households in intermediate years

Persons	1618–20	1620–1	1621–3	1623–4	1624–8
	1618 185 = A 1620 150 = B	1620 150 = A 1621 154 = B	1621 154 = A 1623 174 = B	1623 174 = A 1624 176 = B	1624 176 = A 1628 180 = B
Totals					
Persisting	122	126	131	151	115
Proportion of A	65.9%	84.0%	85.0%	86.8%	65.3%
Proportion of B	81.3%	81.8%	75.3%	85.8%	63.9%
Disappearing	63	24	23	23	61
Proportion of A	34.1%	16.0%	14.9%	13.2%	34.6%
Of those disappearing					
Died	5 (9%)	2 (8%)	1 (4%)	1 (4%)	1 (2%)
Married	1 (2%)	1 (4%)	0	0	3 (5%)
Household members out-migrating	c. 34 (c. 54%)	0	0	0	c. 25 (c.41%)
Servants	19 (30%)	15 (62%)	15 (65%)	7 (30%)	13 (21%)
Unaccounted for	4 (6%)	6 (25%)	7 (30%)	15 (65%)	19 (31%)
Appearing	28	28	43	25	65
Proportion of B	18.7%	18.2%	24.7%	14.2%	36.1%
Of those appearing					
Born	6 (21%)	5 (18%)	6 (14%)	4 (16%)	12 (18%)
Married	0	0	0	0	0
Household members in-migrating	0	2 (7%)	20 (47%)	0	c. 13 (c.20%)
Servants	13 (46%)	8 (29%)	13 (30%)	10 (40%)	20 (31%)
Unaccounted for	9 (32%)	13 (46%)	4 (9%)	11 (44%)	20 (31%)

Households

	1618 33 = A 1620 30 = B	1620 30 = A 1621 31 = B	1621 31 = A 1623 34 = B	1623 34 = A 1624 33 = B	1624 34 = A 1628 33 = B
Totals	29	30	30	32	29
Persisting					
Proportion of A	88%	100%	97%	94%	88%
Proportion of B	97%	97%	88%	97%	88%
Disappearing	5	0	1	1	4
Proportion of A	15%	0	3%	3%	12%
Disappearing households moving out	5 (100%)	0	0	0	4 (100%)
Appearing	2	1	4	0	4
Proportion of B	7%	3%	12%	0	15%
Appearing households moving in	0	1 (100%)	2 (50%)	0	1 (25%)

Note: For turnover categories, see observations in table 2.22, where it is stated that some servants at Cogenhoe have had to be reckoned as members of migrating households.

3. Long-term trends in bastardy in England

I

In the study of family life, as with all other consistencies of behaviour, the irregularities count for a very great deal to the observer, more in fact than they do to the membership of the society concerned. This is particularly true of historical sociology. We can only get to know about the effectiveness or often even the existence of a rule from the records of what happened when this rule was breached. We certainly have to rely to a very large extent on the documents which were written about such unwonted events for our knowledge of the framework of family life, and of the quality of the experience of those who lived within it.

Ordinary, modest, conscientious men and women did not spend much of their time describing for the benefit of posterity the ordinary conventions which they lived by and their everyday relationships with their children or their servants. Least of all were they disposed to record their sexual relationships with their spouses, or their spouses-to-be. When they did set down such things — and the mere fact of the recording may have to qualify the description of the recorder as 'ordinary', since the ability to write in this way was no ordinary accomplishment — what they spelt out was only too apt to be highly conventional, so proper and improving that we do not know how much of it to believe. Only if something outrageous happened, if a son started to steal or a daughter to take up magical rites, and above all if a servant girl produced a bastard child, was it likely that expression would be given to the conventions and regulations which should have been obeyed. When these things happened, there would certainly be considerable discussion of the facts, or alleged facts, and sometimes a written record made. Such a record was most often the work of persons other than the participants, though the words of the actors themselves would frequently be recorded, and usually it would be written out in professional, conventionalized form for legal or quasi-legal purposes.

The social principle in play when such things occurred is familiar enough. The function of deviance from the viewpoint of the established order is to draw a thick, black line around what is permissible. There is a sense in which a set of conventions like those which constituted marriage in the traditional order required the occurrence of illegitimacy and its public acknowledgment in the form of a solemn record, in order that these conventions should maintain their position. However much the troubled parson might have shaken his head when offered a bastard to baptize, he must have been aware of the exemplary use he might make of the event when he came to preach to his flock about the sanctity of marriage. An effective social rule must be capable of being broken if it is to be effective. Those who defy it do something to confirm its importance, and this may be so even if they are very numerous.

If we are to get to know how the family worked, and what its values meant to its members, we must consider very carefully what was said in the Church courts when sexual offences were still an ecclesiastical concern, and the evidence of the secular courts as well, along with the whole body of literary references to such things. Our first important task must surely be to find out, if we possibly can, how often breaches of the familial regulations actually took place. Only if we can gain a fair idea of the frequency with which men and women would set aside these rules and conventions can we judge how strong they were. And only if we can observe these things over time and from place to place can we begin to understand what the limits to familial irregularity must have been.

The larger the period we can study and the greater the number of places, the more confident we should be of our grasp of the reality. In this chapter, therefore, we turn our attention away from what happened in particular places like Clayworth and Cogenhoe over short periods of time and direct it towards large numbers of places over very many years. Individual communities and individual people, even individual bastards and bastard-bearers, will appear, of course, but our object is a general one and quite straightforward. It is to record the figures of sexual irregularity for one country over a really long period of time and for as many of its communities as is practicable.

The discussion inevitably has to be complex in its content because of the formidable difficulties of winning our figures at all.[1] In order to take

---

[1] The original article appeared in *Population Studies* in July 1973, under the authorship of Peter Laslett and Karla Oosterveen, incorporating results of research done at various times since 1966 and even earlier. The version presented here has been corrected and to some extent amended to take account of the analysis of much larger collections of (unchecked) illegitimacy ratios now in process at Cambridge as part of the computerized study of 404 sets of English parish register statistics by my colleagues E. A. Wrigley and R. S. Schofield. My thanks are due to them, to Miss Oosterveen and many others, including Professor David Glass, Professor E. Shorter and Richard Wall. Some of the critical discussion of the original sample of 24 parishes (called here 'the master sample') has been omitted as being of less importance in view of the new figures. A further and much more detailed study of the whole body of evidence now being assembled by the Cambridge Group will appear in the collective volume on the comparative history of illegitimacy in a number of countries to be edited by Peter Laslett and Karla Oosterveen.

advantage of the exceptional length of the reach in time which we possess over English social development it was decided to go back to the earliest possible point, which is to the first part of the sixteenth century when English baptisms, marriages and burials began to be recorded by the Church, and to continue until the present day, using the official figures of the Registrar-General from the time of their inception in the 1840s. The graph on p. 113 (fig. 3.1), therefore, is an attempt to portray the variations in the frequency with which the English produced illegitimate children for the four centuries and more which elapsed between the 1540s and the 1960s.

The term 'illicit love' in the title of this book covers both illegitimacy and pre-nuptial pregnancy, although it is possible to wonder whether all pre-nuptial pregnancy should be described by such an expression. Together they have a significance which goes even further than the study of familial life as such. They have always been of the greatest importance to the individual, for the rules which forbid the begetting of children outside marriage have to a large extent succeeded in ensuring to every person born a mature male protector and provider. This appears to be true for all societies at all times. These rules, moreover, have always been part of that regulatory system which keeps the numbers of a society within its means of subsistence. Their content and operation, therefore, affect the demographer, as well as the anthropologist, the sociologist and the social psychologist. It is easy to show that the demographic importance of irregular conceptions and births was by no means trivial even in the era of traditional life when the Christian Church and its Pauline sexual code were in official control of personal behaviour.

In certain countries, as is well known — in Jamaica for example — the proportion of all births marked as illegitimate now reaches three out of four, and there are seven or eight countries where it exceeds one-half. The rather less startling fact that between 1845 and 1921 5.3% of births recorded in England and Wales were of this type cannot be regarded as insignificant from the point of view of fertility, and in the succeeding fifty years this proportion has risen to 6.6%. Even the knowledge that the mean illegitimacy ratio was something like 3.0% for the two and a half centuries before British official figures begin in the 1840s is of some importance to the historical demographer, especially in view of the variation from time to time and place to place.

The earliest official national figures, those from Sweden starting in 1751, begin with a proportion of over 2% of all baptisms being registered as illegitimate, but the level rose by the decade 1811—20 to 8%. We shall find that nearly two centuries previously, late in the reign of the first Queen Elizabeth, the proportion of bastard births could reach 9% to 10% over whole decades in certain parishes in Lancashire and Cheshire. These figures are of the order of those attained in England during the great industrial revolution, though they were by no means then confined to urban or industrial areas. Indeed, in the early nineteenth century much of our country showed lower levels than those displayed by some places in the early seventeenth century.

It was perhaps inevitable that the extraordinary upsurge in our illegitimacy figures during the 1960s should have come to concern demographers most. But even this conspicuous development need not persuade us that the secular trend in bastardy in this one country, the first for which really long-term figures have so far been recovered, is patternless. There are clear indications of regional differences, some of them showing obstinate persistence over time. This was observed by Albert Leffingwell in 1892 in the first book (so he claimed) ever published in England on illegitimacy and still in some ways the most penetrating.[2] There are interesting indications of rhythmic rise and fall, of something like a wave motion over time with a period of some two hundred years, a phenomenon which is very easy to read into the shape of the curve in the figure mentioned above. The striking inclines and declines in the illegitimacy curve, which it is tempting to regard as unique and revolutionary, in this light begin to look more like alterations in direction which long-term influences might have brought in any case, if not on so large a scale. This pattern of change, moreover, shows signs of being in sympathy with those long-term rhythmic fluctuations in general fertility whose existence has often been suspected by demographers.

The traces which we observe of a secular pattern may themselves invite us to see a more defined shape than the figures will warrant, and to exaggerate the sameness of the phenomenon at different times and in different places. In reading what follows it must never be forgotten that bastardy may have meant various things to an Englishman or an Englishwoman in Tudor times, to a Hanoverian or a Victorian or a citizen of the Lloyd George era. The causes of illegitimacy must have varied as well as its extent, and seem certain to have differed from social class to social class.

II

As might perhaps be expected, no single-cause analysis seems at all likely to be successful, and the simpler, more ambitious generalizations which have been put forward have all to be seriously qualified.

[2] *Illegitimacy and the influence of seasons upon conduct* (London, 1892), in which (pp. 85–7) bastardy in Britain is shown to be a rural rather than an urban phenomenon, to be associated with prosperity and education rather than poverty and ignorance, and not to be directly correlated with religious dogma. On the 1960s see S. F. Hartley, 'The amazing rise of illegitimacy in Great Britain', *Social Forces* 44, 4 (June 1966): 533–45, now supplemented by the same scholar's comparative study *Illegitimacy* (1975).

Changes in the extent of illegitimacy in English history do not appear to be connected in a straightforward way with the growth of towns, or with the progress of industrialization, or with the age at marriage – even with the business cycle – with the sex ratio of the population, or with the relative proportions of married and spouseless women at fecund ages. Perhaps most disconcerting is the contradiction of the natural expectation that when marriage is late, illegitimacy will be high. In English history at any rate, and over the long intervals we deal with here, this cannot have been true. When there was a tendency for the number of children to go down whilst the age at marriage stayed constant or even went up, the number of illegitimacies might fall, sometimes sharply.[3]

As for a direct connection between ideology and non-conforming sexual behaviour, in so far as such behaviour can be measured by registered irregular births, this difficult issue is also found to be fraught with surprises. Nearly everyone would expect that the decade of the 1650s, when the brief reign of the Puritans ran its course in England, would stand out in our illegitimacy curve as the time at which the bastardy ratio was apparently the lowest in the whole four hundred years. And so it turns out in our graph. But the succeeding period, that of the Restoration, often reckoned to be the most licentious in English literary history before our present permissive generation, can there be seen to have been marked throughout its whole half-century by a fairly constant low level, showing a slow, rather even rise but nothing which could correspond to a widespread relaxation of the marriage rules. In fact, the assumption that illegitimacy figures directly reflect the prevalence of sexual intercourse outside marriage, which seems to be made whenever such figures are used to suggest that beliefs, attitudes and interests have changed in some particular way, can be shown to be very shaky in its foundations. Before we consider the meaning of our various diagrams and tables we shall do

[3] This is certainly true for the upsurge of illegitimacy ratios in the late eighteenth century, but it has been questioned for earlier periods; see n. 19 below.

Some of the many theories of illegitimacy are listed in an article by E. Shorter, E. van de Walle and J. Knodel, 'The decline of non-married fertility in Europe', *Population Studies* 25, 3 (November 1971): 375–94. Dorothy Swaine Thomas attempts to correlate illegitimacy with economic fluctuations in *Social aspects of the business cycle* (London, 1925), and finds correlation coefficients of -0.37 to -0.43 for various periods in the later nineteenth and earlier twentieth centuries, with two- and three-year time lags. An ambitious but unpersuasive attempt to account for the sharp rise in illegitimacy in eighteenth-century Europe as brought about by a complete attitudinal change is made by Shorter in 'Illegitimacy, sexual revolution and social change in modern Europe', *Journal of Interdisciplinary History* 2, 2 (Autumn 1971): 237–72, and developed into a theory of two sexual revolutions in his book *The making of the modern family* (New York, 1975; London, 1976). Some of the positions set out above are discussed in Laslett 1965, edition of 1971, in a preliminary way, especially in the notes: compare Laslett 1976b on the Restoration and illegitimacy.

well to discuss quite what the statistics of registered illegitimacy can be supposed to represent.

We may first notice that the abandonment of a single-cause explanation of fluctuations in the number of bastards at all places and at all times is distinct from the claim that no partial explanations can be found, or that a general explanatory model is, in principle, impossible. At the end of this essay, indeed, a suggestion will be made which will have to be developed elsewhere,[4] that the history of bastardy in England may be partially understood on the hypothesis that something like a sub-society of the illegitimacy-prone may have existed over time.

As general fertility rose, the hypothesis states, the fertility of the women in this set of people rose, too, but faster still. It is also possible that at such times the shadowy society of the bastard-bearers itself grew larger and that women not belonging to it also became more liable to have irregular children. We have little evidence at present on these further points, though it is surely very significant that the preliminary consideration of varying levels of illegitimacy so soon raises issues of social structure.

A decision on exactly how much might be explained by the possible presence of a sub-society of this kind will be a difficult matter because there seem to have been so many forces at work. Though, in general, postponement of marriage is not necessarily associated with an increase in bastardy ratios, it could conceivably have accounted for a much greater proportion of bastardy at times when levels were low than when they were high: moreover, such postponement might have continued to have an important effect on those persons who did not share in the widespread relaxation of qualifications for marriage which must have occurred when people began to wed at younger ages. Considerations such as these, we believe, make it wise to be wary of supposing that wholesale, revolutionary attitudinal changes have to be invoked to explain such a phenomenon as the formidable increase in illegitimacy all over Europe in the eighteenth and early nineteenth centuries.

Fluctuations in the statistics of illegitimacy, in fact, like those of fertility as a whole, must be supposed to represent the outcome of an intricate interplay of individual motives, of which rational calculation was

---

[4] These points will be discussed at length in the volume referred to in n. 1 above. In an interesting study in course of publication, 'The social context of illegitimacy in early modern England' (1975), David Levine and Keith Wrightson undertake to provide reasons for the change in the social structure of one English village. They reject any suggestion of illegitimacy's being a 'demographic' occurrence, and insist on the importance of the sub-society of the bastardy-prone analysed by them by the examination of networks of kinship and of collaboration. It is of some significance that their examination of all sources for illegitimacy confirms the parish registers as the most reliable, though always with omissions.

only one, no doubt very restricted in its role for bastard-begetters. This is true of all collective behaviour in its relation to individual decisions. But an hypothesis to the effect that there were sets of circumstances which arose in the past at something like two-hundred-year intervals which affected both legitimate and illegitimate fertility — indeed, every type of reproductive behaviour — has to take account of international, intercultural differences as well as of the problem of individual motivation. No succession of numerical measures stretching over a period of time long enough to check the suggested relationship between wave-like fluctuations in legitimate and illegitimate fertility in England has yet been published for any other national society. But a recent set of figures for the whole of France for the period 1740—1829 shows that, though the illegitimacy ratio rose very sharply after 1750, more steeply than in England, fertility was not as high as in our country, and that neither the number of births nor the total population was increasing. It seems unlikely that changes in fertility could be made to explain any part of the increase in bastardy in France in the later eighteenth century, the years of so-called sexual revolution. But signs of a bastardy-prone sub-society have been found in French communities at the time.[5]

III

It is crucial to recognize that figures for illegitimacy refer to a composite, not a simple, phenomenon; each ratio is the outcome of interplay of factors and circumstances rather than the result of one single 'cause'. The following circumstances had to obtain before any birth could be marked 'spurious' or 'base' or 'natural' (there were many similar phrases) in an English parish register, or be classed illegitimate in the books kept from 1838 by the English Registrar-General.

A man and a woman, both fecund and not married to each other, though not necessarily unmarried, had to be in association. Sexual intercourse had to take place at a time and under circumstances when conception was possible, and without successful contraceptive measures. Spontaneous abortion must not have occurred during pregnancy, and no effective act of deliberate abortion either. No marriage must have taken place between the parties before term — that is, where they were both at liberty to marry each other. The child must have been born alive, and

[5] See a paper by E. A. Wrigley in course of publication, called 'Fertility strategy for the individual and the group' (1974), on rational calculation in procreation. On French eighteenth-century illegitimacy, fertility and population dynamics, see Louis Henry and Yves Blayo in *Population*, 30 (special no., 'Démographie historique') (November 1975) (esp. Blayo, 'La proportion de naissances illégitimes en France de 1740 à 1829'), and on fertility as related to illegitimacy, Shorter 1975, ch. 3.

have survived birth for the period of time (which might be weeks or even months) which elapsed before baptism or registration came into question.[6] This means that the baby must have been in sufficient health to survive the most dangerous days of its existence (especially for unwanted infants) and that no one should have disposed of it, either at parturition or subsequently, by violence or by deliberate neglect. Finally (in the era before official registration) the child must have been taken to the church for the ceremony of baptism and the act of christening. When it came to making the entry in the register the parson or his parish clerk must have felt obliged to set down the tell-tale description of the baby's social and legal status. After civil registration began, the official responsible must have got this information out of the reluctant mother. Sexual intercourse between associating individuals not recognized as spouses to each other cannot have led to a recorded illegitimacy unless every one of these conditions had been satisfied.

Care must be taken not to look upon this series of attitudes, acts and decisions as entirely those of the parties concerned, which means above all the mother of the baby, though it includes the man who impregnated her, and to some extent the families of both of them. For it was public opinion and especially the opinion of the local community, the neighbours, which decided whether any particular association could be called a marriage, and not only the Church and the law. Public opinion on such matters might vary from place to place and alter with time, and so might the attitudes of the clergy and of the civil authorities.

The duty of the student of bastardy figures, therefore, is to try to decide how much each of the elements which have been distinguished could have changed between any two points in time, either independently, or in correlation with other elements. Only thus could it be decided whether an alteration in the numbers might·reasonably be described as mainly due to one particular cause. To make such a decision confidently would require a great deal more evidence about sexual behaviour, marriage and ecclesiastical and/or civil registration than we could ever expect to obtain from the past, even from the recent past. We should have to know, for example, about the following factors before we could decide whether the trough in English illegitimacy figures in the 1650s, so apparent in our graph, was really due to the actions of the triumphant Puritans in reforming the manners of the people.

One would be the reliability of registration generally, for in that time of war and disorder English parish books were worse kept than before and survived in fewest numbers. Another would be the extent to which

---

[6] See B. M. Berry and R. S. Schofield, 'Age at baptism in pre-industrial England', *Population Studies* 25, 3 (November 1971): 453–65.

unmarried lovers became more careful at that time in practising pre-
vention, though the young and inexperienced are always less likely to
do this effectively than married couples. Another would be the number
of guilty mothers-to-be who disposed of their babies before or during
birth, or who concealed what was going on from the stern authorities in
their own villages by moving elsewhere at the critical time, perhaps
being assisted in their attempts by the connivance of others who resented
the regime.[7]

It might in fact have been true that the Puritans did succeed in reducing the amount of actual irregular intercourse in England during the
1650s and enforcing an unwonted chastity. But even this outcome can
be ambiguous, because the parties might have taken refuge to a greater
extent in those bundling practices which some commentators have
found so attractive as an explanation of how sexual deprivation was
endured. In Wales a reference has been found in the mid nineteenth
century to bundling as 'courtship in bed'. But little sign of established
or accepted customary behaviour of this character has come to our
attention for England in the 1650s or at any time, though cases in the
civil and ecclesiastical courts are often quite explicit about what went
on and where between suspected fornicators.

Keith Wrightson, of the University of St Andrews, is researching into
means of social control in seventeenth-century England and is particularly concerned with the repressive action of the Puritans in the 1650s.
He finds that what the American sexologists call petting and heavy
petting are recorded for young people involved in bastardy cases at all
periods (lying on each other's beds is frequently mentioned), but there
is little sign of such courtship customs as lying out in the fields all night
in summer, sharing the same peasant garment, which Wikman refers
to and which even the great Malthus observed in Scandinavia in his
time. The element of collective action, groups of young men engaging
in bundling customs, has also yet to be discovered in England.

It is worth recording here also that the seasonal incidence of illegitimate conception in England shows no significant difference from seasonality in legitimate conceptions. Both sets of statistics, which are also
subject to the error arising from their being based on baptismal rather

---

[7] On limitation, see Wrigley (ed.) 1966: 82–109. His assumption is that with-
drawal was the method used. In France, where the illegitimacy ratio in the villages
until the later eighteenth century was apparently universally at a very low level,
about 0.5%, a further complication has to be reckoned with. Mothers of bastards seem
to have moved to the cities to leave their offspring there as *enfants trouvés*, sometimes on
a considerable scale. This cannot be confirmed to have happened in England on anything
like the same scale, but the literature about foundlings and especially about the foundling
hospital in London shows that abandonment of babies, legitimate as well as illegitimate,
on city streets was certainly widespread.

than birth dates, have some tendency towards singling out the months of May, June and July — the warm, light months — as those when conception was more likely than in the rest of the year, and this effect seems to grow less over the years from the sixteenth to the nineteenth centuries. But no confirmation can be found in illegitimacy registration for believing that the frolicsome English peasantry — when authority could be defied — indeed disported themselves in the hay and along the hedgerows in the leafy month of June, as the sentimentalists suppose. Sexual relations before and outside marriage certainly went on in England under the Puritans and indeed at all times. But bundling may be a misleading guide; it is too picturesque to be resisted.[8]

IV

When, therefore, the reader contemplates the graphs and the tables set out here, we hope that he will bear in mind the composite and complex character of the pattern of behaviour which is shown in them to be varying over time. To look upon them as the record of fluctuation in the extent of fornication alone is a serious misunderstanding. The prime exhibit is of course the graph spread out over page 113, fig. 3.1, which traces out the course of English illegitimacy for something over four hundred years from the mid sixteenth to the mid twentieth century.

We are fortunate to have such a record at all, and it is only possible to take this lengthy perspective over some fifteen generations because of the voluntary research carried on all over the country by the correspondents of the Cambridge Group for the History of Population and Social Structure. The results of their work[9] sustain the series up to the 1830s. The whole period from the 1540s to the 1840s is what we call the parish register era, but although we can be fairly confident of our figures for the major part of that stretch of time, between the 1580s and the

[8] On seasonality and on bundling, see Shorter 1975, ch. 3 and appendix IV. The authority is the Finnish literary historian K. Rob V. Wikman (1937), and there is an excellent, judicious commentary on the Scandinavian evidence in Orvar Löfgren, 'Family and household among Scandinavian peasants', *Ethnologia Scandinavica* (1974): 1—52.

[9] This valuable contribution to historical sociology has created an aggregative file of sets of monthly figures for baptisms, marriages and burials for some 600 English parishes. Many of these sets of figures begin in the later sixteenth century, and all by 1600; they mostly continue until after 1800, often, unfortunately, breaking off in 1812 (Rose's Act), but some go on until 1837, when civil registration began, and a few even continue to 1840 or later. We should like to take this opportunity to register our debt to these hundreds of willing volunteers, and to the many individuals amongst them who have specifically commented on illegitimacy and corresponded with the Cambridge Group about it. It would seem that bastardy was fairly conscientiously set down in a third or a quarter of English parish registers.

1800s, we are much less certain about them in the years between 1540 and 1580 and between 1800 and 1850. The evidence deteriorates so much that no decadal figure at all can be drawn out for the 1840s, after which the official register begins, the era of relative certainty.[10]

The outstanding difference between the two parts of the curve in fig. 3.1 lies not so much in the quality of the data as in the size of the population concerned. In the official register era the population at issue covers the whole English nation, with the Welsh as well, whereas in the parish register era it is confined to those living in less than a hundred places and faithfully christening their babies at the Anglican church, or at least registering them there. In its earlier part the graph is based on 98 of the 10,000 parishes or local ecclesiastical districts which go to make up the whole country represented in the later part. On the face of it, therefore, the later part of our plot is to be presumed more accurate than the earlier, and the level of illegitimacy is more likely to be indicated as too low before the 1840s than after.

Moreover, the figures from the 98 registers which underlie the part of the curve portrayed in fig. 3.1 for the parish register era are, as we shall see, unchecked by us from the original registers. That is to say, they have not been investigated for completeness in the way which was adopted for a smaller, master sample of 24 parishes appearing in fig. 3.2, a sample which we established first so as to make up our minds as to the *prima facie* usefulness of English ecclesiastical illegitimacy recordings and which we shall shortly describe. This is the reason why the ratios represented in fig. 3.1 for the years 1580 to 1810 portray illegitimacy levels as being lower than they are in the graph for our master sample in fig. 3.2: checking always raises the ratio, since more irregular births are recovered. Fig. 3.1, our prize exhibit, as we have called it, may in fact represent bastardy as being as much as a fifth too low between the mid sixteenth and the mid nineteenth centuries. All the lines on fig. 3.2 (we shall explain how they are related in a moment) also err in this direction to a greater extent than those on fig. 3.1, except perhaps in the case of the master sample, which we shall find very probably exaggerates the level between the 1580s and the 1620s. There are smaller differences between the various curves. But it is the case that no set of figures which we have ever derived from illegitimacy registration for ten or more places gives rise to a curve differing in its general shape from that drawn out in fig. 3.1. And these intricacies must not be allowed to distract our attention from the message of that curve for the study of illegitimacy over time, a message which is reinforced by every

[10] For a discussion of the degree of reliability of official illegitimacy registration since the 1840s, see Laslett and Oosterveen 1973 and its references, especially Glass 1973.

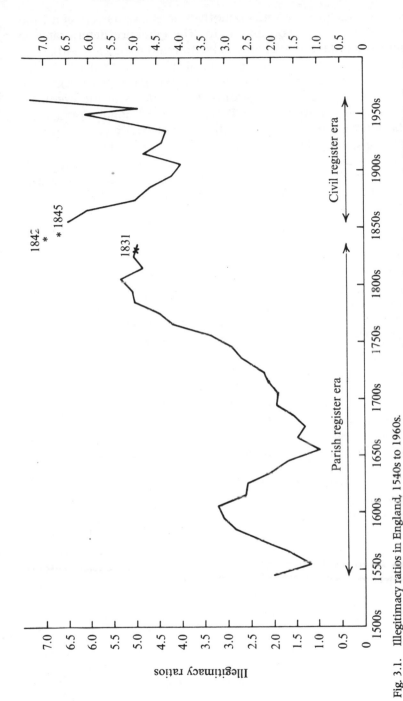

Fig. 3.1. Illegitimacy ratios in England, 1540s to 1960s.

Sources. 1540s – 1830s: sample of 98 parish registers, totals by decades of baptisms and of baptisms marked 'illegitimate', etc. Registration not checked. Consistency qualification: at least 1 baptism marked 'illegitimate' in any 500.
1831: results of Rickman's enquiry into parish registers.
1842, 1845: results of Registrar-General's enquiries for particular years of civil registration.

set of figures we have worked out and every graph we have drawn up.

The peak in the illegitimacy ratio in the early years of the seventeenth century is its salient and its novel feature. Hitherto the conspicuous rise in the eighteenth century to a high point sometime in the mid nineteenth century has been the only change in illegitimacy known to historical sociologists before the beginning of official registration, and then only in rather vague terms. Almost as important is the impression of wave-like movement which appears when a series as long as this is plotted: one quite clearly marked wave seems to have reached its climax about 1600 and a second to have done so in the 1840s. There are even indications of a third with a sharp apex in the 1940s, though this last effect might be better regarded as a function of the Second World War, or of that rapid oscillation which appears to be characteristic of demographic behaviour in the contemporary world.

Another notable feature of the graph is the dip which comes in the 1810s, interrupting over half a century of continuous rise in the illegitimacy level, slow at first but by the end of the eighteenth century almost as fast as at the end of the sixteenth century. The generally downward tendency in the ratio during the years from the 1800s to 1831, together with the very high levels for the individual years 1842 and 1845,[11] must surely interest the historian of industrialization and the social scientist concerned with urbanization, since these were times of critical development in these directions in England. The discussion of these issues will have to be postponed to the fuller study of English illegitimacy now in preparation.

The upwelling which took place in the eighteenth century seems to have been much more substantial than that of the sixteenth. In the course of this second cycle in the secular process, moreover, the general level of the ratio appears to have risen permanently. But we must not forget that the figures before the 1580s are rather sketchy, a fact which has general implications for the whole shape of our graph. The fall in the later part of the nineteenth century which has understandably been interpreted as unique in its character, was certainly not the first of its kind, if our figures for the sixteenth and seventeenth centuries are to be relied upon. Still, too much significance should not be attached to the absolute levels of the graph, not even to the slopes indicating rates of change. It is its overall shape which should occupy our attention.

[11] See appendix 2. The effect of dislocation between the end of the parish register curve in the 1830s and the beginning of the Registrar-General's figures in the 1850s, together with the peaks in 1842 and 1845, may be due to a very sudden, steep increase in the late 1830s, or simply represent better registration.

This overall shape can in fact be accepted as representing with rough and ready accuracy the objective story of bastardy levels in England at least from the 1580s to the 1800s, and since the 1850s. The relationship between the lines in fig. 3.2 seems to confirm this claim with some finality for the years which it represents. In that figure the curve derived from the 98 parishes appears again, but alongside two other curves. One is that from the collection which has already been referred to as the master sample of 24 parishes, in which every single entry for a baptism was investigated by us, and a decision made on its status as to legitimacy and illegitimacy. The other curve in fig. 3.2 is for a considerably larger collection of sets of figures, arising from 165 parishes, but selected after passing a test for consistency and completeness in registration considerably less exacting than that which produced our sample of 98, and of course much laxer than the criteria required for our master sample of 24. Fig. 3.2 has a further feature. Above the lines for the 98 parishes and for the 165 are dotted lines representing inflated totals. At the risk of being tedious, we must describe how this inflation was carried out.

The 24 parishes whose statistics go to make up our master sample were selected for the relative excellence of their recording, for their rough geographical representativeness and for the availability of their

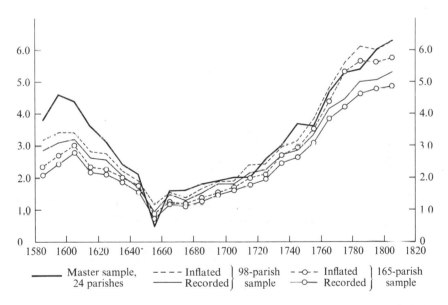

Fig. 3.2 Illegitimacy curves for master sample (24 parishes) and for 98 and 165 parishes, with inflated curves shown.

TABLE 3.1. *Detailed registration figures, ratios and indicators for master sample of 24 selected parishes, by decade, 1581–1810*

Decade	Baptisms	Burials	Marriages	Ratio of baptisms to marriages
1580s[b]	[7,535]	[6,302]	[2,050]	[3.7]
1590s[b]	[8,162]	[7,644]	[2,211]	[3.7]
1600s	9,224	6,868	2,337	3.9
1610s	9,660	7,585	2,223	4.3
1620s	9,607	8,047	2,060	4.7
1630s	10,012	7,997	2,043	4.9
1640s	[8,712]	[8,520]	1,356	[6.4]
1650s	6,981	7,414	1,790	3.9
1660s	7,995	8,234	1,842	4.3
1670s	7,805	8,893	1,766	4.4
1680s	7,905	8,951	1,613	4.9
1690s	8,469	8,732	1,823	4.6
1700s	9,194	7,876	2,336	3.9
1710s	9,247	7,476	2,499	3.7
1720s	9,858	10,236	2,603	3.8
1730s	11,157	8,654	2,963	3.8
1740s	11,002	9,141	3,024	3.6
1750s	11,727	9,240	3,419	3.4
1760s	12,242	10,574	4,011	3.1
1770s	13,508	10,626	4,371	3.1
1780s	14,619	11,516	4,899	3.0
1790s	15,400	12,636	5,012	3.1
1800s	16,217	11,357	6,128	2.6
Total 1581–1810	[236,238]	[204,519]	[64,379]	3.8

Square brackets surround figures which have had to be slightly amended to allow for periods of interrupted registration.

registers.[12] We extracted from their baptismal entries not simply those births marked with a sign of illegitimacy, but also those attributed to a mother only, with no father mentioned, or those with some cryptic indicator such as 'alias', and those born to widows. The actual criteria used are set out in appendix 1, and in table 3.1 are set down the figures for

[12] The 24 parishes are named in the table in appendix 1, which contains a brief discussion of their adequacy as a master sample. Since it was out of the question for us to travel to the areas concerned and go through the documents in the places where they were preserved (sometimes in the churches themselves), we had to confine our choice to those registers which had been printed or of which publicly available transcripts had been made. It will be understood that the figures used for all graphs and tables other than those for the master sample were worked out by the volunteers who analysed the parish registers for the purpose of aggregating monthly totals of baptisms, marriages and burials, and who entered the illegitimacy recordings only incidentally.

Index of increase or decrease[a] (%)	Bastards				Overall bastardy ratio (%)
	Named	Inferred	Inflation coefficient	Total	
16.36	249	29	112	278	[3.7]
6.35	326	37	111	363	[4.6]
25.54	381	28	107	409	4.4
21.48	324	26	108	350	3.6
17.28	278	21	108	299	3.1
20.12	232	19	108	251	2.5
2.20	151	16	111	167	[1 9]
−6.20	31	7	123	38	0.5
−2.99	120	6	105	126	1.6
13.94	118	6	105	124	1.6
−13.23	133	12	109	145	1.8
−3.10	157	4	103	161	1.9
20.86	175	10	106	185	2.0
19.15	166	22	113	188	2.0
−3.83	241	20	108	261	2.6
22.43	300	31	110	331	3.0
16.91	363	39	111	402	3.7
21.20	364	56	115	420	3.6
13.62	500	76	115	576	4.7
21.33	567	147	126	714	5.3
21.22	655	141	121	796	5.4
17.95	791	143	118	934	6.1
29.97	867	153	118	1,020	6.3
	7,488	1,049		8,538	3.6

[a] Difference between baptisms and burials in each decade expressed as a percentage of baptisms in that decade. Where burials exceed baptisms, index has a minus sign.
[b] 23 parishes only.

the illegitimacy ratio for each decade from 1581 to 1810 which were finally established for these 24 parishes.

It will be noticed that the other columns in the table record burials, marriages and the ratios of baptisms to burials, along with indications of increase or decrease of population for each decade, as well as bastards recorded and bastards inferred as such by us. The digits in the last column but two are inflation percentages, describing the amount by which the figures of bastards named have to be increased by allowing for inferred bastardies so as to make up the final total. We have used these decadal inflation multipliers so as to produce the dotted line in fig. 3.2 above the curves for the 98 parishes and for the 165 parishes. These secondary lines represent, therefore, what we estimate would have been the illegit-

imacy levels in the samples concerned if we had been able to check all
the recordings in the same way as was done in the case of the master
sample.

It is the satisfactory and perhaps somewhat surprising correspondence
between the curves in fig. 3.2 which encourages us to suppose that the
behaviour of bastardy is indeed quite well described by the portion of the
graph in fig. 3.1 which covers the parish register era for our 98 parishes.
The coincidence between the decadal values in the master sample and
those in the 98 is particularly impressive between the 1660s and the
1760s. In fact, over the years from 1660 to 1730, the period of the
stable low in the history of English illegitimacy, the percentage was
only slightly less in the sample of 98 sets of uncorrected figures than
it was in the master sample of 24 corrected sets of figures, 1.78% as
against 1.97%. Indeed, if we take the complete run of decades when
these two lines are at their closest, between the 1660s and the 1760s,
we find that the two ratios were actually identical, at 2.48%. This
is especially reassuring since it is has often been assumed that this
was a century of lax ecclesiastical administration and hence of poor
registration. The places in our collection of 98 may well have had rather
higher levels of illegitimacy over these decades than those in our master
sample: this is because, as we have seen, checking their registers in detail
must have yielded more bastardies. It will be noticed that throughout the
same period the largest of the three collections represented, that for
165 parishes, must have behaved in a very similar way.

It is easy to see why the general level goes down, and the bastardy
curve flattens out, as the size of the sample grows larger. The 98 sets of
figures were arrived at by requiring that no run of five hundred baptisms
should go by without one illegitimate being recorded, whilst for the 165
sets the condition was relaxed to 1 in a thousand. This must mean that
in the bigger collection many parishes are present where illegitimacy
registration was indifferent to bad.[13] But there are areas of the graph
where the correspondence is not so close. Since these represent the time
when the level was at its highest and lowest, and therefore are the most
interesting, they require further consideration.

The two times of high illegitimacy in the parish register era, around
1600 and around 1800, show substantially lower levels in the case of the
98 parishes than in the master sample: this is especially so during the
early high. The discrepancy can be partially accounted for by the fact

---

[13] The whole body of parishes now being analysed automatically has been made to
yield several other bastardy curves by varying tests for consistency of registration.
Every one of these curves has the same shape as those in figs. 3.1 and 3.2. A plot of the
same statistic for the whole number (404) gives this shape again, but flatter in profile,
of course, since very many of the parishes concerned were recording no bastards at all.

that the master sample is known to contain one parish, Rochdale in Lancashire, of quite disproportionate size[14] where exceptionally large numbers of bastards were born at the turn of the sixteenth century. But the composition of the master sample may not explain the whole difference, and the earlier high could conceivably have in fact been more impressive in size than appears in fig. 3.1. If this was so, it was perhaps due to a general reluctance to record illegitimate births, at least as such, in the later sixteenth century. Registration conditions were so complicated in the later part of the parish register era, after 1770, that it is difficult to say whether the later rise is also too low in fig. 3.1, but this could well be so. In general, however, the provisional conclusion would seem to be that the *relative* heights of the two peaks cannot be far out as we represent them, whatever the *absolute* heights may have been. The comparison given by the semilog curve in fig. 3.3, a form of representation calculated to bring out the relative rates of change, is probably a just one.

Fig. 3.3 exaggerates in a rather unfortunate way the further conspicuous discrepancy between the curves compared in fig. 3.2, a discrepancy relating to the 1650s — the lowest point in the whole series, as has been

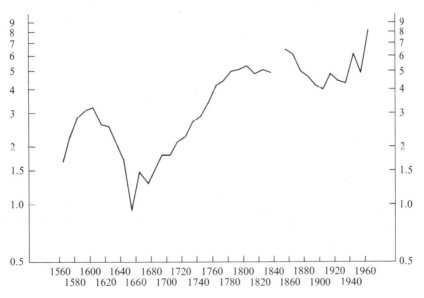

Fig. 3.3   Illegitimacy curve for 98 parishes, 1560s — 1960s, semilog plot.

[14] About 40% of the whole population of the master sample lived in this parish; see appendix 1.

said, usually referred to as the Cromwellian or the Puritan nadir. It seems best to record all available readings for this period of ten years. They are: 404 parishes (largest available sample), 0.4%; 24 parishes (select master sample), 0.5%; 165 parishes (laxest consistency conditions), 0.73% (inflated 0.87%); 98 parishes (more stringent conditions), 0.94% (1.14%); 67 parishes (more stringent still), 1.25% (1.53%); 61 parishes (most stringent), 1.33% (1.63%). The better the registration, therefore, the higher the level during the 1650s, illustrating the general principle laid down. But it will be seen that when registration is best of all, in the master sample, the level in the 1650s falls back very conspicuously. The obvious explanation is that the master sample is faulty during the 1650s; and perhaps our best estimate for this nadir is between 1.0% and 1.5%. It is a pity that we have to be so vague on this particular point, because so much in the way of historical explanation may turn on the angle of the descent preceding the Puritan low.

V

All the figures so far quoted have referred to the percentages of baptisms or births described as illegitimate in our sources, a statistic which is conventionally referred to as the illegitimacy ratio. This is an important and indeed an essential item of information for the historical sociologist, because it indicates the numbers of babies who may be present at any time or during any period with no recognized mature male protectors, as well as being some sort of measure of the propensity of women to produce them. But the illegitimacy ratio, as is well known, is inappropriate as a gradation of this last propensity. The only women who can bear bastards are those not married to their partners; therefore, the proportion of all children who are born illegitimate, the ratio, can vary with the proportion of women in the population eligible to bear such children, without the propensity towards illegitimacy changing at all. It is obvious also that the number of births in any one year will always affect the illegitimacy ratio very directly: if it goes up sharply, for example, because married women have more children, the ratio will go down even though the unmarried women have the same number of bastard children as before.

These disadvantages of the bastardy ratio were recognized quite early, and it has been conventional to prefer the bastardy *rate* as a measure of illegitimacy, that is, the number of irregular births as a function of the women at risk, generally those unmarried, widowed or divorced aged 15 to 44. We now know that a rate reckoned in this way may also be deceptive to some extent, in our day, anyway. This is because a significant proportion of all illegitimate births can occur to married women, that is to women of married status becoming pregnant by men not their legal husbands.[15]

In the era of parish registration in England, when divorce was an impossibility for any other than highly privileged people, consensual unions between partners indissolubly married to other persons may well have been fairly common. This was, after all, the only choice open to spouses whose marriages broke down and who were unwilling to live for ever alone: there is evidence in lists of inhabitants that such partnerships existed. Here is an example from a Welsh parish, listed successively

[Listing of 1685]   [Listing of 1686]

---

[15] The Registrar-General stated in 1970 that 'the conventional use of the single, widowed and divorced female population as the denominator for the rate could be misleading, particularly for women over 25; nearly one child in three might have been born to a married woman, or one who would describe herself as such in the Census'. See the *Statistical Review* for 1966, Part III, referring to its counterpart for 1964, pp. 65–8, where the results of tracing 1,059 mothers reporting bastards in April 1961 to the 1961 Census are given: 26% of all illegitimate births were found to have occurred to women stated to be married in the Census. I have seen no reference by demographers to a further type of irregular birth within marriage, the one to a woman who does not acknowledge the fact in registering the baby, and may even be unaware of it herself. L. E. Schacht and H. Gershowitz reported in 1961 to the Second International Congress of Human Genetics that a blood-group match of children to their parents in the Detroit area of the U.S.A. revealed a minimum of 1.4% of all white children ($n = 1,417$) and of 8.9% of all Negro children ($n = 523$) who could not have been the offspring of their legal fathers, although not described as illegitimate in any context (*Proceedings* 2 (1963): 994-7; I owe this reference to Professor Michael Lerner). Births of the last kind escape both the rate and the ratio, and their occurrence is one more indication of the danger of arguing from either to the extent of extra-marital intercourse. It seems dubious whether the rate could be amended so as to add to the denominator those married women who produce children whom they register as illegitimate, since they need not be living with their lovers; only 65% said they were doing so in the 1961 sample, and in any case declarations to this effect would be very difficult to obtain. It is obviously impossible to allow for the births engendered by non-spouses discovered by the geneticists; such births are not illegitimate at all from the social point of view.

in the years 1685 and 1686. Edward Parry and his concubine were presumably living in a stable, consensual partnership.[16]

An illegitimacy rate, then, of the conventional kind for all or for any part of the parish register era might be a somewhat misleading measure, as it can be in the England of our own day. Nevertheless, the rate is clearly the only available direct indicator of the propensity to produce illegitimates, and it is known that under certain circumstances rate and ratio can differ markedly in their pace and direction of change. We should be considerably better placed in comparing illegitimacy over time if we could calculate both statistics over the whole range of our data. This is out of the question, because we can get no national figures for the distribution of the population by age, sex and marital status before official registration began.

We do not know, therefore, how far the ups and downs of the illegitimacy ratio during the parish register era could be accounted for by fluctuations in the proportions of the population eligible to produce bastards, by changes in the age at marriage for women, for example, or changes in the sex ratio and the number widowed. We can, however, compare the course of illegitimacy ratios with the course of illegitimacy rates over nearly the whole era of official statistics. These two curves are presented in fig. 3.4. Logarithms of the values have been used again here, so as to bring out the relationship between the rates of change of the two statistics over time. A plot of the course of the gross reproduction rate during the same period has also been added.

This figure is not discouraging about the relationship of the rate and the ratio from our point of view, which is rough, rather than refined, historical comparison for England alone. Clearly the two statistics could occasionally move independently of each other over short periods, and even go in opposite directions. The movement of the ratio, as must be expected, was more volatile than that of the rate, since the rate is dependent on factors like age composition which are unlikely to change overnight. No one would venture to estimate the absolute level of the one statistic from a knowledge of the other alone, but safer inferences between the two might be made about the direction if not the speed of change. On the whole the two statistics have followed each other reasonably well, if sometimes at a distance, over the last 120 of our 400 years. The two or three occasions when they have travelled in divergent directions may be explained, at least to some extent, by the exceptional circumstances of the two world wars.

---

[16] Parish of Llanelian, in Denbighshire; reference supplied by Eric Sheldon. At Eccleshall in Cheshire a clerical listing was drawn up during the 1690s which, with obvious scepticism, described some of the women heading households as *claiming* to be married to a husband then absent, and some unions as 'stated' to consist in marriage.

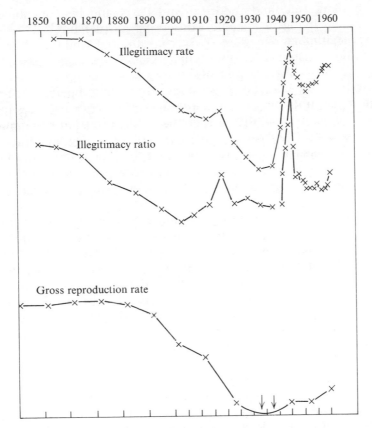

Fig. 3.4   Illegitimacy ratio, illegitimacy rate and gross reproduction rate, 1840s–1960s. *Source*: reports of Registrar-General.

Allowing for these incoherencies, and stressing our interest in long-term development rather than in short-term oscillation, we cautiously maintain that ratios alone are a reasonably adequate indication both of the extent of bastardy and of the propensity to produce illegitimate children. Given the record between the 1840s and the 1930s, it would be astonishing if it turned out that a major part of the gross movement we are interested in was due to changes in fertility, in the age composition, the sex composition and the level of marriage in the population at large. We should like to have more revealing measures for the parish register era, but we believe that the ratio alone is adequate for our over-riding object of setting out the record as to the frequency with which illegitimate children were born in the past. We are also concerned with the logically distinct phenomenon of the propensity of women to produce them, but we shall have to accept rather distant and oblique indications of that.

A much more interesting feature of fig. 3.4, both for the demographic and for the sociological study of illegitimacy, is the association which it may suggest between the behaviour of gross reproduction rates and that of illegitimacy rates and ratios over the period from the 1840s to the 1950s. They all three seem to change together, with a time lag of about a decade between the illegitimacy ratio and the illegitimacy rate, and two decades or three between them and the gross reproduction rate.

It is even possible to advance the hypothesis that a direction of change in illegitimacy is to some degree *predictive* of a direction of change of fertility. On this suggestion the well-known peak in English fertility in the 1870s would correspond to the high point of illegitimacy in the 1840s: the sharp decline of the rate of reproduction in the 1880s and 1890s to the outstanding fall (the fastest since the 1650s) of illegitimacy in the 1860s and 1870s. Even the upsurge of fertility in the 1950s and 1960s could conceivably be said to have its premonition in the behaviour of the illegitimacy statistics in the 1910s and 20s.

Against such a somewhat unlikely proposal is the possibility that the relationship between the curves is merely coincidental. This cannot be tested until we have comparable curves for other societies. There is in any case no need to go as far as to hint at prediction in this way in order to agree that these similarities of direction bear out in some detail for England over a long period a suggestion made by Shorter, van de Walle and Knodel in 1971. The fall in illegitimacy between 1880 and 1940 all over Europe, they tentatively propose, was entailed by the fall in fertility during that period, which demographers often refer to as that of the European demographic transition.

But can it be shown that the same effect was present in the first half of our four-hundred-year interlude in English history? Can the wave motion which may characterize illegitimacy throughout these fifteen generations be supposed to be linked to a similar shape in the fertility curve over the same time span? In order to explore this hypothesis, it will be necessary to look at the figures for the course of demographic change during the parish register era.

Table 3.2 makes it possible to compare the decadal ratios of baptisms to marriages and indexes of increase or decrease in the population given in table 3.1 for the master sample of 24 parishes with similar ratios for the largest collection of such statistics we have, those for 404 aggregated sets of figures now under analysis by the Cambridge Group. The bastardy ratios underlying fig. 3.1, for 98 parishes, have been added. The relationship between the two sets of numbers in tables 3.1 and 3.2 is fairly close, though those in table 3.1 are more erratic, as would be expected, since

TABLE 3.2. *Decadal ratios and indexes*

Date	Ratio of baptisms to marriages (404 parishes)	Index of increase/ decrease (404 parishes)	Bastardy ratio (98 parishes)
1580s	3.69	27.26	2.84
1590s	3.68	13.34	3.08
1600s	3.93	28.92	3.20
1610s	4.04	17.35	2.61
1620s	4.41	18.63	2.54
1630s	4.35	14.02	2.06
1640s	5.62	17.12	1.70
1650s	4.24	6.89	0.94
1660s	4.86	5.19	1.48
1670s	4.84	4.31	1.30
1680s	4.57	−0.07	1.52
1690s	4.80	8.99	1.82
1700s	4.26	16.00	1.80
1710s	3.94	10.70	2.12
1720s	3.82	−3.49	2.24
1730s	3.89	16.23	2.69
1740s	4.06	11.23	2.85
1750s	3.77	20.42	3.35
1760s	3.39	15.80	4.17
1770s	3.63	24.19	4.45
1780s	3.63	22.74	5.00
1790s	3.75	28.18	5.07
1800s	3.66	32.96	5.32
Mean of ratios 4.12		Mean of ratios 2.79	

the sample is so much smaller. They agree in suggesting that baptisms were increasing up to the 1630s, fell rather sharply after that and, like the illegitimacy ratio, were at a minimum in the 1650s.[17] The index of increase or decrease follows roughly the same course over the whole of the early period of booming population, and over the succeeding half-century when baptisms increased only very slowly, or even fell below burials, and when the general tendency was itself towards a static or even a declining population.

[17] The actual decadal totals for baptisms, marriages and burials will be separately published from the Cambridge Group. Close examination of them cautions against treating the data for the 1640s and 50s too seriously, however, since the yearly totals for the 404 parishes show evident signs of a sudden collapse in registration after 1643, which may not have been put right until after 1662. This is understandable in view of the disturbed state of the country and the Church during the Civil War from 1642 onwards, and under the various civil and ecclesiastical regimes which intervened before the restoration of Charles II in 1660.

Not until the 1730s, a good century after the population arrest had set in, did steady increase begin again, though the actual numbers from the smaller collection give a more pronounced impression of demographic decline than the indicators from the larger one. It is interesting that both should agree in selecting the 1680s and the 1720s as particularly unfavourable decades; even more so that the spurt which seems to have started in the 1750s was interrupted in both series during the 1760s, and did not give way to the rapid rise which is always associated with the great industrial revolution until the 1770s. The interplay between economic and demographic vicissitude over this crucial interlude of social mobilization, the first occasion on which any society experienced that process, was evidently rather complex.

But our concern here is with illegitimacy particularly in relation to fertility, and it is important to notice that in both sets of figures bastardy ratios did seem to change over this whole series of decades in sympathy with the index of surplus or deficit in the population. A rank order correlation by decade of the illegitimacy ratio with this index is highly significant indeed (Spearman $r = 0.778$, $Z = 3.647$ for the index and ratios in table 3.2). A crude indication of population increase tells us very little, of course, about the actual story of demographic dynamics over this period. Nevertheless, it is perhaps worth pointing out that this index follows the course of the illegitimacy ratio, but is offset by a decade or two. Thus the low point in bastardy in the mid seventeenth century *precedes* the period of demographic stagnation in its later decades, and illegitimacy rises in the eighteenth century *before* the era of steady increase established itself, although the picture is not very clear-cut. Imaginative inference about illegitimacy as a predictor of demographic change should not be pushed beyond this point.

As for actual demonstration of fertility change from family reconstitution, we know from Wrigley's study of Colyton, which is, after all, one of our 24 communities, when fertility was high and when it was low in this single village. He specifies the years 1646—1719 as the interlude of lowest fertility, as measured by completed family size; this was, as we can see, also the interlude of lowest numbers of bastards and of lowest illegitimacy ratios. His two interludes of very high completed family size, 1560 to 1609 and 1770 to 1837, are, on the other hand, just the periods when our figures and statistics show the illegitimacy ratio also to be in its upper reaches.

But reconstitution makes possible absolutely direct measures of marital fertility, and we may quote Wrigley's discussion of his remarkable table of age-specific measures of that tendency broken down into rather different date intervals, though all of them interestingly related to the changes in our illegitimacy graph.

'In the first period 1560—1629, the age-specific marital fertility rates were high. There is a marked decline in the last 15 years before the plague [in Colyton] of 1645—6 and this became pronounced after 1646. Fertility remained low throughout the period (1640—1719) which was marked also by an exceptionally high average age at first marriage for women. During the period 1720—1769 there was some recovery in fertility rates, while during the final period 1770—1837 the rates were much higher, though still not quite at the level attained in the sixteenth and early seventeenth centuries. There was therefore a cycle in marital fertility, passing from high through low to high once more during the three centuries under review.'[18]

The reference to a rise in the age of marriage for women at the time when fertility was low should not escape us, for this was also the time of low illegitimacy. When taken along with the evidence on the point from other reconstitutions now in progress, the facts about women's ages at first marriage at Colyton — rising from a mean of 27.0 in 1566—1619 to 29.6 in 1647 1719, falling to 26.8 in the succeeding sixty years and to 25.1 in 1770—1837 — relate to our illegitimacy ratios in an unmistakable fashion. It is not justifiable, it would seem, to suppose that when the parishioners of pre-industrial England married late, illegitimacy amongst them was always high, and when they married early, the number of bastards inevitably went down. This we believe falsifies any argument which supposes a necessary positive connection between sexual deprivation and the procreation of children outside marriage.[19] The figures could also be said to provide something in the way of numerical confirmation of our view that illegitimacy rates in the parish register era were not seriously out of line with illegitimacy ratios. For when the marriage age was high and the number of bastards stayed low — and both seem to be true between the mid seventeenth and the early eighteenth century — the illegitimacy rate must also have been low, since its denominator consists largely of women below the average age at marriage.

[18] Wrigley 1966 : 88—90; see his table 4 for age-specific marital fertility with its graphical representation in fig. 2, and his table 11 for completed family size. The corresponding statistics for fertility now becoming available for other parishes being reconstituted at Cambridge confirm this pattern of development.

[19] Levine and Wrightson (1975) have questioned whether the inverse relationship between illegitimacy ratios and age at first marriage for women can always be sustained for the earlier high (c. 1590—1610). Taking medians rather than means. they calculate that of 9 reconstituted parishes the inverse relationship holds in 4 only. No such question has arisen about the later high, where the inverse relationship is more pronounced. This revision may perhaps qualify the emphasis placed on the point in the original study, but does little to justify the dogma there under criticism — that a positive relationship between postponed marriage and level of illegitimacy is always to be expected.

These considerations place a great deal of weight on the accuracy of our figures on numbers of illegitimates born and baptized in the century from the 1640s to the 1730s. We shall have to consider an argument which can be used to question the value of the totals of illegitimate baptisms during this period. But before we do this, we may turn our attention to another type of irregular birth, that which results from conception taking place before the partners concerned are actually married, married in church, that is, and registered as married. The relation of such births to illegitimacies is an interesting and important one.

Although there is evidence on pre-nuptial pregnancy for a number of English parishes during the sixteenth, seventeenth and eighteenth centuries, no series over a term of years like the one we are examining for illegitimacy itself has yet been worked out for a sample of parishes. We have not undertaken to prepare such a file for our present purposes, though it would certainly have been possible to do so for our 24 parishes, given the effort necessary for a tedious task. But pre-nuptial pregnancy is logically distinct from bastardy: in fact two contrasting types can be distinguished, one of which can have nothing to do with illegitimacy whatever. In the first type no arrangement for an eventual marriage has been settled, or even perhaps proposed, when intercourse leading to pregnancy occurs; the decision to marry is taken after the arrival of a child looks certain. In the second type the partners have decided on marriage and engage in intercourse in confidence that a wedding will take place. The act may have been in fact an accepted part of the marriage process itself, a process which took several days or even weeks to complete, and in which what happened in church (service and registration) was the public celebration and confirmation.[20]

The first of these types is close to bastardy though separable from it. Its presence can readily be descried in the shotgun weddings which seem to have been responsible for the greater part of the births which family reconstitutions disclose before the mother was aged 20. Such pre-nuptial pregnancy differs from illegitimacy in that the child never seems to have been registered as a bastard; this in spite of the fact that the partners could be brought under ecclesiastical discipline for an offence somewhat grotesquely described as 'fornication before marriage with his own wife'. In Scotland, in the eighteenth century, punishment was ordered by the Kirk Session if the pastor found that the marriage had been put into the book less than nine months before the man and wife came to have their first child baptized. But even the stern Scottish minister accepted the birth as legitimate.

[20] For a brief description of traditional marriage processes, where the wedding came after the point at which sexual intercourse was permitted, and for some discussion of its probable distribution in the seventeenth and eighteenth centuries in England, see Laslett 1965 (1971 ed.: ch. 6).

The second type of pre-nuptial pregnancy appears when both partners have the intention of marrying one another at the time of the sexual act. On one interpretation of the marriage practices of traditional English society there was a form of matrimony quite widespread at the time, though probably varying from place to place, where each partner was at liberty to go to bed with the other directly a match had been definitely decided upon, although the church wedding was still in the future. Under such circumstances both the man and the woman can be assumed to have had the intention of accepting the risk of pregnancy during the interval between the decision to marry and the nuptial celebration in church. Pre-nuptial pregnancy arising in this way, our second type, must be held to be entirely distinct from bastardy. It would be interesting to know how far the irregular incidence of ecclesiastical action against the offence was due to the recognition that such anticipations of the church ceremony did not qualify for correction.

A variant of this situation, which could perhaps be called a third form of pre-nuptial pregnancy, is one which might well have been common. This is where only one of the partners, perhaps usually the woman, intends to marry the other partner, and ensures that conception is risked in order to induce the other to accept marriage as inevitable. No presumption that the form of marriage permitted cohabitation before registration need necessarily be in question here. This type must certainly be regarded as closer to illegitimacy in (irrecoverable) intention, but it is nevertheless quite distinct, and further away than pre-nuptial pregnancy of our first type.

Although there are these important differences between illegitimacy and pre-nuptial pregnancy, there are persuasive reasons for believing that the two were linked together as forms of sexual behaviour. Measures of pre-nuptial pregnancy in England over time seem to have varied in a way generally similar to measures of fertility of other kinds, legitimate and illegitimate. The tendency for the level to rise between Tudor and Victorian times has recently been shown by Hair (1966, 1970) to be qualified by a further tendency for the seventeenth century to have lower records than the eighteenth: our curve all over again. In the reconstitution evidence now being studied at Cambridge the familiar pattern seems to be rather clearer, as is plain from the figures set out in table 3.3 for seven parishes. The figures in the first column under each period are pre-nuptial pregnancies, and those in the second column total first pregnancies, with the percentage for the period for all parishes given in the last line.[21]

[21] From the reconstitution file of the Cambridge Group. A substantial but variable proportion (up to 40%) of all pre-nuptial pregnancies occurred to the youngest brides, those under 24. When these are disregarded, the level falls to 28% in 1550–99, but the overall contrast between periods remains clear.

TABLE 3.3. *Pre-nuptial pregnancy in seven parishes, by period*

| | 1550—99 | | 1600—49 | | 1650—99 | | 1700—49 | | 1750—99 | | 1800—49 | |
	A	B	A	B	A	B	A	B	A	B	A	B
Aldenham (Herts.)	6	27	12	75	8	48	9	45	17	51	25	63
Colyton (Devon.)	31	79	41	163	14	64	15	50	41	128	53	121
Hartland (Devon.)	13	48	32	138	43	176	48	153	95	207	56	132
Easingwold (Yorks.)	0	—	5	26	4	41	8	62	32	108	11	38
Alcester (War.)	1	6	18	75	7	80	16	89	19	82	14	73
Banbury (Oxon.)	10	33	23	140	8	81	43	162	73	237	0	5
Hawkshead (Lancs.)	0	—	25	116	19	95	16	70	44	97	44	95
Total	61	193	156	733	103	585	155	631	321	910	203	527
Proportion of live births less than 9 months after marriage	31.6%		21.3%		17.6%		24.6%		35.2%		38.5%	

A = Baptisms before 9 months.   B = Total baptisms.

The importance of these facts about pre-nuptial pregnancy to our discussion of the relationship of illegitimate to legitimate fertility is that they may help to buttress a general thesis that all forms of fertility changed together in response to the same set of influences, but that irregular conceptions leading to registered illegitimacies were affected more powerfully than any of the others.

VI

If what was accepted as marriage could alter over time, then children born of any particular type of marriage might be recorded as bastards at one period but not at another. If illegitimacy varied drastically from region to region, moreover — and we have already hinted at evidence of local peculiarities — the communities represented in our tables and figures may not stand for *English* bastardy history at all. Taken together, these considerations go to make up the obstacle in the way of accepting our full case about the behaviour of English illegitimacy over four hundred years.

Close examination of the figures in tables 3.1 and 3.2, especially those in the columns headed 'Ratio of baptisms to marriages', shows that there may be an argument for believing that the definition of marriage changed during the period of parochial registration. The value might be expected to be low during the later seventeenth century because fertility was low: in fact, the ratio of children to marriages is often used as a rough estimate of the marital fertility rate. In these figures, however, it will be seen that the number of children to a marriage was markedly *higher* during the later seventeenth century, the earlier part of the period of arrested growth of population, than it was over the whole spread of years from the 1580s to the 1810s. It appears that in these collections of data there were actually more children to a marriage when fertility was low than when fertility was high, which is quite against expectation. Only one explanation of this seems possible, that marriages are missing from church registers during this period of low fertility and must therefore have taken place outside the regular parish institutions. Here, then, we are faced with what amounts' to a change in the definition of marriage and hence perhaps in the definition of what should be accepted as a legitimate birth.

Now the full consideration of this argument against accepting the fall in registered bastardies in the later seventeenth century at its face value cannot be our present concern. Our preliminary descriptive commentary is already much weighed down with essential details of the methods used to extract illegitimacy figures from our recalcitrant material. We must content ourselves with noticing here that the period of low ratios of baptisms to marriages by no means coincides completely with the period of low legitimate and illegitimate fertility. The baptism/marriage ratio is high during the later part of the peak in bastardy early in the seventeenth century, and returns to normal well before the level of illegitimacy began its sharp rise in the eighteenth century. It could perhaps be argued that bastardy was increasing, if marginally, at the time that the baptism/marriage ratio fell, and this would attribute a residual influence to the practice of clandestine marriage. But it would seem unjustifiable to go further than this.

There are other interesting facts and circumstances which bear upon this issue. The later seventeenth century is well known to have been a time when clandestine marriage was widespread. Dr Wrigley has found a parish, Tetbury in Gloucestershire, where such irregular weddings were openly referred to in the register during the 1690s. The children of these unions were not baptized as bastards.[22] Indeed, there is no

[22] See *Local Population Studies*, no. 10 (Spring 1973), and for the first discussion of the paradox of high baptism/marriage ratios in the late seventeenth century, no. 3 of the same journal (1969). Close comparison of tables 3.1 and 3.2 above shows that in the late eighteenth and early nineteenth centuries these ratios were abnormally *low* in the master

clear evidence that a priest or a parish clerk would mark a baby as illegitimate even if he were uncertain whether the mother had undergone any form of matrimony at all. The criterion seems simply to have been whether or not the father was recognized as the husband of the mother at the time of the birth. This being so, it is difficult to see how the greater or lesser prevalence of irregular marriages should give rise to differing degrees of willingness on the part of parsons to accept as legitimate children whose mothers did not 'produce their marriage lines'.[23]

For the strength of the argument for supposing that the illegitimate registrations of the century 1620–1719 are not greatly out of line with illegitimate births in that period is positive rather than negative. It rests on the attitude to bastardy of parishioners as well as of the clergy. However various the forms and practices of marriage, it is claimed, it would usually be publicly known whether a couple should be recognized as man and wife, and their offspring as legitimate. When all the evidence is in view, it seems to us that we are not obliged to suppose that any temporary decline in regularly registered ecclesiastical marriages led to such pronounced uncertainty about the status of candidates for baptism at this time that they were less often described as bastards than they should have been.

As for the issue of the representativeness of our figures, the outcome of the discussion of the 24 parishes going to make up our master sample, set out in appendix 1, is indeed the detection of a clear bias due to geography. Rochdale, which has already been mentioned, and Oswestry, the 2 largest parishes in the 24, turn out to have exaggerated the rise-and-fall effects in the bastardy curve not because of their relatively large size but because they were situated where they were. Now that we have the larger samples represented in figs. 3.1 and 3.2 to compare with the

sample as compared with the 404 parishes. This seems to have been due to an under-registration of baptisms, perhaps as a result of the growth of nonconformity in the large parishes, which are so considerable a part of the 24-parish sample. Without Rochdale the statistic would have been higher at that time, and in the seventeenth century, too, for that parish never experienced exaggerated figures of this kind.

The ratio of baptisms to marriages returned in the 1700s to its level in the 1600s, and it would seem that clandestine marriage declined markedly at that time. Half a century later the Hardwick Marriage Act (1753) put the whole set of practices outside the bounds of civil law, irrespective of the ecclesiastical. There was no consequent rise in marriages detectable in the parish registers, certainly not outside London, and no sudden effect on the number of illegitimates.

[23] References to such documents, presumably certified copies of entries in the marriage register, are not uncommon, especially in imaginative literature. But I have never seen one, nor an instance of a priest demanding that one should be produced before he would accept a baby as legitimate.

24 parishes, the extent of this distortion can be estimated, and the fact that they did yield the proper general course of bastardy over time can be confirmed, in spite of the exaggerations. But the tendency of illegitimacy to vary because of locality alone, a tendency which has now been borne out in other countries and for other periods, is obviously of importance in its own right. A collection of 24 parishes such as those comprising our master sample is of little use by itself for studying regional variation. The much larger numbers in the computer-based collection cannot yet be exploited for the purpose, and may never yield very impressive results, since the registration of illegitimacy varies so much within these collections. Accordingly, further sets of bastardy recordings have had to be brought in.

VII

For the purpose of making a rough general survey of geographical variation in English illegitimacy ratios over time we extended our collection of parishes by choosing 100 other sets of recordings. It was out of the question to check the entries of bastards in these registers as was done for the master sample.[24] Many of the 100 sets of recordings appear only in the original parish books held in the churches themselves, or at various local repositories, and the purpose we had in mind did not in any case justify the effort. This gave us a little more freedom in the places we could take, but we were still obliged to pay as much attention as possible to continuity and completeness of recording.

To this end, as will be seen from tables 3.4−10, we have divided the 100 sets of passable recordings quite arbitrarily into five areas of the country. These areas were dictated to us far more by the availability of the figures than by such knowledge as we had of 'natural' divisions of this kind, or even by considerations of the distribution of the population. The counties in each *bastardy region* can be read off from the tables themselves. There was little point in working out illegitimacy ratios in each decade at each parish, and we satisfied ourselves with obtaining figures for every place and every region for the four select periods to be seen in the column headings of the tables, together with a final column for the whole set of decades. Three of these sets of decades are easily recognizable as the developmental periods of our discussion so far. The first (1581−1640) is the time of the early high, the early illegitimacy wave. The second (1661−1720) is that of the middle low, omit-

---

[24] There are a number of places common to the master sample, the samples of 98 and 165, and the full set of 404, the last of which does not, however, contain quite all even of the original 24. We have checked the 98 parishes represented in the curve displayed in fig. 3.1 for regionality and found them to be reasonably representative.

TABLE 3.4. *Illegitimacy ratios by select periods (countrywide collection of 24 checked sets of figures)*

Parish	Period 1: decades 1—8 1581—1640			Period 2: decades 11—16 1661—1720		
	No. of bastards	Total baptisms	%	No. of bastards	Total baptisms	%
(1) Woburn, Beds. (−1810)	22	1,285	1.7	18	1,720	1.0
(2) Gawsworth, Ches.	20	854	2.3	19	909	2.1
(3) Bridekirk, Cumb. (−1810)	84	1,519	5.5	18	1,402	1.3
(4) Crosthwaite, Cumb. (−1810)	184	5,225	3.5	9	1,855	0.5
(5) Colyton, Devon.	98	3,505	2.8	62	2,050	3.0*
(6) Hartland, Devon.	84	2,158	3.9	50	1,791	2.8
(7) Aldenham, Herts. (−1810)	27	2,171	1.2	15	1,738	0.9
(8) Speldhurst, Kent	15	1,090	1.4	17	1,153	1.5*
(9) Hawkshead, Lancs.	47	2,407	2.0	16	1,670	1.0
(10) Rochdale, Lancs.	696	11,660	6.0	261	12,493	2.1
(11) Norwich St Giles, Norfolk	12	839	1.4	21	1,711	1.2
(12) Oswestry, Salop (−1810)	358	6,478	5.5	140	6,165	2.3
(13) Pitminster, Somerset	34	1,403	2.4	67	1,335	5.0*
(14) Wedmore, Somerset (−1810)	88	2,922	3.0	37	2,404	1.5
(15) Alstonfield, Staffs. (−1810)	32	737	4.3	35	1,224	2.9
(16) Barton-under-Needwood, Staffs. (−1810)	12	753	1.6	6	1,081	0.6
(17) Horringer, Suffolk	4	504	0.8	5	509	1.0*
(18) Abinger, Surrey (−1810)	4	381	1.0	3	580	0.5
(19) Tanworth-in-Arden, War.	16	1,990	0.8	33	1,965	1.7*
(20) Bishops Canning, Wilts. (1601—1810)	15	901	1.7	21	1,567	1.3
(21) Marske-in-Cleveland, Yorks. N.R. (−1810)	37	900	4.1	9	979	0.9
(22) Gisburn, Yorks. W.R. (−1810)	48	2,209	2.2	47	2,202	2.1
(23) Linton-in-Craven, Yorks. W.R. (−1810)	11	1,217	0.9	3	1,461	0.2
(24) Thornton-in-Lonsdale, Yorks. W.R. (−1810)	2	751	0.3	18	656	2.7*
Overall ratio	1,950	53,859	3.6	930	50,620	1.8
Less Rochdale and Oswestry	896	35,721	2.5	529	31,962	1.7
Mean of ratios			2.5			1.7
Range			0.3—6.0			0.2—5.0
Median			2.1			1.4
124 parishes Overall ratio	8,776	230,794	3.80	3,617	226,265	1.60

*Ratio exceeds that in period 1. See text.

	Period 3: decades 17–26 1721–1820			Period 4: decades 23–26 1781–1820			1581–1820		
	No. of bastards	Total baptisms	%	No. of bastards	Total baptisms	%	No. of bastards	Total baptisms	%
(1)	129	3,275	3.9	51	1,079	4.7	173	6,716	2.6
(2)	163	2,944	5.5	71	1,321	5.4	204	5,018	4.1
(3)	81	2,226	3.6	49	941	5.2	200	5,548	3.6
(4)	193	4,074	4.7	113	1,532	7.4	406	12,430	3.3
(5)	214	3,864	5.5	83	1,891	4.4	389	10,324	3.8
(6)	300	3,771	8.0	165	1,733	9.5	446	8,379	5.3
(7)	115	3,004	3.8	45	1,075	4.2	161	7,518	2.1
(8)	211	3,028	7.0	142	1,639	8.7	245	5,392	4.5
(9)	277	3,555	5.0	106	1,576	6.7	246	8,359	2.9
(10)	2,381	47,690	5.0	1,406	25,225	5.9	3,393	74,484	4.6
(11)	133	2,815	4.7	91	1,120	8.1	168	5,707	2.9
(12)	449	10,791	4.2	180	4,046	4.4	948	23,780	4.0
(13)	113	2,502	4.5	50	1,057	4.7	224	5,771	3.9
(14)	176	4,456	3.9	85	1,853	4.6	319	10,788	3.0
(15)	113	2,926	3.9	63	860	7.3	184	5,262	3.5
(16)	79	2,038	3.9	39	818	4.8	101	4,206	2.4
(17)	74	1,375	5.4	46	622	7.4	84	2,547	3.3
(18)	58	1,516	3.8	30	525	5.7	68	2,650	2.6
(19)	211	4,483	4.7	105	2,047	5.1	260	8,681	3.0
(20)	191	2,958	6.5	97	1,046	9.3	234	5,964	3.9
(21)	64	2,099	3.0	27	858	3.1	113	4,316	2.6
(22)	169	4,398	3.8	85	1,625	5.2	274	9,626	2.8
(23)	153	4,321	3.5	97	1,707	5.7	173	7,450	2.3
(24)	126	2,758	4.6	77	1,177	6.5	146	4,348	3.4
	6,073	126,867	4.8	3,383	57,373	5.9	9,130	243,482	3.7
	3,243	68,386	4.7	1,448	21,357	6.8	4,818	146,910	3.3
			4.7			6.0			3.3
			3.0–8.0			3.1–9.5			2.1–5.3
			4.5			5.5			3.3
	26,628	710,439	3.75	15,111	335,201	4.51	37,557	1,297,441	2.89

ting the decades 1641—60 because, as must be expected, the figures are here so fragmentary as to be meaningless. The third period (1721—1820) is that of the later high, that is, the second, perhaps tidal, illegitimacy wave. The fourth period (1781—1820), however, has been inserted to select out the years when illegitimacy could be expected to be at its very highest for the whole parish register era.[25]

With this introduction we shall allow our 124 sets of English illegitimacy figures, a checked countrywide collection and five unchecked regional collections, to speak for themselves. We shall comment only on those points which seem to us to be relevant to our general discussion, and which are mostly salient features on table 3.10, the summary table.

These arrays of figures demonstrate that regional variation has been a well-marked feature of English bastardy and that it is present both in the summary statistics covering the whole set of decades under consideration and in the differential development of each bastardy region. As for the average over the centuries, our arbitrarily nominated West and North-west region stands out as the most bastardy-prone; it is notable that the overall percentage of its 20 sets of figures should be so close to that of our master sample. Bastardy region South comes second, well above the North, which is also clearly ahead of region East and region Middle: these two cannot be distinguished from each other. This is not the occasion to go into the possible reasons for such differences, and we have not marshalled such evidence as has so far become available so as to broach the subject.[26] Let it simply be recorded that the western and north-western counties were the counties of high illegitimacy during the parish register era: Gloucestershire, Herefordshire and Shropshire were amongst them, Lancashire and Cheshire being very

[25] In table 3.4 of this series the relevant figures from table 3.1 for the 24 select parishes have been rearranged so as to make direct comparison possible with tables 3.5—3.9. Extra lines have also been added so as to show the effect of the omission of Rochdale and Oswestry. A similar addition has been made to table 3.5, that for bastardy region East, but in this case to bring out the particular characteristics of two eastern counties, Norfolk and Suffolk. Measures of dispersion have been added at the foot of each column of the tables; range, median and a mean of ratios in contrast with the overall ratio. This should help in estimating the within-region variation. More exact measures seemed unnecessary, because our bastardy regions are so arbitrarily constructed, as is evident when they are compared to those of the Registrar-General; see appendix 2. The large array of figures in this series is mainly the work of R. A. Laslett, and I should like to acknowledge his help.

[26] The descriptive characteristics attached to the 24 parishes in the table in appendix 1 give us little help in beginning an ecological analysis of this phenomenon. North and North-west England were in what is sometimes called the Highland Zone, and grazing rather than crop-growing dominated the economy. But this variable does not explain the other rankings in the figures. Blayo (see n. 5 above) demonstrates regional variation in France in the eighteenth century.

TABLE 3.5. *Illegitimacy ratios by select periods (22 unchecked sets of figures): bastardy region East*

Parish	Period 1: decades 1–8 1581–1640 %	Period 2: decades 11–16 1661–1720 %	Period 3: decades 17–26 1721–1820 %	Period 4: decades 23–26 1781–1820 %	1581–1820 %
(1) Dedham, Essex (−1812)	0.5	0.5*	1.8	1.3	1.0
(2) Dengie, Essex	2.6	5.0*	3.9	2.8	3.0
(3) Writtle, Essex (1634−)	1.4	1.6*	4.0	4.4	3.1
(4) Edmonton, Middx.	2.5	0.2	1.4	1.5	1.3
(5) Berkhamsted, Herts.	0.8	0.7	3.2	3.2	2.5
(6) Hemel Hempstead, Herts.	0.6	0.1	1.2	1.2	0.7
(7) Hitchin, Herts. (1589−)	0.7	0.3	2.2	2.7	1.3
(8) Ampthill, Beds. (1602−)	1.2	1.1	2.5	2.7	1.8
(9) Kempston, Beds.	1.0	0.9	2.2	2.6	1.4
(10) Sawston, Cambs. (1601−)	1.7	0.3	1.5	1.6	1.7
(11) Framlingham, Suffolk	0.9	1.4*	6.3	6.3	3.6
(12) Hadleigh, Suffolk	0.7	1.2*	3.6	4.6	1.9
(13) North Elmham, Norfolk (−1812)	2.3	1.1	5.3	7.2	3.1
(14) Swaffham, Norfolk (16(8−)	0.8	1.5*	7.1	8.5	4.7
(15) Wells, Norfolk	0.5	1.6*	3.3	4.3	2.2
(16) Wymondham, Norfolk (1615−)	2.2	1.0	3.8	5.2	2.6
(17) Norwich St James, Norfolk	1.1	1.8*	3.8	3.8	2.7
(18) Norwich St Margaret, Norfolk	0.7	0.7*	2.6	6.1	1.7
(19) Grimsby, Lincs. (−1812)	1.6	0.7	2.0	2.8	1.8
(20) Ropsley, Lincs.	2.0	1.4	1.9	3.7	1.7
(21) Wrangle, Lincs. (1601−)	1.8	1.3	6.1	8.4	4.7
(22) Wyberton, Lincs.	2.4	1.9	3.4	6.0	2.5
Overall ratio	1.2	1.0	3.3	4.0	2.2
Mean of ratios	1.4	1.2	3.3	4.1	2.3
Range	0.5–2.6	0.1–5.0	1.2–7.1	1.2–8.5	0.7–4.7
Median	1.3	1.1	2.9	4.0	1.8
Norfolk and Suffolk (8 parishes)					
Overall ratio	1.1	1.3	4.2	5.8	2.7
Mean of ratios	1.2	1.3	4.9	6.1	2.6
Range	0.5–2.2	0.7–1.8	3.6–7.1	3.8–8.1	1.7–3.6

* Ratio equals or exceeds that in period 1.

TABLE 3.6.   *Illegitimacy ratios by select periods (23 unchecked sets of figures): bastardy region South*

Parish	Period 1: decades 1581–1640 %	Period 2: decades 1661–1720 %	Period 3: decades 1721–1820 %	Period 4: decades 1781–1820 %	1581–1820 %
(1) St Columb Major, Corn. (–1780)	2.8	0.7	2.8	—	1.9
(2) Branscombe, Devon.	3.9	1.0	4.6	4.0	3.2
(3) Chardstock, Devon. (1599–)	3.1	2.7	6.5	5.9	4.4
(4) Ottery St Mary, Devon. (1601–)	1.5	1.9*	4.4	1.2	2.7
(5) Stoke Gabriel, Devon. (–1812)	0.9	1.3*	4.4	4.5	2.1
(6) Widecombe, Devon.	1.3	1.4*	5.2	5.8	3.1
(7) Thorncombe, Dorset	1.3	1.0	5.1	6.7	3.2
(8) Frome, Somerset (–1812)	2.9	1.7	2.2	1.6	2.0
(9) North Cadbury, Somerset	3.0	2.3	5.9	2.3	4.5
(10) North Petherton, Somerset	2.7	2.2	4.7	5.2	3.6
(11) Bromham, Wilts. (–1812)	1.3	1.8*	5.0	8.1	3.1
(12) Sonning, Berks. (1592–1812)	0.4	1.1*	3.7	6.4	3.0
(13) Winkfield, Berks.	0.9	2.1*	4.7	5.5	3.4
(14) Boldre, Hants (1596–)	3.4	1.9	4.7	4.5	3.5
(15) Ringwood, Hants	2.0	1.8	4.1	5.8	3.0
(16) Romsey, Hants	2.1	1.0	3.2	3.4	2.4
(17) Selborne, Hants	2.1	0.7	4.9	6.7	3.0
(18) Salehurst Sussex	0.8	1.0*	5.5	5.6	3.6
(19) Ashford, Kent (1796–1812 missing)	1.0	0.4	5.3	6.7	2.3
(20) Eltham, Kent (1584–)	2.3	1.7	4.0	3.7	3.1
(21) Sittingbourne, Kent	2.6	2.1	5.7	6.4	4.4
(22) Sevenoaks, Kent (–1812)	2.9	0.7	5.2	6.1	3.1
(23) Tonbridge, Kent (1585–1812)	2.5	1.7	2.2	2.6	2.0
Overall ratio	2.1	1.4	4.0	4.5	2.9
Mean of ratios	1.9	1.5	4.5	4.9	3.1
Range	0.4–3.9	0.4–2.7	2.2–6.5	1.2–8.1	1.9–4.5
Median	2.1	1.7	4.7	5.5	3.1

* Ratio exceeds that in period 1.

138

TABLE 3.7. *Illegitimacy ratios by select periods (20 unchecked sets of figures): bastardy region West and North-west*

Parish	Period 1: decades 1–8 1581–1640 %	Period 2: decades 11–16 1661–1720 %	Period 3: decades 17–26 1721–1820 %	Period 4: decades 23–26 1781–1820 %	1581–1820 %
(1) Dymock, Glos.	2.1	0.7	6.1	9.1	4.0
(2) North Nibley, Glos.	2.4	1.2	5.2	6.2	3.3
(3) Westbury-on-Trym, Glos.	3.4	0.9	2.0	2.7	2.1
(4) Wotton-under-Edge, Glos.	0.4	1.1*	4.2	5.5	2.6
(5) Llantilio Pertholey, Mon. (1591–)	1.1	2.5*	6.1	7.5	3.7
(6) Ledbury, Herefs. (–1812)	3.7	0.9	5.8	8.4	3.6
(7) Wellington, Herefs. (1601–)	2.8	1.1	6.5	9.4	4.3
(8) Albrighton, Salop (–1812)	2.3	1.8	3.8	4.0	2.9
(9) Baschurch, Salop	3.7	1.5	3.4	4.2	2.9
(10) Cleobury Mortimer, Salop (1601–1812)	1.1	1.5*	2.7	4.9	2.0
(11) Wem, Salop (1583–1812)	2.3	2.4*	7.5	11.1	4.5
(12) Sandbach, Ches.	5.0	1.7	5.5	5.1	4.5
(13) Frodsham, Ches. (–1808)	3.3	1.0	4.3	5.4	3.3
(14) Lancaster, Lancs. (1601–1800)	4.0	1.3	3.1	3.9	2.8
(15) North Meols, Lancs. (1601–1812)	6.2	1.2	5.1	7.9	4.4
(16) Eccles, Lancs. (–1808)	7.2	1.5	5.1	7.3	4.8
(17) Warton, Lancs.	1.2	1.2*	4.0	5.4	2.9
(18) Whittington, Lancs. (–1800)	3.1	3.3*	3.8	8.0	3.3
(19) Radcliffe, Lancs. (–1812)	1.3	2.2*	4.4	5.5	3.7
(20) Sefton, Lancs. (1601–1780)	7.0	1.7	2.1	—	3.1
Overall ratio	3.6	1.4	4.6	6.2	3.6
Mean of ratios	3.2	1.5	4.5	6.4	3.4
Range	0.3–7.2	0.7–3.3	2.0–7.5	2.7–11.1	2.0–4.8
Median	2.9	1.4	4.3	5.5	3.3

* Ratio exceeds that in period 1.

TABLE 3.8. *Illegitimacy ratios by select periods (17 unchecked sets of figures): bastardy region Middle*

Parish	Period 1: decades 1–8 1581–1640 %	Period 2: decades 11–16 1661–1720 %	Period 3: decades 17–26 1721–1820 %	Period 4: decades 23–26 1781–1820 %	1581–1820 %
(1) Aylesbury, Bucks. (–1812)	0.8	1.6*	4.0	4.4	2.4
(2) Banbury, Oxon. (–1812)	1.0	1.2*	2.2	2.9	1.5
(3) Standlake, Oxon.	1.6	1.3	4.2	5.4	2.6
(4) Kings Norton, Worcs. (–1812)	1.1	1.9*	4.7	4.6	2.7
(5) Alcester, War.	3.0	0.8	2.0	3.3	1.7
(6) Rowington, War. (1613→)	0	1.3*	4.1	3.8	2.8
(7) Tredington, War.	0.5	1.5*	2.8	3.5	1.8
(8) Bottisford, Leics. (1601→)	1.2	0.8	2.4	3.4	1.8
(9) Castle Donnington, Leics. (1584→)	1.0	1.4*	2.9	2.4	2.3
(10) Hinckley, Leics.	0.9	0.7	1.7	1.3	1.3
(11) Loughborough, Leics.	1.0	0.8	2.6	2.9	1.8
(12) Market Harborough, Leics. (1601→)	1.8	1.2	2.5	2.1	1.8
(13) Melton Mowbray, Leics.	1.0	0.7	2.7	4.3	1.6
(14) Prestwold, Leics.	2.3	1.3	3.2	4.8	2.6
(15) Ellaston, Staffs. (–1812)	4.8	3.3	6.7	8.6	5.1
(16) Sedgley, Staffs.	2.5	1.1	2.5	1.8	2.2
(17) Stowe-by-Chartley, Staffs.	1.9	2.3*	4.8	6.6	3.6
Overall ratio	1.6	1.3	2.9	3.1	2.1
Mean of ratios	1.5	1.4	3.3	3.9	2.3
Range	0–4.8	0.7–3.3	1.7–6.7	1.3–8.6	1.3–5.1
Median	1.1	1.3	2.8	3.5	2.2

* Ratio exceeds that in period 1.

TABLE 3.9. *Illegitimacy ratios by select periods (18 unchecked sets of figures): bastardy region North*

Parish	Period 1: decades 1–8 1581–1640 %	Period 2: decades 11–16 1661–1720 %	Period 3: decades 17–26 1721–1820 %	Period 4: decades 23–26 1781–1820 %	1581–1820 %
(1) Arnold, Notts. (1601–)	2.4	1.8	2.4	2.8	2.3
(2) Warsop, Notts. (–1812)	1.9	0.7	3.0	4.5	1.9
(3) Dronfield, Derby.	3.4	2.6	4.3	5.7	3.4
(4) Wirksworth, Derby. (1613–)	2.9	1.2	3.0	2.5	2.3
(5) Addingham, Yorks. W.R. (–1812)	2.4	1.0	2.7	3.2	2.2
(6) Adel, Yorks. W.R. (–1812)	2.8	0.7	1.7	1.7	1.4
(7) Almondbury, Yorks. W.R.	3.0	0.4	2.9	4.4	2.7
(8) Bolton Percy, Yorks. W.R.	2.7	1.5	4.7	5.2	2.7
(9) Conisborough, Yorks. W.R.	2.1	1.7	4.5	7.0	3.2
(10) Ilkley, Yorks. W.R. (1597–1812)	2.7	3.3*	6.3	9.5	4.5
(11) Keighley, Yorks. W.R. (1597–)	4.3	4.5*	3.0	3.4	2.7
(12) Skipton, Yorks. W.R.	5.4	2.3	4.5	5.6	4.0
(13) Thornhill and Flockton, Yorks. W.R.	2.8	1.5	1.9	1.8	2.0
(14) Bridlington, Yorks. E.R. (1601–1812)	0.6	0.7*	4.1	5.3	2.5
(15) Easingwold, Yorks. N.R. (1603–)	1.8	1.5	3.6	5.2	2.8
(16) Earsdon, Northumb. (1607–)	2.9	0.4	2.5	3.1	2.1
(17) Tynemouth, Northumb. (1607–)	1.2	0.7	1.3	1.5	1.1
(18) Wigton, Cumb. (1605–)	3.8	1.2	3.8	4.9	3.8
Overall ratio	2.9	1.3	2.9	3.5	2.5
Mean of ratios	2.8	1.6	3.5	4.3	2.6
Range	0.6–5.4	0.4–4.5	1.3–6.3	1.5–9.5	1.1–4.5
Median	2.7	1.5	3.0	4.4	2.6

* Ratio exceeds that in period 1.

TABLE 3.10. *Regionalism in the history of English illegitimacy 1581–1820: summary of statistics of overall ratios for the country and five bastardy regions*

Region	Period 1 (early high)	Period 2 (middle low)	Period 3 (later high)	Period 4 (final peak)	Total
Nationwide collection (24 checked sets)	3.6	1.8	4.8	5.9	3.7
Bastardy region East (22 sets)	1.2	1.0	3.3	4.0	2.2
Bastardy region South (23 sets)	2.1	1.4	4.0	4.5	2.9
Bastardy region West and North-west (20 sets)	3.6	1.4	4.6	6.2	3.6
Bastardy region Middle (17 sets)	1.6	1.3	2.9	3.1	2.1
Bastardy region North (18 sets)	2.9	1.3	2.9	3.5	2.5
100 sets	2.3	1.3	3.5	4.2	2.7

conspicuous. Comparison with the rank orders of counties in the 1840s set out in appendix 2 shows that these counties did not lose their propensity towards high illegitimacy levels, but were joined by others.

Convention requires that our aim in this preliminary exploration of the history of English bastardy should be a set of statistics which best approximates to truly national figures. The more such an object is pursued, of course, the more elusive it becomes. Given such a requirement, however, it is important that any collection of figures claiming representativeness should allow for these quite marked regional variations. If it contained too many places from the North, and especially from the North-west and West, its overall level would be too high, and its development over time rather overdrawn, as seems to have happened with the master sample.

Moreover it cannot be claimed that every parish with tolerably good illegitimacy registration actually displays the pattern of an early high, a middle low and a later high in the parish register era. A perusal of the columns of our geographical tables, parish by parish, makes this quite clear. For there are 39 parishes marked with a star where period 2 was not lower in its illegitimacy ratio than period 1, and 6 of them appear amongst our selected 24. In nearly one-third of the places we have examined, therefore, the overall temporal pattern we are describing at such length was not in evidence at all. In every single set of recordings except one, there is a rise from period 2 to period 3; at Dengie in Essex, low-lying and malarial, the home of what was once called Dengie fever, where burials always seem to have exceeded baptisms, the ratio actually fell. Dengie apart, a countrywide rise is clearly sanctioned, therefore, for the later eighteenth century, and perhaps an overall tendency to secular increase from the mid sixteenth century onwards, with some interruption in the seventeenth century. But the wave motion we have discussed, with peaks in 1600 and 1800, is less well borne out by these rough indicators.

No one with any experience of data of this kind, however, would expect even as simple a relationship as the one in question to be shown by every instance; even in region West and North-west, where the pattern is at its strongest, stronger, in fact, than it is amongst our 24 parishes, 4 places conradict the predicted fall from period 1 to period 2. We consider that to find 85 parishes out of 124 which demonstrate a principle of this kind in figures so inexact and wavering is about as much as we could have hoped for. The impressive feature of our tables, we believe, as it is the impressive feature of the whole body of figures we have collected on the subject, most of them too fragmentary, too restricted in their temporal range to have been included here, is the way in which each new parish can be expected to behave as has been predicted. Such a submission could only be justified by a mass of fragmentary statistics, but we shall content ourselves with one such partial set of recordings standing all alone. The bastardy figures from the parish of Prestbury in Cheshire in table 3.11 can justifiably occupy such a position, for they have a strong claim to be the most remarkable in all of England during the era of parochial registration.

Even these detailed figures do less than justice to the record of this parish, for in the calendar year 1590 there were 41 baptisms and 9 illegitimacies (all named as such), giving a bastardy ratio of 22%; there were in addition 4 bastards among the 42 burials. The disconcerting irregularity of the registrations should be noticed, as well as the oddities of description which make so much inference necessary. In all these respects Prestbury is only too representative of the scores of further parishes for which we possess fragmentary records, and which have therefore had to be omitted from our estimates. But Prestbury, like so many of the others, shows forth that part of our bastardy curve which we should expect it to do between the 1560s and 1630s. This, let us stress again, is the circumstance which makes us convinced of the reality of the pattern over time in English illegitimacy which we have been analysing.

We cannot allow an interest in exceptionally high figures to let us linger in bastardy region West and North-west.[27] The final feature of our geographical tables which requires comment is perhaps the most interesting of all, and the most surprising. Bastardy region West and North-west has the highest ratios in all the columns of the summary table, 3.10, except in the middle low when the southern region equals it. Region West and North-west in fact has both a distinguishing overall feature, its general high level, and also a temporal pattern, for the rhythmic shape of its curve over time is the most pronounced, 'classical', as we might say.

Bastardy region East has a pronounced individual pattern, too, one which can be seen to be at its most marked in the two counties of Norfolk and Suffolk. Here ratios are low throughout, for we are in the part of the country where bastardy seems to have been least prominent in the parish

[27] The ratio was as high as 5.6% at Standish, Lancs., in 1551–70, 7.3% in 1571–90, and 5.6% in 1591–1610. It was 6.4% (14 out of 219) as early as 1541–60 at Whittington in that county, 9.1% at Eccles in 1581–1600, 7.4% at North Meols in 1621–40. The affected area spread over from Lancashire and Cheshire into parts of Staffordshire, as can be seen from table 3.8. The ratio was 6.0% at Eccleshall in 1574–60, 6.1% 1588–95 and 1601–11: even in Herefordshire the ratio could rise quite a lot, quite early, as at Ledbury 1561–80, when it was 4.2%. The highest ratio in the parish register era does not in fact belong to the early high or to this group of counties, but to Cumberland during the later high; at Arthuret it was 9.1% in 1761–80, 16.4% 1781–1800, 19.4% 1801–20 and 14.4% 1821–37; it was 15.3% there over the whole period 1781–1837.

TABLE 3.11. *Illegitimacy ratios at Prestbury, Cheshire, 1561–1636 (by baptism and burial)*[a]

Decade	Baptisms	Burials	Baptisms of illegitimates		Bastardy ratio (baptismal)		Burials of illegitimates	% of all burials
			Max.	Min.	Max. (%)	Min. (%)		
1: 1561–1570	354	336	16	13	4.5	3.7	8	2.1
2: 1571–1580	443	433	71	61	16.0	13.8	42	9.7
3: 1581–1590	454	566	72	28	15.9	6.2	12	4.3
4: 1591–1600	415	625	66	7	15.9	1.7	16	2.6
5: 1601–1610	422	576	45	27	10.7	6.4	16	2.8
6: 1611–1620	446	559	29	19	6.5	4.3	14	2.5
7: 1621–1630	542	628	37	7	6.8	1.3	2	0.3
8: 1631–1636	358	497	2	2	0.6	0.6	1	0.2
Total 1561–1636	3,434	4,270	338	164	9.8%	4.8%	111	2.6%

[a]Communicated by Mr J. R. Harrison, who has made a special study of illegitimacy in this parish. His maximum and minimum figures correspond to *bastards named* and *bastards inferred* in table 3.1 above Inference was made from the presence of the word *alias*, sometimes abbreviated *als*, and the fact that when this expression appears, no father's name is given.

145

register era, but the level was rising all the time, with only the slight drop in one or two places during the middle low to interrupt the steady progress. We may notice from appendix 2 that Norfolk had risen to be second in order of the counties by 1842, and was third in 1845. Whereas, therefore, in this predominantly agricultural area widespread bastardy under Victoria was comparatively new with little historical root, in industrializing Lancashire it had a history behind it continuing back for as long as we have as yet any recordings. The historical pattern of the other three bastardy regions is not so pronounced, but traces of local individuality can be discovered in the tables.

In the South, ratios were high in general, but relatively low in period 1. The figures for the actual parishes in table 3.6 show that those in the centre of the region, in Hampshire, Berkshire and perhaps West Kent, are those which pull down the mean, and as in the East variation may be based on quite small areas. This seems also to be the case in the Middle region, which is both intermediate and mixed. Leicestershire was evidently a county of low recordings, but, as we have seen, parts of Staffordshire can provide very high ones. The North was marked by highish levels, but a curious shortfall comes at the time of the later high; like the rest of these effects, this may be due only to oddities in registration from parish to parish at that time of increasing clerical laxity and of growing nonconformist sects. In early Victorian times Cumberland, with a ratio of 11.1% in 1842 and 11.4% in 1845, had the highest recordings in the country, and with Westmorland showed markedly more illegitimacy than the mining county of Durham. It is regrettable that we cannot yet confirm that the very low levels of London and the South-east, which come out in appendix 2 and in all the nineteenth-century records, were a continuation of historical trends. I myself believe this to be so (see n. 28).

[28] The computer-based sample of 404 parishes has been shown to possess marked regional characteristics as to illegitimacy even though its recordings of that variable are so erratic.

As Levine, Wrightson and others have shown, bastardy can also be studied very profitably in various other classes of documents, such as court records detailing the prosecution of bastard-begetters and -bearers, poor-law records showing payments to mothers of bastards and so on. It seems unlikely, however, that any exact notion of numerical variation from area to area will be forthcoming from such sources. The reader will have noticed that no consideration has been given to the possibility of urban/rural differences in the bastardy ratio. This is because our aggregative file is deficient in urban recordings, especially in those specifying bastards. What evidence there is, however, seems to imply low illegitimacy in English cities, lower than in the English countryside. This is what Leffingwell found in the 1890s and what is quite evident in Appendix 2. Even the exceedingly low recordings for the Metropolitan area to be seen there cannot be dismissed out of hand. The trifling figures appearing in the full returns for London slum areas must be wrong, but it is not improbable that the city shared to some extent in the habits

Here we must reluctantly abandon our hasty sketch of regional variation in the history of English illegitimacy in the parish register era. Far larger numbers of relatively reliable recordings would be necessary to make a serious investigation possible. In fig. 3.5 the geographical pattern of English illegitimacy is presented for its nineteenth-century peak, almost, but not quite, the pattern which we believe obtained over all four hundred years. Norfolk and Suffolk are the great exceptions.

VIII

We cannot go very far here towards justifying the remarks made at the outset about the existence of a sub-society of the bastardy-prone in English villages in the parish register era. Almost the whole body of the rather tangled and somewhat miscellaneous evidence, which is probably all that we are entitled to expect to have, must be reserved for a separate occasion. One fairly straightforward statistic, however, can usually be recovered from any register consistently recording illegitimacy. This statistic has to do with the relative numbers of bastard births which are due to mothers known to have had more than one illegitimate child.

We shall call baptisms of this kind 'repeaters', which we admit is scarcely logical because it is the actions of the mother which are repetitive, not those of the children. The principle we think we have found to be at work is as follows. When the bastardy ratio goes up, the proportion of repeaters amongst the baptisms tends to go up too, at an even faster pace. The inference we provisionally draw is that an increase in the proportion of illegitimate births is disproportionately due to those prone to such a form of childbearing having a greater number of confinements. In table 3.12, we illustrate this principle from three parishes.

In presenting this table we have made use of the information already surveyed, that is to say, we have headed our columns for periods 'early high', 'middle low', 'later high', in spite of the fact that at Wem the ratio actually rose in the middle period; we have been somewhat arbitrary in our datings, too.[29] We have ventured, in fact, to illustrate our suggested

of its hinterland, where illegitimacy was low in the 1840s and seems always to have been so, in comparison with, say, Cheshire or Lancashire. In this, England provides a quite startling contrast to the French situation between Paris and other great towns with their enormous illegitimacy totals, and the rural areas where illegitimacy was low.

[29] At Colyton the middle low is taken to be the years 1640–89, the period 1661–1720 not being readily recoverable — unfortunate, since there was an unparalleled rise in bastardy there over the period 1690 to 1739. Values are so small at Bolton Percy that they have little significance, especially in periods 1 and 2. The figures from this parish are due to Bernard Ayre, and those from Wem are due to R. A. Laslett.

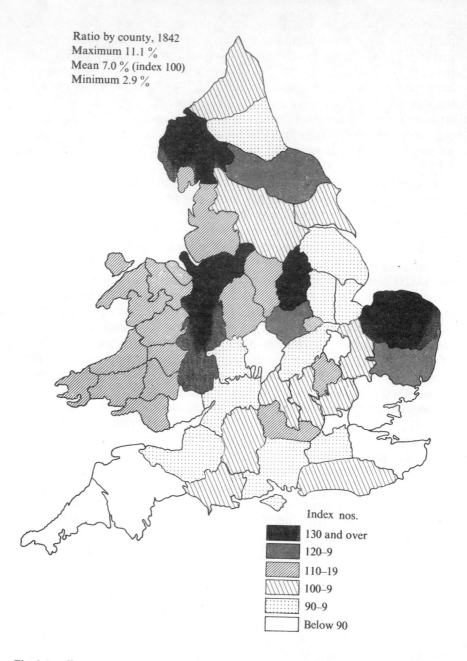

Ratio by county, 1842
Maximum 11.1 %
Mean 7.0 % (index 100)
Minimum 2.9 %

Index nos.

- ■ 130 and over
- ▨ 120–9
- ▧ 110–19
- ◿ 100–9
- ⋯ 90–9
- □ Below 90

Fig. 3.5 Illegitimacy levels in England and Wales at their high point before the twen-tieth century (figures from appendix 2).

principle by taking the first three sets of figures to become available for publication and requesting the reader to consider a particular interpretation of them to be the most likely. Their strong point for this purpose is the clear contrast they show in the proportion of repeaters between what we believe to be generally high and generally low periods both of illegitimacy and of pre-nuptial pregnancy, a contrast which is striking for the eighteenth-century rise. The further work to appear in our later study will, we expect, substantiate to some degree the interpretation and free it from the regional bias which might affect table 3.12.[30]

At Colyton there were baptisms, marriages and burials in the name of Hoare from the early seventeenth until the early nineteenth century, and six women of that name were mothers of bastards between the dates 1616 and 1808. Some of these women were sisters; some got married, mostly to men who were themselves illegitimate, or who had fathered bastards, sometimes on the girl named Hoare whom they in fact later married. There could be no more appropriate name for a family selected as an instance of a situation which could be succinctly described as the claim that when illegitimacy increased it was due more to the activities of whores, or to women whose procreating activities look unmistakably like those of whores, than to any other identifiable influence. The Hoares of Colyton married with the Abbots of the same parish, and as for the name Abbotte or Abbot, to quote our preliminary research findings, 'it persists throughout three centuries. There are marriage dates for eight Abbots who took their brides from the Dommett, Hoare and Vye families, all of which produced bastards.' A volunteer student of illegitimacy from Hemyoke in Somerset, Mrs Lodey, writes this of her chosen parish: 'It is clear from the work I have done already that the problem is common to certain families throughout many generations.'

Reliable argument from this evidence would be possible only if we were able to demonstrate how much more probable it was that a woman would bear a bastard if she herself was a bastard, or if either of her

[30] Both Colyton and Wem are in bastardy region West and North-west. Miss Oosterveen is engaged in an analysis of all the parishes, reconstitution materials of which are becoming available at Cambridge from the point of view of bastardy, which has been traditionally omitted from the reconstitution process, because without marriages so little is derivable from the entries in the registers. The parishes in question include Hawkshead, Colyton, Aldenham, Alcester, Warwickshire (for which the late Peggy Ford analysed illegitimacy). The Alcester figures show the same repeater effect as we observe for the three parishes in table 3.12, which has also been observed at Banbury in Oxfordshire and at Hartland by Susan Stewart and at Ash in Kent by Anthea Newman. All these studies will be published in the volume in preparation; and it will be noticed that Aldenham, Banbury and Ash are outside the areas where high bastardy levels have been reported above.

TABLE 3.12.   *Proportion of repetitive bastard-bearing*

	Period 1 (early high) 1590—1639	Period 2 (middle low) 1640—1689	Period 3 (later high) 1740—1839
Colyton (Devon)			
Illegitimacy ratio	3.3%	2.4%	5.6%
No. of bastards	90	49	243
No. in groups of 1	70	47	154
No. in groups of 2	14	2	54
No. in groups of 3	6	0	35
% repeaters	22%	4%	37%
	1581—1640	1641—1720	1721—1812
Wem (Shropshire)			
Illegitimacy ratio	2.3%	2.4%	4.9%
No. of bastards	60	85	374
No. in groups of 1	48	76	242
No. in groups of 2	12	9	132
% repeaters	20%	11%	35%
	1570—1639	1640—1739	1740—1812
Bolton Percy (Yorkshire, West Riding)			
Illegitimacy ratio	4.3%	2.0%	4.7%
No. of bastards	57	41	80
No. in groups of 1	55	39	65
No. in groups of 2	2	2	15
% repeaters	4%	5%	19%

parents or any of her grandparents had been bastards, and how much more probable it was that she would marry a man who was himself a bastard than another man, or a man who had a bastard in his ancestry, or who had actually begotten a bastard. This is not a stage we have as yet reached, and we cannot pursue this subject here beyond this point. The social status of bastard-bearers, men and women; the ages at which women had their illegitimate children; the numbers who were widowed; the numbers who might have been living in consensual unions with spouses whom they could not marry because one or other was already married — all these subjects and many more must be left over for our further study of illegitimacy in England over four centuries.

To have gone thus far in establishing the possibility of differential illegitimate fertility between sections of the community is nevertheless to raise a number of very interesting questions about the facts we hope we have been able to establish with greater probability in this essay. For if the Cromwellian regime was able to extinguish illegitimacy pretty well, or at least bring it down to the standards of the hated Catholic French, maybe it was the traditional bastard-bearers who were disciplined — identifiable, controllable to some degree because, being poor and dependent, their activities were perhaps open to regulation and temporary repression. When the age of marriage went up and bastardy went down, then it could be again that these were the women most affected by the stringency of the times. It was perhaps their fertility that fell, whilst what happened to the more settled and respectable, those who would be almost certain to appear on the forms for the reconstitution of families, was that they had to wait longer to be married.

We must end by stressing as strongly as we can that this so far ill-defined sub-society never produced all of the bastards, all of the bastard-bearers. Most illegitimate children in traditional times were brought to baptism by mothers who appear on that occasion, and on that occasion only, in the registers. These evanescent women are like the famous sparrow of the Nordic story, which flies through the one door out of the dark, traverses the tiny area of light, and passes out of the other door into the dark again. About them we shall never know anything more. Indeed, in view of the evidence we have had to be so painstaking in describing, it seems remarkable to us that we already know so much about long-term trends in illegitimacy amongst the English.

Appendix 1. Master sample of 24 parishes

The parishes selected for the study of illegitimacy in detail and for checking with our larger collections of figures are listed in table 3.13. Registration data are given with the particulars which seemed to us important in judging of their representativeness and in deciding why the illegitimacy rates recorded for them should be high or low.

It will be seen from the column for population in 1811 in the table that we were hardly successful in distributing the inhabitants of our parishes over the country in units of reasonably equal size. One of our select places, no. 10, contained over half the people, and together with one other, no. 12, no less than 60%. What is more, both are situated in the West and North-west region of the country, which we now know is that with the highest illegitimacy. The parishes we had to use, more-over, cannot be said to have been free of bad recording. The years 1561—90 and 1641—60 stand out in this respect, the second being the period first of civil war and political revolution and then of control by the Puritans. This confirms that the rapid ascent of the bastardy ratio under Elizabeth and its dramatic descent under Cromwell could scarcely be called well documented in the master sample.

In order to see how far the figures from Rochdale and Oswestry

TABLE 3.13. *Master sample of parishes: registration data*

Parish and county	Period of full registration	No. of decades with registration gaps 1561–1610		Population 1811	Market town (✓)	Economic character	Illegitimacy ratio 1561–1810 (%)
		Wanting	Imperfect				
(1) Woburn, Beds.	1561–1830	0	1	1,506	✓	Sheep and corn	2.6
(2) Gawsworth, Ches.	1561–1830	0	2	757		Fattening	4.0
(3) Bridekirk, Cumb.	1585–1810	2	2	1,552		Mixed (corn and stock)	3.6
(4) Crosthwaite, Cumb.	1571–1810	0	1	3,656	✓	Grazing	3.2
(5) Colyton, Devon.	1541–1840	0	0	1,774	✓	Mixed (corn and stock)	3.9
(6) Hartland, Devon.	1561–1830	0	0	1,734	✓	Grazing	5.2
(7) Aldenham, Herts.	1561–1830	0	2	1,127	✓	Mixed (corn and stock)	2.1
(8) Speldhurst, Kent	1561–1830	0	2	1,901		Fattening	4.1
(9) Hawkshead, Lancs.	1568–1830	1	4	1,710	✓	Grazing	2.7
(10) Rochdale, Lancs.	1581–1830	2	1	46,156	✓	Woollen town: grazing area	4.3
(11) Norwich St Giles, Norfolk	1538–1840	0	4	1,043	✓	City parish in mixed area	2.7
(12) Oswestry, Salop.	1581–1810	2	2	6,751	✓	Fattening	4.0
(13) Pitminster, Som.	1541–1830	2	2	1,206		Mixed (corn and stock)	3.8
(14) Wedmore, Som.	1561–1810	0	1	2,480		Fattening	2.8
(15) Alstonfield, Staffs.	1541–1810	1	3	4,171		Grazing	3.6
(16) Barton-under-Needwood, Staffs.	1570–1810	1	3	1,225		Mixed (corn and stock)	2.4
(17) Horringer, Suffolk	1561–1830	0	4	523		Dairying and pigs	2.9
(18) Abinger, Surrey	1561–1810	0	2	629		Fattening	2.5
(19) Tanworth-in-Arden, War.	1561–1830	0	2	1,682		Dairying and pigs	2.9
(20) Bishops Canning, Wilts.	1601–1810	5	0	1,339		Mixed (sheep and corn)	3.9
(21) Marske-in-Cleveland, Yorks. N.R.	1570–1810	1	4	890		Mixed (corn and stock)	2.6
(22) Gisburn, Yorks. W.R.	1561–1810	0	0	2,530	✓	Grazing	2.8
(23) Linton-in-Craven, Yorks. W.R.	1561–1810	0	1	179		Grazing	2.3
(24) Thornton-in-Lonsdale, Yorks. W.R.	1581–1810	2	1	1,152		Grazing	3.3
Total		17 (3%)	44 (8%)	87,673			3.6

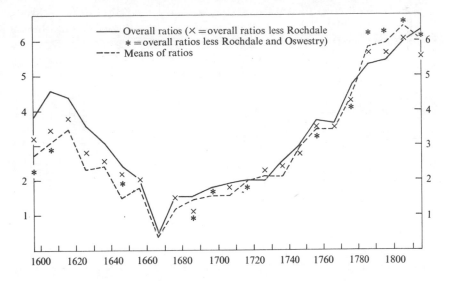

Overall ratios (× = overall ratios less Rochdale
* = overall ratios less Rochdale and Oswestry)
---- Means of ratios

may have distorted the graph for the whole collection of 24, we have drawn up the accompanying figure.

These facts suggest that there may be a relationship between size of community and level of bastardy, but the figures of table 2.1 do not bear this out, since the bastardy ratio does not seem to increase with the level of figures for baptisms etc. A scattergram showed no visible sign of any co-variation in this collection of parishes. The operative influence at work therefore seems to have been mainly geographical. The points and lines in the figure appear to be related as they are to each other because Rochdale and Oswestry come from that area of the country which had high overall illegitimacy. Though markedly higher at the time of the first rise in the ratio, bastardy in these two large parishes was quite distinctly lower at the time of the second rise, the famous upsurge associated with industrialization and so with that same English region. Because of their disproportionate size, it is clear that these two parishes palpably affected the impression created by the 24 parishes in the master sample. At the foot of table 3.4 will be seen the overall ratio for this collection without these two, nearly 10% lower than our original statistics. This is not a closed issue, of course, and our 24 parishes would have been unrepresentative without some communities from the West and North-west.[31]

[31] The sample would also have been faulty if it had lacked the largest possible proportion of figures from meticulously kept registers where illegitimacy was carefully recorded. The Rochdale register is a model of this kind, and we are duly grateful to the Rev. M. Potter for the equally meticulous work he did on it for the Cambridge Group, paying

It remains to record the principles used in checking the illegitimacy recordings found in the 24 parish registers. They have been applied as consistently as possible, but it is possible that in some instances we have counted as bastards children actually conceived within marriage between a widowed mother and her husband.

Principles used in checking illegitimacy recordings in parish registers

1. A child shall be counted legitimate at baptism unless he or she is described as:
    (*a*) illegitimate;
    (*b*) bastard;
    (*c*) base;
    (*d*) base born;
    (*e*) spurious;
    (*f*) son of the people;
    (*g*) having a father described as *reputed* or given some equivalent description;
    (*h*) natural.

    These descriptions rank as always marking illegitimacy, and the presence of any is taken to certify illegitimacy, whatever else appears in the entry. Such illegitimacies are counted 'above the line'.

2. A child shall be counted illegitimate who is *inferred* to be so from one or other of the following circumstances:
    (*a*) Where the child has name 'son of' or 'daughter of' the mother only, and the father's name is not mentioned. This is to be reckoned even where no surname is given for the child itself.
    (*b*) Where the child is given a surname other than that of the mother.

    Such illegitimacies are regarded as 'below the line' and are to be recorded separately on the illegitimacy registration forms. Separate ratios including illegitimates below the line and excluding them will be prepared when illegitimates below the line are common.

3. Children of widows described as posthumous and foundlings are not regarded as illegitimate.

particular attention to bastardy registration at our request. The Oswestry register is not so impressive in these directions, but part of the explanation of high numbers coming from these two communities must be that they seemed to let few bastardies escape the recording quill, and our other 22 registers, select as they are for our purposes, do not always give the same degree of confidence.

4. Foundlings should, however, be registered separately in the appropriate column of the bastardy registration form by year.[32]

[32] Illegitimacies 'below the line' appear in the column for 'bastards inferred' in table 3.1. The description of illegitimates under principle no. 1 above cannot cover all such ways of indirectly referring to the baptism of bastards. In some registers (as at Prestbury in Tudor times; see above) the word 'alias' before a baby's name evidently marks bastards and in others Latin descriptions appear, e.g. *filius terrae* 'child of the earth'. It is well known that foundlings were given odd names by hard-pressed and unimaginative parish officials, who christened them after the parish itself or the place of abandonment ('Porch' for church porch is an example) or the day of the week. Even the families of bastard children showed exuberance in this way; in 1806 'Nimrod' Laslett was baptized as a member of the husbandman-farming family of Laslett at Ash in Kent, and marked illegitimate by the priest, though appearing in the family genealogy as in no way irregular (information from Anthea Newman).

Appendix 2. Geographical variation of illegitimacy at the nineteenth-century peak

Ratios by division and county for 1842 and 1845, from the eighth *Annual Report* of the Registrar-General

Rank order of divisions	Illegitimacy ratio	Index (7.0 = 100)
England and Wales, 1842	7.0	100
(1) Eastern (Essex, Suffolk, Norfolk)	8.7	124
(2) North-western (Ches., Lancs.)	8.4	120
(3) North Midland (Leics., Rutland, Lincs., Notts., Derby.)	8.3	118
(4) Northern (Durham, Northumb., Cumb., Westmorland)	7.9	113
(5) Welsh (Mon., N. Wales, S. Wales)	7.7	110
(6) York (W. Riding, N. Riding, E. Riding)	7.5	107
(7) Western (Gloucs., Herefs., Salop, Worcs., Staffs., War.)	7.2	103
(8) South Midland (Middx., Herts., Bucks., Oxon., Northants., Hunts., Beds., Cambs.)	6.9	99
(9) South-eastern (Sussex, Kent, Hants., Berks.)	6.6	94
(10) South-western (Wilts., Dorset, Devon., Corn., Som.)	6.1	87
(11) Metropolis (Middx., Surrey, Greenwich)	3.7	53

	Illegitimacy ratio	Index (6.7 = 100)
England and Wales, 1845	6.7	100
(1) North-western	8.8	131
(2) Eastern	7.9	118
(3) North Midland	7.7	115
(4) Northern	7.4	110
(5) York	6.8	107
(6) Welsh	7.2	101
(7) Western	6.8	101
(8) South Midland	6.7	100
(9) South-eastern	6.4	96
(10) South-western	5.7	85
(11) Metropolis	3.2	48

Illegitimacy ratios: rank order of counties in 1842 and 1845

1842	Illegitimacy ratio	Index (7.0 = 100)	1845	Illegitimacy ratio	Index (6.7 = 100)
(1) Cumberland	11.1	157	(1) Cumberland	11.4	170
(2) Norfolk	10.8	154	(2) Herefordshire	10.6	158
(3) Shropshire	10.5	150	(3) Nottinghamshire	9.9	148
(4) Westmorland	10.2	146	Norfolk	9.9	148
(5) Nottinghamshire	9.8	141	(5) Cheshire	9.6	143
(6) Herefordshire	9.7	139	(6) Westmorland	9.3	139
(7) Cheshire	9.3	133	Shropshire	9.3	139
(8) Yorkshire N. Riding	9.0	129	(8) Yorkshire N. Riding	8.9	133
(9) Suffolk	8.9	127	(9) Lancashire	8.7	130
(10) Leicestershire	8.7	124	(10) Suffolk	8.1	121
(11) Bedfordshire	8.3	119	Derbyshire	8.1	121
Derbyshire	8.3	119	(12) Bedfordshire	7.7	115
(13) Lancashire	8.2	117	(13) North Wales	7.5	112
North Wales	8.2	117	Oxfordshire	7.5	112
(15) South Wales	8.1	116	(15) Staffordshire	7.4	110
Berkshire	8.1	116	(16) Berkshire	7.3	109
(17) Rutland	7.7	110	Buckinghamshire	7.3	109
Staffordshire	7.7	110	Wiltshire	7.3	109
(19) Northumberland	7.6	109	(19) Leicestershire	7.2	107
(20) Wiltshire	7.4	106	Cambridgeshire	7.2	107
Yorkshire E. Riding	7.4	106	(21) Yorkshire W. Riding	7.1	106
Hertfordshire	7.4	106	(22) Hertfordshire	7.0	104
(23) Yorkshire W. Riding	7.3	104	(23) Yorkshire E. Riding	6.9	103
(24) Buckinghamshire	7.2	103	South Wales	6.9	103

(25)	Sussex	7.1	101	(25)	Sussex	6.8	101
	Dorset	7.1	101		Rutland	6.8	101
(27)	Oxfordshire	7.0	100		Northumberland	6.8	101
	Cambridgeshire	7.0	100	(28)	Dorset	6.7	100
(29)	Lincolnshire	6.8	97	(29)	Northamptonshire	6.4	95
(30)	Somerset	6.7	96		Hampshire	6.4	95
(31)	Gloucestershire	6.6	94	(31)	Kent (excludes London)	6.3	94
(32)	Surrey (excludes London)	6.5	92		Lincolnshire	6.3	94
	Worcestershire	6.5	92	(33)	Somerset	6.2	92
(34)	Hampshire	6.3	90		Worcestershire	6.2	92
	Northamptonshire	6.3	90	(35)	Gloucestershire	6.1	91
	Durham	6.3	90	(36)	Durham	5.6	84
(37)	Kent (excludes London)	6.1	87	(37)	Essex	5.3	79
(38)	Essex	5.7	81	(38)	Surrey	5.2	78
	Huntingdonshire	5.7	81	(39)	Huntingdonshire	5.1	76
(40)	Middlesex (excludes London)	5.6	80		Devonshire	5.1	76
	Warwickshire	5.6	80		Warwickshire	5.1	76
(42)	Devonshire	5.5	79	(42)	Monmouthshire	4.6	69
(43)	Cornwall	5.1	73	(43)	Middlesex (excludes London)	4.4	66
(44)	Monmouthshire	5.0	71	(44)	Cornwall	4.2	62
(45)	Metropolis – Middlesex	3.8	54	(45)	Metropolis – Middlesex	3.4	51
(46)	Metropolis – Surrey	3.5	50	(46)	Metropolis – Surrey	2.8	42
(47)	Metropolis – Kent	2.9	41	(47)	Metropolis – Kent	2.7	40

4. Parental deprivation in the past

A note on orphans and stepparenthood in English history[1]

Parental deprivation is a term typical of the social observation which goes forward in our day, perception of a body of facts diffused through a strong sympathy for the position of those to whom the facts relate. Illegitimate children are likely to be parentally deprived, because they are brought into the world without proper fathers: they arouse our interest because of that circumstance, for they appear as the helpless victims of a powerful social and familial convention. We have seen that the numbers of children born outside wedlock were sometimes quite large in the past, and the numbers so conceived considerably larger. In our day the proportion of children alive who were registered as illegitimate at birth must be substantial. But bastard children cannot be anything like a majority of the parentally deprived, now or at any time in history. Those who suffer the actual loss of the father — or of either parent — have always far outnumbered those who never had recognized fathers at all.

In spite of the fact that so many conceptions and births took place outside marriage in the past, few, or very few, of the children alive at any time were illegitimate. This is because bastards died so quickly and because some of them ceased effectively to be bastards by the marriage of their mothers, sometimes, though not always, to the men who had procreated the children in question.[2] In England in the 1970s the marriage of parents of illegitimates has been fairly common, and so many of the remaining bastards are adopted by quite other parties that the concept of parental deprivation has to be modified for the whole body of children in this class. But the loss of the father, and to a lesser extent

[1] A somewhat modified and extended version of an article in *Local Population Studies* 13 (Autumn 1974).

[2] The numbers of bastard-bearers who got married, in England, in France (especially in the nineteenth century) and in other countries are discussed in the volume on the comparative history of illegitimacy in preparation by Laslett and Oosterveen (see ch. 3, n. 1 above). It would seem that having had a bastard child was never a disqualification for marriage, any more than being divorced is a disqualification today. It must be remembered, therefore, that a small addition should perhaps be made to all proportions of stepchildren discussed in this chapter, to cover illegitimate children whose mothers got married to a man other than the biological father.

of the mother, through the breakup of the marriages of parents with children, has become substantial and is growing all the time. Parental deprivation has accordingly become a subject of considerable importance, and parentally deprived children a preoccupation of the concerned observer.

There is undoubtedly a great deal in the situation of these young people to be concerned about. The psychologists insist that parental loss has a significant effect on the development of the personality, and this is true whether it comes about by rejection, estrangement — as through divorce — or death. Rejection need not be accompanied by physical separation between parent and child, but there can be no doubt that such separation can be very widespread. In the United States at the present time something like a sixth or more of all children under the age of 18 may well have suffered departure of a parent from the home. It is probable that less than a quarter of these parentally deprived persons have actually lost father or mother because of death, for orphans so defined only make up something over 4% of all children of these ages. The rest, that is, some 12% to 15% of American children who are 17 or younger, have been cut off either from father or from mother because of divorce or because their parents are living apart as separated couples.

We can take this as the highest proportion of parentally deprived children we are likely to find in our time, since estrangement, divorce and remarriage are so much commoner in the United States than they are elsewhere.[3] Nevertheless, there is growing concern in other highly industrialized countries, including our own, about the increase in the breakup of families, with its regrettable effects on children, especially young children. There seems, moreover, to be the same tendency here as the historical sociologist has observed for other issues: to look on our own generation as burdened by the problem to an extent never paralleled in the past. Arguments in support of such self-sympathetic views are seldom advanced, and I am not aware that any previous work has ever been done of a properly historical kind on the breakup of vertical family links. The only exception is an interesting set of numerical calcu-

[3] It seems peculiarly difficult to find numerical calculations for such proportions, and the estimates for children of divorced and separated parents are based on the figures given in H. Carter and P. C. Glick, *Marriage and divorce* (1970), referring to the 1960s; see chs. 8 and 9 and esp. the notes on pp. 432–3. I have increased the proportions suggested by the figures appearing there by 25% to allow for growth in the number of broken families in the last ten or fifteen years. It is true that a good part of this parental deprivation in the U.S. occurs amongst blacks and that in black ghetto society separation from the biological parent, even the mother, may not mean separation from the effective parent, who can be quite another person. These complications, however, do not seem to me likely to alter the gross comparative effects with which we are concerned in this note.

lations about grandparenthood, great-grandparenthood and orphanage in France in the 1970s as compared with three villages in the Paris basin in the eighteenth century published by the French demographer Le Bras in 1973 which I shall be quoting below.

In this chapter I want to try to give a provisional answer to the following question: are there more parentally deprived children today than there were in traditional, pre-industrial England? The answer cannot of course be very definite at this stage, since estimates of the proportion of children in such a position two or three hundred years ago are subject to so much error. But the evidence we do have for England, when prompted by the French figures I have referred to, seems to me to suggest that we may not be justified in believing that parental deprivation is commoner now than it has ever been before. There were so many orphans present in the seventeenth- and eighteenth-century English communities that they must have equalled or surpassed the proportion of children who have lost a parent by death, divorce or separation in England at the present time. Indeed, there are indications that the number of orphans in pre-industrial English society – children who had lost either father or mother or both – was very likely to have been of the same order as the maximal figures I have quoted from the United States, or even larger. This certainly seems to be true for individual communities at particular points in time, although, as must be expected, orphanage levels varied very widely from place to place.

Such a circumstance need not surprise us, because the demography of pre-industrial times required that high proportions of all children should have lost one or other of their parents by the age at which they ceased to be children, which in the traditional social order means the time when they got married. With the expectation of life varying, as we shall see in the next essay, between the late 20s and the late 40s – with perhaps a tendency to fluctuate about the early and middle 30s at ordinary times[4] – anything from about two-fifths or perhaps as much as two-thirds of girls, for example, could be expected to have

---

[4] For expectation of life, see table 5.1 below. Some idea of the proportions likely to be orphaned at early ages and at marriage can be gleaned from model life tables. Taking model West, level 8, from Coale and Demeney's *Regional model life tables* (1966), with the expectation of life at birth for males as 35, and assuming an average age of the father at the birth of his children of about 35, 9% of all children aged 5 would be fatherless, 17% aged 10 and 27% aged 15. Some 46% of girls would be fatherless at age 25, which can serve as an estimate of mean age at marriage for them. All these average figures, of course, conceal a considerable spread of figures on either side. When we come to consider such age material as we have for England (see below) we have used the calculations of Le Bras, but we hope finally to make detailed and realistic estimates of such statistics as proportion orphaned below a certain age by microsimulation, where variance is taken into account.

lost their fathers by the time of marriage. When losses of mothers are added to these proportions, it can be seen how few young women were likely to have had both parents alive when they themselves became wives. Boys married a year or two later, of course, so being orphaned whilst 'children' was even more likely for them.

The proportion orphaned at a particular age is considerably greater than the proportion of all persons of that age and younger who are orphaned. The two statistics are related in a rather complicated way, not all that easy to estimate with the vital statistics so far available to us for pre-industrial populations. For this reason it is of considerable interest to see how many orphaned *children*, defined as those orphaned at the age at which they got married or of younger age, are actually described as such in our usable sources. These sources are lists of inhabitants which provide such descriptive detail, and provide it accurately enough to inspire credibility.

It has to be admitted that children are rather uncomfortably defined by taking them in this way to be all unmarried persons, and this makes the proportionate or comparative statistics of this essay somewhat ambiguous. The difficulty arises because it is essential to be able to reckon for the most part without ages in years, since numerical details of age are so rare in the evidence we have about the past persons who concern us, in England at least. But it is also due to a fundamental difference, as we shall see, as to who counted as a child in traditional society in contrast to who counts as a child today.

This issue is at its sharpest when it comes to the servants, whose position in the household we have already had to discuss. Servants were certainly in some senses children in that era. They were young and nearly always unmarried, as we have seen, a fair proportion of them in their early teens and a half or more under 21. They were in some ways treated like children by their masters and mistresses, even when they were rather older, because you had to be married in that society to be accepted as fully grown up. If they went back home to visit their parents, as we have seen them doing at Cogenhoe, or to stay with them, they became resident 'children' once again. How many persons called servants were mature in the physiological sense it is difficult to say, and we shall return to the issue of sexual maturity in chapter 6. It is not improbable that a reason for young persons leaving home and going into service was in fact that they had reached puberty. This makes it obvious that it is impossible to look on servants as children in all senses; they could be men and women in the prime of life, in their 30s or even 40s. Moreover, in their capacity as servants, away from the parental home and perhaps without any connection with it, they were quite independent of their families of origin. This ambiguity about servants will recur

TABLE 4.1. *Resident orphans, Clayworth, Nottinghamshire, 1676 and 1688*

	1676 (Pop. 401) No.	% of all orphans	1688 (Pop. 412) No.	% of all orphans
Orphans living with widowed mother	32	64	19	34
Orphans living with widowed father	11	22	5	9
Orphans living with widowed mother and stepfather	4	8	14	25
Orphans living with widowed father and stepmother	3	6	18	32
Total	50	100	56	100
Number of resident children	154	—	162	—
Proportion of all children orphaned	32%	—	32%	—
Number and proportion of all resident children bereaved of mother	14	9%	23	13%
Number and proportion of all resident children bereaved of father	36	23%	33	19%

Note: Servants not taken as 'children' in this table; see text.

as our theme develops. Sometimes we shall have to regard servants as children, children of a particular kind, and sometimes not as children at all.

We may start with such totals for resident orphans as we have been able to recover from the analysis of the lists of inhabitants of settlements in the seventeenth and eighteenth centuries which has been made by the Cambridge Group. We can construct, for example, a table for orphans on the basis of the two documents written out for his parish by that exceptionally intelligent, well-informed and accurate observer, our familiar friend, William Sampson, rector of Clayworth in Nottinghamshire during the 1670s and 80s. Such is table 4.1 above.

This shows that a third of all resident children present in Clayworth at these two points in time had lost one or other parent by death. It is interesting to see that many more of them were fatherless than motherless, well over double the number in 1676, and that no child was recorded as deprived of both parents. The rector tells us nothing in the lists of his parishioners about the other young unmarried individuals he mentions which would enable us to recognize them as having lost their fathers or their mothers. These others were servants for the most part, of whom there were 67 in 1676, and 65 in 1688 (see table 2.13). If we look at the evidence of the parish register which Sampson kept so conscientiously over these years, we find that at least 4 of the servants in 1688 were in fact offspring of fathers who had been living in the village in 1676 but who had died.

No doubt there were other orphans amongst the servants in 1688 whom we cannot recognize as such. Coming from outside the village, as we have seen most servants did, they had family histories not accessible in the Clayworth documents. There may indeed have been a higher proportion of orphans among servants than among resident children everywhere, if the loss of the father or the breakup of the family group by further bereavement led to offspring going into service, as happened in the four cases we know about. Adding these other orphans to the total of 56 at Clayworth in 1688 we arrive at a proportion of well over a third of all unmarried persons there as being bereaved of parents. Even this is a lower limit, for Sampson might not have been able to identify every individual resident offspring of a broken marriage. A closer estimate might be something over 40%, allowing for orphans disguised as resident relatives or as lodgers — sometimes billetted on a household by the Poor Law authority — or even as solitaries. A good two-fifths, therefore, of all unmarried dependent young persons had suffered parental deprivation in that village in that year. We learnt in chapter 2 that the death rate had been high in Clayworth over the preceding twelve years, but cannot regard its situation in 1688 as being at all unusual.

We may notice that quite a number of the orphans at Clayworth, 7 in 1676 and no less than 32 in 1688, were stepchildren living with a remarried parent. Psychologically these children may have been in an even more difficult position than those living with their widowed mothers or fathers, whatever the economic situation, which is always worst for the families of widows.

The inaccessibility of the emotional experience of our ancestors is brought home to us when we realize how little we know, how little we can imagine, of what it can have been like for the young son or daughter of a husbandman or a craftsman to confront the woman whom the father introduced into the home after the death of the mother. The new wife and mother-substitute might have brought children of her own with her, as so frequently happened in Clayworth and Cogenhoe. This would have meant, of course, that there were new brothers and sisters to get used to as well, new rivals for the father's affection. The attention of the mother would be unequally divided, too, between her own boys and girls, those of the man she had married and the ones she might herself have by him.

If we had reliable information on how young children were reared amongst the English peasantry, we might be less baffled, and perhaps

TABLE 4.2.   *Resident orphans in 19 English communities, 1599—1811*

	No.	%
Orphans living with widowed mother	720	52.1
Orphans living with widowed father	333	24.1
Orphans living with stepmother only	0	0
Orphans living with stepfather only	1	0.1
Orphans living with father and stepmother	105	7.5
Orphans living with widowed mother and stepfather	173	12.5
Orphans living with two stepparents	5	0.4
Known orphans living with persons other than parents or stepparents	46	3.3
Total orphans	1,383	100%
Total children	6,668	
Orphans as a proportion of all resident children	20.7%	
Living with {widowed parents not remarried	76.2%	
{remarried widowed parents	20.0%	

less disposed to sentimentality. It seems very likely from such evidence as has been surveyed that the child of peasant parents was brought up with a bevy of other children, caressed and attended to by a knot of other mothers and other adults, too, as is known to be the situation in many 'primitive' societies today, rather than being nurtured in the privacy of the cottage, the shack or the boarded-off rooms which the family inhabited.[5] A little boy or a little girl with such a plurality of parental figures would seem likely to have felt the deprivation and the sudden change rather less keenly than the one who, like the children in the supposedly isolated cell of the late-twentieth-century conjugal family, had been exclusively tied to two parents, and especially to the mother.

But we should not exercise our sympathy by thinking of the children alone. There are very large numbers of stepmothers and even of stepfathers represented in table 4.2, which sets out figures for all 19 of the English places, including Clayworth in 1676 and 1688, for which we have what looks like fairly complete information as to orphanage.

Brenda Maddox has recently demonstrated how difficult and ambiguous is the position of the stepparent in our own society, ambiguous in respect of the law and conventions of marriage, ambiguous in respect of the relatives of the parties to the union contracted, ambiguous above

[5] The sources cannot be said to be certain on this important point. For an assemblage of references to child rearing in the literary sources, see deMause 1974 and the articles in *History of Childhood Quarterly*. Compare also the discussion on pp. 20—4 above with its references, esp. Laslett 1976a. Criticism of the view that ... one mother figure is universal — a view often associated ... possible is to be found in M. P. M. Richards ... (ed.), *The integration of the child into a social world* (1974).

all in respect of the children for whom he or she suddenly becomes responsible.[6] She insists, however, that the difficulties of a man or a woman who marries a spouse whose previous partner has died are worse than those which arise after a divorce, where the former parent is still alive. Let us not forget that the first was the plight, if plight it can be called, of a high proportion of all the married persons at the head of the households in the village of Clayworth in 1688 (see p. 58 above). A long time must go by, once again, before we have much insight into how their situation resembled that of the late-twentieth-century successor to the position of a man's divorced wife. There is a great deal which we do not yet know about family life and illicit love in earlier generations, and much of it may well remain closed to us for ever.

The figures in table 4.2 put the facts from Clayworth into a somewhat more general context, though they are a poor basis on which to generalize about pre-industrial English society as a whole. In this larger sample some circumstances are found which are absent at Clayworth, including the occurrence of full orphans, for children living with two stepparents must have been in this position. There were only five of these out of 1,383 orphans and nearly 7,000 children. It is to be expected that the minimum proportion of resident orphans in these less carefully counted places should be less than at Clayworth, 21% as against 32%. Though we can be certain only that one in five of the children in this larger sample was parentally deprived we may believe that in fact a much greater number were in this plight. When the names of the settlements are written out in date order, it becomes apparent that the determinable level of resident orphanage must vary quite considerably with the quality of the data. It seems, moreover, to have varied with time as well, which is much more interesting.

As for the quality of data, the documents for Cardington, Puddletown and Ealing are all superior in the detail they contain and in the consistency of their entries. In this they resemble the file for Clayworth, and it must be significant that these places have the highest recorded proportions of resident orphanage, along with St Nicholas-at-Wade. Registration is not particularly good at this last place, and its high figure demonstrates that variation must also have been due to causes other than the quality of the data. The documents for Chilvers Coton and for Harefield are also high in standard, and it would seem that their low levels of resident orphanage represent genuine variation downwards.

---

[6] See *The half-parent* (1975). The extraordinary position of stepparents described in this book, in relation to the laws of incest, for example, cannot be new in our time. Such laws are of considerable importance in a situation where sexual attachment can easily arise between a stepfather and his mature stepdaughter. The history of stepparents needs to be recovered as well as its sociology worked out.

TABLE 4.3. *Settlements with recorded proportions of orphans, in date order*

	%
(1) Ealing, Middx., 1599	25
(2) Cogenhoe, Northants., 1624	25
(3) Clayworth, Notts., 1676	32
(4) Chilvers Coton, War., 1684	12
(5) Clayworth, Notts., 1688	32
(6) Norwich St Peter Mancroft, 1694	7
(7) Lichfield, Staffs., 1695	21
(8) Harefield, Middx., 1699	16
(9) Stoke-on-Trent, Staffs., 1701	25
(10) Monkton, Kent, 1705	16
(11) St Nicholas-at-Wade, Kent, 1705	36
(12) Puddletown, Dorset, 1724	26
(13) Cardington, Beds., 1782	34
(14) Corfe Castle, Dorset, 1790	17
(15) Ardleigh, Essex, 1796	14
(16) Barkway and Reed, Herts., 1801	16
(17) Binfield, Berks., 1801	13
(18) Littleover, Derby., 1811	7
(19) Mickleover, Derby., 1811	16

The modest proportions at Norwich and at Littleover are more likely to have been the result of incomplete identification.

This small sample, therefore, can be taken to reveal the expected variability in orphanage from place to place. The impression of variation over time is also conveyed by the listings of proportions according to date. If this effect is a real one, it presumably arose because of shifts in demographic rates, particularly in mortality, by far the strongest influence on orphanage. The mean of mean proportions of identifiable resident orphans for the 19 places is 20.5% or 22% omitting the two lowest figures; the median, a more realistic marker, is 18% (25%). But the first 11 places, which are dated between 1599 and 1705, have a median of 25% (mean of 22.5%), whereas the last eight, dated between 1724 and 1811, have a median of 16.5% (mean of 17.9%). The seventeenth century is becoming known as a period of high mortality over much of England, especially after 1650, and it could be that the effect of this in maintaining higher proportions of orphaned children shows itself in these recordings in spite of variation due to locality and to quality of document. We must remember that all the figures for the 19 places would have to be increased to obtain a total proportion which would include servants and others not being children resident in their families of origin. There must also have been some grandchild orphans in these 19 places, children sent back to the parents of their fathers or their mothers after the death of one or other of them or of both. None happened to be present at Clayworth, but we believe they were not uncommon elsewhere.

This is about as far as it is possible to get with information from lists of inhabitants lacking figures for ages, the usual case, unfortunately, with English materials. Our information can be supplemented, however, with one further set of facts derived from the exceptional entries made during the seven years from 1653 to 1660 in the marriage register for St Mary's, Manchester. Here the names of the fathers of both bride and bridegroom are given, and marked 'dec' where appropriate to indicate deceased. Between 52% and 59% of all brides at first marriage were described in this way as fatherless.[7] This proportion, which covers all brides, of course, and not simply those resident with their parents or stepparents at the time of the ceremony, is about what we might expect in girls of age to be married, if a fifth of *all* unmarried girls had lost their fathers, and a third had lost either father or mother, or both. The rare recordings for Manchester may accordingly be taken as generally confirming our estimates for the mid and late seventeenth century, and especially Clayworth.[8]

We must recognize, of course, that it is not entirely realistic to compare the class of unmarried, dependent young persons of that generation in England with the class of all persons under 18 years old in the United States in our generation if we want to get an idea of the relative prevalence of parental deprivation then and now. But it is also evident that no direct comparison of like with like would ever be possible, not even one contrasting those of identical age and marital status at the two

---

[7] Lancashire Parish Record Society, registers of Manchester, vol. 3 (1949), pp. 47–93. Three samples of girls marrying for the first time were taken, yielding 53/93 or 57% orphans, 83/140 or 59%, and 100/192 or 52%. Obviously variability was high. Corresponding proportions for bridegrooms were 37/78 (47%), 64/130 (49%) and 85/178 (48%), much less variable and against expectation, since bridegrooms and so their fathers were presumably some years older. Less trouble seems to have been taken to discover whether the fathers of men were alive, since it was less important. I should be delighted to hear from any reader who knows of other registers giving such information.

[8] In reconciling proportions orphaned at marriage with proportions of resident orphans, the age at marriage for women is assumed to be 22–25, and proportions orphaned at those ages, and at those ages and younger, are taken from the calculations made by Le Bras (see below). A further confirmation of the Clayworth reckonings, based on a collection larger than that used in table 4.3, the Marriage Duty Act returns for the city of Bristol for 1696, can now be added. J. R. Holman, writing in *Local Population Studies* 15 (Autumn 1975), concludes 'that one child in three living in Bristol in the late seventeenth century had lost one or both parents'. The detailed further findings of this little study make interesting comparisons with the present essay and it is a pity it appeared too late to be taken fully into account.

TABLE 4.4.   *Resident orphans: proportions in various age groups*

Age group	Ealing, 1599 (pop. 427) %		Lichfield, 1697 (pop. 2,861) %		Ardleigh, 1796 (pop. 1,145) %		Census of 1921 %
0—3	3/27	11.1	18/214	8.4	10/130	7.7	4.5
0—5	7/43	16.3	30/348	8.6	18/190	9.5	6.1
0—9	17/81	21.0	79/642	12.3	31/315	9.8	8.7
All resident orphans	33/133	24.8	268/1,146	21.5	87/598	14.5	(0—14, 11.3%)
Orphans 0—9 as a proportion of all orphans	17/33	51.5	79/268	29.5	31/87	35.6	—

chosen points in time. Assumptions about maturity, childhood, dependency, subordination were simply different in the earlier society. To discover, however, that a third or considerably more of all unmarried dependants could be parentally deprived in traditional society when mortality was high, and that the figure seldom dropped below one-fifth even at times and in places with more favourable conditions, does make possible the rough comparison which we have in mind. Considering that in our day the very highest proportion of parentally deprived amongst those under 18 is a sixth or somewhat over, it cannot be said that parental deprivation is commoner under the conditions of the late twentieth century in high industrial society than it was in the seventeenth and eighteenth centuries in traditional society. It looks as if the reverse must be true. We are hardly justified, in historical terms, in sympathizing with ourselves for the prevalence of broken marriages in our time and its deplorable effects on our children.

We may complete our note with a glance at such age evidence as we do possess. For England the historical data at present can only be called crude, and not much worked over, but for France the situation is a little better. For the twentieth century we have one very useful set of English statistics, compiled by the Registrar-General from the national Census of 1921 — England and Wales. In table 4.4 will be found proportions of resident orphans in 3 English settlements up to age 3, up to age 5 and up to age 9, set out alongside the corresponding proportions of orphans recorded in the Census of 1921.[9] The first of these age groups has been

[9] It must be borne in mind that the Census figures are for *all* orphans in the national population, not simply those resident in a particular set of households. The figures seem to have been worked out for the Census of 1921 because of the considerable mortality amongst fathers caused by the First War, and so must be regarded as high for an early-twentieth-century industrial society.

TABLE 4.5. *Calculated proportions of orphaned offspring, eighteenth-century France (3 villages) and twentieth-century France*[a]

Age group	Eighteenth century %	1960s %
0—3	4.5	0.3
0—5	7.1	0.8
0—9	12.5	1.9
All orphaned offspring[b]	32.1	8.5
Orphans 0—9 as a proportion of all orphans[b]	21.1	8.5

[a]Estimates from Le Bras 1973.   [b]All orphaned offspring taken as those aged 0—25.

used because of the great vulnerability of children in their first 3 or 4 years to parental loss, particularly to the loss of the mother. During the next 2 years of life, ages 4 and 5, infants remain very dependent, and even amongst the very poor in pre-industrial society were extremely unlikely to be sent out of the home, although they might begin to do a little work. By the age of ten, however, the prospect of leaving the family as servants began to be tangible, and we have to reckon with the fact that only up to that age can figures for resident orphans be taken to indicate approximate figures for all orphans. A comparison between the last two rows of the table in the columns for pre-industrial communities gives some idea of how many orphaned children left their families of origin between the age of ten and marriage, since the percentages seem to increase far too little.

Some notion of how much greater the growth in the proportion of orphans would be if we had information on all parental losses after age ten can be gathered from the next table, constructed, of course, on entirely different principles and for French pre-industrial communities rather than English.[10] Although these figures would seem to imply that fewer children up to age 5 were orphaned in the French eighteenth-century villages concerned than in any of the English, the very different bases of calculation make comparison hazardous.[11] The contrast

[10] See H. Le Bras, 'Parents, grand-parents, bisaieux', *Population* 28, 1 (1973): 9–38. He draws his historical data from the reconstitution of *Trois villages de l'Ile de France, c. 1700–1800*, by Jean Ganiage (Paris, 1963).

[11] The object of the article by Le Bras was to estimate probabilities of having surviving parents, grandparents and great-grandparents at given ages rather than of estimating orphanage as such, using vital rates derived from reconstitution rather than lists of inhabitants. The figures in my table have been derived from *graphiques* 11 and 13, printed on pp. 32 and 34. Le Bras is now engaged on work on orphanage itself and tells me that his results will take account of variance rather than simply being based on averages.

between the eighteenth century and the 1960s is certainly a startling one, and underlines the enormous difference between ourselves and our ancestors in respect of the risk of death. We may 'lose' our parents at a rate comparable to that which they experienced, or at least the Americans may do so, but nearly all of those parents go on living. It should not escape us that the difference between the English census figures of 1921 and estimates for France in the 1960s are considerable, too. Most of the change in orphanage, as in so many other matters of population and social structure, has come recently, within the lifetimes of our older contemporaries. If we knew as much about the history of orphanage in recent times as is reported in our next chapter on the history of aging, we might be able to tell a similar story of swift and sudden change taking place within living memory.

In our last table we venture on a direct comparison between orphanage worked out from lists of inhabitants and orphanage worked out from demographic statistics.

These final details serve to draw attention to the instability of the proportions we have been dealing with and warn us against accepting any of them as anything other than a rough estimate. They bring out, however, two points we have stressed more than once in this note. The first is how much more likely you were to lose your father than your mother, and still are, indeed; in this respect the French figures for the eighteenth century seem to be an aberration. The second is how rare it always has been to lose both your parents when a child. In common parlance the word 'orphan' seems to mean one who is entirely bereft of the father who begat him and the mother who brought him into the world, and Cinderella is the archetypal orphan. But a Cinderella was a rarity, in the traditional world where the story — that influential piece of mischievous make-believe — is set.[12]

[12] In the 'original' version of Cinderella in Grimm's fairy tales the neglected child does have a father, and he seems to appear, though a dim and distant figure, in most of the other multifarious versions, too. But it seems that the general belief nowadays is that Cinderella was a complete orphan, even though this rather blunts the edge of the story. For the 345 variants of the Cinderella story, see M. R. Cox, *Cinderella* (London, 1892).

TABLE 4.6. Observed resident orphans (England) and calculated orphaned offspring (France)

Age group	Ealing[a]			Lichfield[a]			1921 Census			
	Father-less	Mother-less	Both lost	Father-less	Mother-less	Both lost	Father-less %	Mother-less %	Both lost %	Un-known %
0–3	3	0	0	17	1	0	2.4	0.9	0.1	1.2
0–5	7	0	0	24	8	1	3.7	1.3	0.2	1.3
0–9	13	0	0	61	24	3	5.8	2.1	0.3	1.2
All resident orphans	31	4	1	191	71	5	—	—	—	—
Motherless as a proportion of fatherless	13%			37%			36%			

Age group	Eighteenth-century France[b]			France in the 1960s[b]		
	Father-less	Mother-less	Both lost	Father-less	Mother-less	Both lost
0–3	7	4	0	0	0	0
0–5	14	10	0	3	2	0
0–9	40	31	2	12	4	0
All orphaned offspring[c]	242	203	55	139	47	3
Motherless as a proportion of fatherless	83.9%[c]			33.8%[c]		

[a] The totals differ from those given in table 4.4 because those who had lost both parents have also been included amongst the numbers fatherless and motherless.

[b] Estimates from Le Bras 1973.
[c] Taken as those aged 0–25.

5. The history of aging and the aged

The twentieth-century Englishman and indeed everyone living in an advanced industrial society seems to have a guilty feeling about the elderly and aged. We uneasily suspect that most of our millions and millions of old people live in reduced circumstances, not much cared about by such children and such kin folk as they have left to them and rather distant from the life of any family; solitary, very many of them, and as they grow to be really aged, miserably relegated to institutional living. The peasant and the craftsman of traditional England, so the common sentiment seems to be, provided far better for the familial life of the old than we do today. It is for us to learn from them.

Aging in our society and aging in the traditional world

Gerontology, the study of aging as a process and of the old as a social group, is the next most recent of the social sciences, the newest of all being historical sociology itself. An early achievement of the gerontologists, an achievement which could be said, as we shall see, to be itself historical in its character, is the demonstration that the beliefs which are so widely held in late-twentieth-century high industrial society about the situation of the aged are scarcely well founded. Gerontological publications in print or in progress[1] show that the majority of the aged are not in the position just described.

[1] See for example Shanas et al., *Old people in three industrial societies* (1968), the countries in question being Britain, the United States and Denmark. A recension of gerontological work on the familial situation of the aged is contained in vol. 1 of the *Handbook of aging and the social sciences*, general ed. James E. Birren, vol. eds. Ethel Shanas and Robert Binstock, in course of publication in New York by Van Nostrand. This chapter is an adaptation and modification of a section contributed by the present writer to that volume and entitled 'Societal development and aging'. I am grateful to the publishers and editors for permission to reproduce parts of the text and a slightly modified form of the tables here. Information and analysis as to the position of the aged in Estonia is due to Dr Heldur Palli; for Japan, to Professor Akira Hayami of Keio University, Tokyo; for Germany, to Dr Hans Medick of Göttingen and to Gabriele Wilson, student of the Open University. Ann Nettley, New Hall, Cambridge, has worked on the aged in the nineteenth century at Puddletown in Dorset. Whilst this chapter was in course of preparation for the press, Professor H. C. Johansen, of the University of Odense in Denmark, circulated his valuable unpublished paper 'The position of the old in traditional society' (see n. 6 below) analysing the situation of the aged in eighteenth-century Denmark. I am grateful to all these associates and collaborators for the results they have communicated to me.

174

Retirement, so often regarded as a declaration of the unfitness of older people to perform what is required of a contemporary citizen,[2] is certainly widespread and peremptory, and clearly distinguishes industrial society from pre-industrial society in respect of aging. But its effect varies with the job that has to be abandoned, with the skill of the individual concerned, with his health and his economic position. The old are not so drastically bereft of prestige and respect as the stereotypes imply; they have recognized functions, especially in relation to their children and grandchildren; they are supported emotionally and otherwise, by their offspring, sometimes by their siblings, and even by more distant kin. They manage to live quite often in association with the families of their children, so combining what they most want to combine, interchange and independence. We must not suppose that the sufferings of some of the aged, and the miseries of the minority of the anomic amongst those who come into contact with the welfare services, are a proper indication of the condition of old people generally in our own society.

Nor must we suppose that there has been a single transition between pre-industrial, peasant society in which the aged were socially valued and enjoyed full family membership, and industrial, modern or even post-modern society where they have been exiled from the familial group. It is particularly inaccurate to identify such a change with the general process by which traditional societies become advanced societies. It is true that some traditional societies have in fact undergone a process during which the transition to industrial living was accompanied by a crucial change in the proportion of the aged in the social structure. Several of the many ethnic and economic regions which go to constitute the present U.S.S.R. are possible examples, as well as others in Central and Eastern Europe. Japan is another. In none of these, it may be noted, was the coincidence at all precise; and in the case of Western societies, in the case of England and Wales particularly, the two developments have been almost entirely separate in time.

One of the reasons why aged persons are thought to have been better appreciated in pre-industrial society is that there were fewer of them. But when we look at what actually happened when industrialization occurred, we find that the increase in the number of the old did not always or even usually coincide with technological and economic change. In France, the U.S.A. and especially England the really extensive changes in the proportions of the aged in the population took place a century or more after the onset of the dissolution of traditional society.

[2] See the number of the Austrian periodical devoted to historical social science particularly directed to the subject of aging: *Beiträge zur Historischen Sozialkunde* 5,1 (Jan. – March 1975), entitled *Die Alten*, especially the contribution of Reinhard Siedel.

This was because the demographic transition, during which the regime of high fertility and high mortality characteristic of traditional society gives way to the regime of low fertility and low mortality characteristic of modern industrial society, was not contemporaneous with the start of industrialization, but came some time afterwards.

In any case the sustained continuance of low fertility, which is responsible for the very high proportions of the aged in all advanced countries, could not in principle have had its full effect until fifty years or so after fertility began its definitive fall.[3] In England and Wales, we shall see, the decline in fertility commencing in the 1870s did not issue in a substantial rise in the proportion of the aged until the years after 1911 and did not bring about an outstanding alteration until the 1920s, 1930s and 1960s.

We shall also observe, to make matters more complicated, that England cannot be taken as necessarily typical of Western experience, except only during the final stages; certainly not as indicating in detail what happened in France. Indeed, we shall consider indications that the actual behaviour of old people in respect of residence may have differed from area to area in traditional European society, and that England may have been somewhat exceptional in its uniformity. This is what we might expect as a corollary to the homogeneity of English household structure which we observed in chapter 1.

But if it is unjustifiable to think of the aged as being always neglected and contemned in our world, it is equally unjustifiable to assume that they were always cherished by their families and by their kin folk in the pre-industrial era. It is true that the fragmentary though suggestive evidence which we shall cite indicates that the aged in pre-industrial England were more frequently to be found surrounded by their immediate family than is the case in the England of today. It is possible that they were given access to the families of their married offspring more readily than is now the case. This may be thought surprising in view of the infrequent occurrence of multigenerational and of complicated households of all kinds, which we have several times remarked upon as characteristic of an earlier England. But we shall find that these cir-

[3] See Roland Pressat, *Demographic analysis* (1972), ch. 9, esp. pp. 277–82, for a demonstration that an increase in the numbers of the old in a population is almost entirely due to a decline in fertility leading, as cohort succeeds cohort, to a progressive diminution in the size of the younger age groups in relation to the older age groups. Increase in length of life (either as mean age at death or expectation of life, which are distinct in all historical populations and certainly in aging populations) is of little importance in this development. If mortality falls and fertility increases, or even if fertility stays constant, the proportion of older persons may actually go down. These are circumstances which it seems rather difficult to grasp without some very elementary demographic knowledge, but are essential to the understanding of how societies grow older.

cumstances can be persuasively accounted for without having to suppose that in the traditional era in our country deliberate provision was made for the physical, emotional or economic needs of aged persons, aged relations or aged parents in a way which was in any sense superior to the provisions now being made by the children, the relatives and the friends of aged persons in our own day, not to speak of the elaborate machinery of an anxiously protective welfare state.

It cannot be shown, for example, that the English family group before the nineteenth century had any socially or legally recognized duty to give succour or family membership to aged relatives other than the parents of the head. The famous Elizabethan Poor Law of 1601 specifically confined responsibility for the relief of the elderly to their children alone. In Scotland, apparently, grandparents and grand-children, perhaps sometimes the wider kin, could be required to repay Poor Law authorities for money spent on the relief of aged persons. In our own country, in spite of the supposedly bilateral character of English kinship, case law developed by the judges succeeded in confining such duties to 'natural' connections, and thus excluded all relatives by law, even stepfathers and stepmothers.

The behaviour of children in the matter of marriage does not seem to have been markedly affected by consideration of the welfare of their own parents. Family reconstitution reveals little or no disposition to wait until the parents died before their sons and daughters took spouses: in fact the marriage of orphaned children appears to have been later than that of those whose parents were alive. No doubt most daughters and some sons did conduct themselves so as to assure the comfort and se-curity of their aging parents as far as they could, but we have found it difficult to confirm that they would return home for that purpose from their jobs or their holdings in other localities. Movement of failing fathers and mothers into the households of their married offspring un-doubtedly occurred, but it was decidedly not a universal pattern in the evidence we have so far surveyed. Nor does it seem to have gone on at the demand of the parents themselves, certainly not at their command.

The authority of the father in traditional England was real enough, especially amongst the elite. He could order his children to marry or not to marry, and could decide where they should live, although his prospects of getting obedience depended to a large extent on whether they had property expectations from him. In practice, as we shall try to demonstrate numerically here, English parents showed little dis-position to keep children at home after marriage, or to require them to return after marriage or after being launched in the world else-where. The ordinary story of the family household after the child-rearing stage was of offspring leaving successively, though not necessarily in order of age, until, if the parents survived, they finally found themselves alone.

There is a telling contrast here with the traditional familial system of an area like South China, for example. There no child left the parental household except under clearly specified conditions, because the recognized rules of familial behaviour required co-residence wherever possible, and no father or mother of grown offspring would ever live alone. In China it would seem that the concept of the family group implied that there should be few persons who lived in what might be called unfamilial situations. It has not proved possible to identify such a concept in the English social structure.

If the stem-family arrangements so widely assumed, at least until recently, to have been common or even universal in traditional Europe had in fact existed in England, then the patriarch in charge, or even his widow, might have had the sanctions at hand to require a grown and often a married child to live at home, and to provide a supporting circle of family members when retirement arrived. But as we saw in our first chapter, this form of the domestic group seems to have been of little importance amongst the English in the generations just before traditional society began the process of transformation.

Where membership of the domestic group was conferred upon solitary, necessitous or infirm parents or kin folk in England in earlier times, therefore, it may be supposed to have been done for quite other reasons. The advantages of the presence of elderly relatives, or the dutifulness, the affection of the charitable disposition of the heads of the households concerned, seem to have been more important than any socially sanctioned expectation that such an action should take place. As for the advantages, they must have existed even before the rise of the factory took the working mother some distance away from the home during the whole of the day and created the need for perpetual child-minders. Many fathers of young children married with what seems to us like unfeeling alacrity when they lost their wives, but Janet Griffiths, who is studying remarriage, does not find that all of them did so. Sometimes, as we saw in chapter 4, a widower sent his orphaned youngsters to live with their grandmother, and occasionally he packed up and took the whole family back there until a new wife could be installed. These things confirm what common sense suggests, that the older generation were of use in child rearing. There are signs that widowed mothers were imported into the households of young and growing families; perhaps some widowed fathers were, too.

But so little was it the accepted thing that the parents of married persons should live with them that we have found such co-residents described as 'lodgers' rather than as family members, and even as 'lodger, receiving parish relief' (Laslett in Laslett and Wall (eds.) 1972: 35 n. 50; the lodger concerned was the aged father of the head of the household). We may recall from the study of what happened in Clayworth in the 1670s and 1680s that it was possible for a son to succeed to the family occupation and to the family dwelling and actually allow his widowed mother and his sister to live in the poor-law institution (see pp. 59—60 above). But it would be unwise to judge the whole social system from the actions of such poverty-stricken individuals, as Jean-Louis Flandrin seems inclined to do (1976: 73, 77).

Nevertheless, it must not be overlooked that the legal duty of a child to assist his parents never seems to have been construed as an obligation to receive or to maintain him or her in the household. Nor did society require the compulsory joining together of families in order to make subsistence cheaper — society, that is to say, in the persons of the administrators of poor relief. These hardpressed volunteers would billet needy people on householders who could give them shelter, like 'Ruth Hurst, lodger upon charge of the town' in the house of Anne Scales, a widow of modest substance in Clayworth in 1688. The *town*, that is, the village acting through the parish officers, would perhaps even have proceeded in this way so as to place the needy with neighbours, members of the community, rather than with relatives where relatives were likely to be unsatisfactory.

It would certainly not be justifiable, however, to suppose that the story of welfare relationships between the young and the old, between children and their aging or infirm parents, in traditional English society was one of indifference or neglect. There is convincing evidence that in medieval England the landholding peasant family had something like a set arrangement for the maintenance of old men, their wives and their widows no longer able to work for their livings. Such picturesquely named customs as 'widow's bench' indicate the extent to which these provisions were sanctioned by community tradition, which must surely have continued well beyond medieval times. Even in areas where partible inheritance was customary, there was apparently an expectation that the family plot would maintain successive holders in the family line throughout their lives.

This was so in spite of the fact that the man in possession seems to have been at liberty to sell on the market as suited his convenience, and can sometimes be seen to have done so in circumstances which suggest that his object was to ensure himself a living in his final years. In the sixteenth century and later the wills of such landed individuals, mostly with small or very small possessions, of course, but some of them fairly substantial, not infrequently provide for the remaining members of the generation about to relinquish possession and control, and even specify the houseroom to be set aside for widowed mothers. It has not been found easy, in fact, to trace these little old ladies dwelling in their allotted living spaces in those lists of inhabitants and residential arrangements which we have been able to study.[4]

But we can say little as yet about the everyday relationship between old people and their grown-up, independent children for any period earlier than recent times, at least in the matter of welfare and support. We are certainly in no position to estimate how much money was transferred, how often children visited their parents and how frequently and strenuously they exerted themselves to live near them or to find accommodation which would enable the parents themselves to come within easy reach. The wisps of evidence we have suggest that in some families elderly persons and children did live in close proximity, in others not. But we cannot hope to decide from the present state of our knowledge how successful our ancestors were in making such provisions.

Account would have to be taken of the very different situation of younger, independent people in that era of exiguous resources, poor communications and widespread illiteracy, which made keeping in touch with home and relations generally so much more difficult. The most likely conjecture from what we do know is that they behaved very much as we behave now in these respects, no better and no worse. In the list of the inhabitants of Corfe Castle, Dorset, as they were in the year 1790, a list which is one of the important sources for the present analysis of aging, the following entry appears for one of the households:

> 'Abner Croker, labourer   73
> Mary Croker, wife   73

'Abn. Croker is blind. He is maintained by his children etc.'
The Croker children, who do not seem to have been living in the village, may have been typical, or they may have been exceptional; we simply do not know.

Superficial as the comparision between past and present has to be, our knowledge is sufficient to show that the position of the elderly in late-twentieth-century social structure is historically novel. If the aged

---

[4] For the interesting issue about retirement and provision for the aged in Tudor and Stuart times, with reflections on the rarity of the retired old in listings of inhabitants, see Margaret Spufford, *Contrasting communities* (1974), esp. pp. 114–15. References in the thirteenth century to payment for the support of old age and of needy family members, whether or not they had ever been responsible for working the plot, can be found in the doctoral dissertation of Richard Michael Smith, 'English peasant life-cycles and social–economic networks' (1974) and its references, particularly to the work of Ambrose Raftis and others. All these scholars insist that the evidence as to the aged is at present scanty, but that much remains to be analysed in the rolls of the manor courts, which continue right up to the seventeenth century and beyond. Sources of this kind for Suffolk manors in the thirteenth century provided Dr Smith with his remarkable information.

in our generation and in our society present a 'problem to be solved', it is a problem which has never been solved in the past, because it did not then exist. The value of historical sociology to the creation of policy in the present is in denoting how far we differ from past people and how much we are the same. With respect to aging, it is maintained that we are in an unprecedented situation: we shall have to invent appropriate social forms, for they cannot be recovered from our history. It could be said, with greater conviction if our knowledge had been greater, that the familial history of peoples other than the English, or of those in areas other than the Western European, does provide examples of the treatment of the aged and aging which might give us guidance and provide precedents. But in all of these areas and at all of the times we know about, the numbers of the aged were very much less than in high industrial society today. Our situation remains irreducibly novel: it calls for invention rather than imitation.

The facts which underlie the statements we have made about aging in the past and aging in the present have had to be painfully recovered, and must be described as few and somewhat desultory. They could be, and no doubt soon will be, enormously extended and enlivened by a search for references to the aged in the literature of the pre-industrial and industrializing West, and especially of England. Such a work has already been undertaken for the literature of France, and for classical literature as well, with the addition of anthropological evidence, by one of the most sensitive of the literary commentators of our day, Simone de Beauvoir in *La vieillesse*. The anthropologists themselves have written works on the comparative situation of the aged in differing cultures.[5] In presenting the first available instalment of the evidence from lists of inhabitants of English villages and towns, I shall pursue the practice of the other chapters of this book. A series of tables and one figure will be set out with a commentary.

Life expectation and proportion of the elderly in traditional societies in the past

A selection of the few available estimates of the expectation of life in some traditional societies in the past is presented in table 5.1. The variations in these estimates from period to period are sometimes surprising to those to whom the demography of earlier societies is unfamiliar. It is now a commonplace in historical sociology, however, that in the

[5] Simone de Beauvoir's work was published in Paris in 1970, and translated into English as *Old age* by Patrick O'Brian (London, 1972). The work of the social anthropologists is commented upon with great acuteness by Jack Goody in his contribution to the *Handbook of aging*, 1 ('Aging in non-industrial societies' and its references).

TABLE 5.1. *Expectation of life in some traditional societies of the past*

Country	Date	Expectation of life at birth (years)	Expectation of life at (age) (years)
England			
Colyton, Devon.	1538–99	45	—
	1600–49	42.5	—
	1650–99	34	—
	1700–49	c. 40	—
	1750–99	c. 45	
Colonial America			
Plymouth colony	17th century	'as high as 50 years in some places' (Wrigley 1969)	—
Massachusetts and New Hampshire	18th century (Wigglesworth)	28.15	— (10) 49.23 (20) 34.21 (30) 30.24 (50) 21.16 (60) 15.43 (70) 10.06 (80) 5.85

France			
Crulai, Normandy	1675–1775	30 ± 2	—
Whole country	Late 18th century	28.8	—
	1821	c. 41 (women only)	—
Switzerland	Late 18th century	20–30	—
Spain	Before 1797	26.8	—
Germany			
Breslau	1690s	27.5	(10) 40.2
Japan			
One village	1671–1725	—	(10) 50.0 (males)
			38.3 (females)
	1726–75	—	(10) 49.9 (males)
			48.1 (females)
Another village	1717–1830	—	(10) 46.9 (males)
			50.7 (females)
Italy			
Verona	1761–6	28	—
Milan	1804–5	30	—
Bologna	1811–12	26	—
India	1891–1901	23.8	—
	1901–11	22.9	—
	1911–21	20.15	—

SOURCES: The figures for Colyton are a free adaptation from Wrigley 1972; for Massachusetts and New Hampshire from M. A. Vinovskis, 'The 1789 life table of Edward Wigglesworth', *Journal of Economic History* 31, 3 (1971). The other estimates come from the standard historical demographic works for the countries concerned or from the U.N. demographic yearbooks. The Japanese estimates were kindly communicated by Professor Akira Hayami.

183

same village, county or even country, fertility, nuptiality and mortality can be expected to change quite drastically between generation and generation, up and down. For this reason the exceptionally high figure reported for the Plymouth colony is not particularly surprising, although the early American settlers may well have lived longer than their European contemporaries. We do not have anything like enough evidence to estimate the limits of such variation, but it is clear that no single figure for life expectation in pre-industrial times generally would make sense.

On the whole, figures for the duration of life are higher rather than lower than might be thought probable, and this is particularly the case with estimates for later ages, as is illustrated by Wigglesworth's famous figures for New England in the later eighteenth century. It may well turn out, in fact, when the evidence is all in, that the life expectation of Western European peasants in the middle and later years of life could be quite high under satisfactory economic, nutritional and climatic conditions, not 'all that much inferior to what it is generally today. Some of the historical statistics compare favourably with those for early-twentieth-century India, for example.

This is important to the question of aging in relation to social change not only because it may mean that the experience of being old came to more people — that is, persons no longer children — than might be supposed, but also because it implies that the family group lasted rather better. The duration of marriage in pre-industrial England was of the order of twenty years for most couples, but could last for thirty-five years or more for a fifth or a quarter of them (see Laslett 1976a, differing from the view of Ariès and others that married life was too brief to ensure familial stability). This in turn improved the chances of old people made solitary or helpless having the home of one or other of their children to go to and stay in.

The Cambridge Group for the History of Population and Social Structure cannot at present provide any very useful estimate of the proportions of elderly English persons, that is of 60 years and over, or aged persons, those of 65 and over, who had at least one married son or a married daughter alive to go and live with, given marriage ages, number of children and so on, prevailing in pre-industrial times. Clearly there must have been considerable variability from family to family, place to place and time to time, and even greater variability when England is contrasted with other cultural areas. Neither can we say how many relatives of any kind such people would have; how often, for example, an elderly or aged spinster might be able to rely on having a similar sister or brother she could live with. It is highly probable, however, that the numbers of old people with no living relative, or even with no living child, married or unmarried, was always small, although liable to fluctuate regionally and temporarily. Without larger, more precise knowledge on this matter, such as is becoming available for Denmark in the eighteenth century from the work of Professor H. C. Johansen, our evidence is less useful than it might be, especially when we compare the situation then with the situation now. The intention, however, is to make estimates for differing demographic rates and so on, once more with the use of microsimulation.[6]

Even with this information to hand, however, we shall still have to try to determine, or to guess, how many of the surviving children of an elderly person would be in contact with him or her, in a position to give houseroom, with the resources to do so, and with a motive as well, of a child-minding character or of any other. These circumstances underline once more how preliminary our present knowledge is and how much there is yet to do to get any *precise* notion of the situation of the aged today in comparison with the situation in earlier times.

Tables 5.2 and 5.3 contain a collection of figures which have been recovered from lists of inhabitants for individual cities, towns and villages, together with those from several national or provincial censuses, and one outcome from palaeodemography — the estimation of the ages of the skeletons excavated from an eleventh-century graveyard. A noteworthy feature of the results of calculating the proportions in the higher age groups of the populations concerned is that they are also nearly all relatively high in relation to what one might expect in traditional societies. Only seven of the fifty-six figures for the percentage of persons aged 60 and above are as low as the percentage reported in Tunisia in 1966 or Brazil in 1970, two contemporary industrializing societies (compare table 5.8: only two are as low as the figure for Indonesia in 1964—5). The variation from place to place, though noticeable, is certainly rather less than might be expected. These variations do not seem to be entirely the result of the smallness of the population studied, since that of Venice was in the tens of thousands. England, with the

---

[6] Johansen in his unpublished paper of 1976, 'The position of the old in a traditional society', does report on such outcomes, using analytic methods rather than microsimulation. He presents a series of interesting results parallel to those derived from the data used here (see table 5.12), and is able to compare his estimates of persons over 60 in certain household positions with those actually recorded in the Danish Censuses of 1778 and 1801. His conclusion, that a half of the elderly who can be calculated to have had married children were actually living in the same household with them, seems to show that the Danish rules were similar to the English ones but may have encouraged more co-residence. He also insists that where old persons had unmarried children, they continued as heads of their own households. Johansen has not interested himself in other familial situations (living as lodgers etc.) and only a few of his outcomes are directly comparable to those reported here.

TABLE 5.2. *Proportions of elderly and aged persons (by sex) in some traditional societies in the past*

Place	Date	Pop.	Aged 60 and above			
			M	F	Both	Sex ratio
South-east Europe						
11th century						
(excavated graveyard)		—	—	—	9.9	—
Italy						
Arezzo	1427	—	15.9	15.9	15.9	104
Venice	1601–10	—	—	—	10.7	
	1691–1700	—	—	—	11.6	
France						
Mostejols	1690	439	9.6	8.9	9.3	123
Longuenesse	1778	332	8.5	9.7	9.1	76
	1790	387	10.2	5.5	7.7	191
Belgium						
Lisswege	1739	796	4.5	5.1	4.8	100
	1748	702	3.6	3.4	3.9	117
Denmark						
Bjorre Is.	1650	1,032	—	—	7.7	—
Zealand Province	1650	129,000	—	—	7.0	—
(National census)	1787	—	8.0	9.3	8.7	85
	1801	—	8.8	9.8	9.4	87
Iceland						
(National census)	1703	—	5.8	9.2	7.7	52
	1729	—	12.4	16.7	14.7	82
	1787	—	6.5	8.7	7.8	58
Germany						
Löffingen Gemeinde	1777	2,500	—	—	8.7	—
Switzerland						
Meltmenstetten	1634	—	—	—	5.1	—
Zürich St Peter	1637	—	—	—	7.2	—
Albisrieden Zumiken	1634	—	—	—	3.4	—
Wiesendangen	1721	—	—	—	6.3	—
(Ober- u. Unter-)	1764	—	—	—	9.9	—
Bern	1764	—	—	—	10.3	—
Austria						
Abtenau	1632	4,000 +	—	—	5.4	—
Estonia						
(Village census)	1782	—	6.8	5.7	6.3	118
	1795	—	4.3	4.7	4.8	89
Hungary						
Kölked	1816	638	5.7	4.6	5.0	113
Serbia						
Belgrade	1733	1,357	5.2	3.4	4.7	133
Japan						
15 places	1671–90	—	6.7	6.8	6.7	100
15 places	1711–40	—	8.9	8.4	8.7	115
	1761–90	—	11.5	11.8	11.7	107
	1811–40	—	8.6	9.7	9.1	93
Nishinomiya	1713	653	9.2	9.9	9.7	106
Colonial U.S.A.						
Bedford and New						
Rochelle	1698	385	—	—	5.7	—

Note: These figures come from a series of specialist studies in historical demography, and in most cases the calculations of percentages and sex ratios have been undertaken by the present writer. The paucity of entries for the later ages is due to numbers not being specified in the sources; where they are present they are often so small as to make sex ratios meaningless.

Aged 65 and above				Aged 70 and above				Aged 75 and above				Aged 80 and above			
M	F	Both	Sex ratio	M	F	Both	Sex ratio	M	F	Both	Sex ratio	M	F	Both	Sex ratio
—	—	2.5	—	—	—	—	—	—	—	—	—	—	—	—	—
10.0	10.2	10.1	105	8.1	8.6	8.4	109	—	—	—	—	—	—	—	—
—	—	—	—	—	—	—	—	—	—	—	—	—	—	—	—
—	—	—	—	—	—	—	—	—	—	—	—	—	—	—	—
5.7	6.9	6.1	93	4.3	3.9	4.1	126	1.8	1.8	1.8	100	1.3	1.5	1.4	100
5.9	8.0	7.0	104	2.0	5.1	3.7	25	—	—	—	—	—	—	—	—
6.4	4.5	5.4	133	3.2	3.0	3.1	100	—	—	—	—	—	—	—	—
—	—	—	—	—	—	—	—	—	—	—	—	—	—	—	—
—	—	—	—	—	—	—	—	—	—	—	—	—	—	—	—
—	—	—	—	—	—	—	—	—	—	—	—	—	—	—	—
—	—	—	—	—	—	—	—	—	—	—	—	—	—	—	—
—	—	—	—	2.6	3.4	3.0	74	—	—	—	—	0.4	0.7	0.6	56
—	—	—	—	2.9	3.6	3.2	79	—	—	—	—	0.5	0.8	0.7	69
3.6	6.1	4.6	48	2.2	4.1	3.3	44	1.2	2.5	1.9	40	0.8	1.6	1.2	45
9.0	12.7	11.0	60	5.8	8.6	7.3	57	3.2	4.9	4.2	55	1.4	2.2	1.9	54
—	—	—	—	1.6	2.5	2.1	48	—	—	—	—	—	—	—	—
—	—	—	—	—	—	—	—	—	—	—	—	—	—	—	—
—	—	—	—	—	—	—	—	—	—	—	—	—	—	—	—
—	—	—	—	—	—	—	—	—	—	—	—	—	—	—	—
—	—	—	—	—	—	—	—	—	—	—	—	—	—	—	—
—	—	—	—	—	—	—	—	—	—	—	—	—	—	—	—
—	—	—	—	—	—	—	—	—	—	—	—	—	—	—	—
—	—	—	—	—	—	—	—	—	—	—	—	—	—	—	—
—	—	—	—	—	—	—	—	—	—	—	—	—	—	—	—
—	—	—	—	—	—	—	—	—	—	—	—	—	—	—	—
2.8	3.3	3.1	82	2.2	2.1	2.2	100	1.3	0.9	1.1	—	—	—	—	—
2.6	1.5	2.1	77	1.8	1.3	1.5	137	—	—	—	—	—	—	—	—
—	—	—	—	—	—	—	—	—	—	—	—	—	—	—	—
—	—	—	—	—	—	—	—	—	—	—	—	—	—	—	—
—	—	—	—	—	—	—	—	—	—	—	—	—	—	—	—
6.3	6.9	6.6	104	4.3	3.6	4.0	136	—	—	—	—	—	—	—	—
—	—	1.8	—	—	—	0.8	—	—	—	—	—	—	—	—	—

TABLE 5.3. *Proportions of elderly and aged persons (by sex) in certain places in England before 1800*

Place	Date	Pop.	Aged 60 and above				Aged 65 and above				Aged 70 and above				Aged 75 and above				Aged 80 and above			
			M	F	Both	Sex ratio	M	F	Both	Sex ratio	M	F	Both	Sex ratio	M	F	Both	Sex ratio	M	F	Both	Sex ratio
Ealing	1599	427	7.0	4.5	5.9	133	1.7	1.0	1.4	–	0.4	1.0	0.7	–	–	–	–	–	–	–	–	–
Chilvers Coton	1684	780	6.6	6.7	6.7	104	3.6	2.4	3.0	130	1.9	1.0	1.4	175	–	–	–	–	–	–	–	–
Lichfield	1695	2,861	6.4	9.4	8.1	87	3.4	4.6	4.1	61	2.1	2.5	2.3	71	–	–	–	–	–	–	–	–
Stoke-on-Trent	1701	1,627	8.2	9.1	8.6	160	5.0	5.3	5.2	86	2.6	3.6	3.1	66	–	–	–	–	–	–	–	–
Corfe Castle	1790	1,239	9.8	9.5	9.7	100	6.6	6.3	6.4	100	3.4	3.5	3.3	98	–	–	–	–	–	–	–	–
Ardleigh	1796	1,126	7.2	4.4	5.9	215	3.4	1.8	3.1	133	2.4	2.0	2.2	127	–	–	–	–	–	–	–	–
Grasmere	1683	310	8.4	10.3	9.4	81	3.9	7.1	5.5	81	3.2	5.2	4.2	–	–	–	–	–	–	–	–	–
Buckfastleigh	1698	1,111	6.4	5.7	6.0	116	2.6	2.4	2.5	–	1.6	1.7	1.6	–	–	–	–	–	–	–	–	–
Ringmore	1698	188	19.3	19.4	19.1	80	10.8	11.6	11.2	75	6.0	7.8	6.9	–	–	–	–	–	–	–	–	–
Trent	1748	375	6.6	10.3	8.0	60	–	–	–	–	1.7	3.6	2.7	43	–	–	–	–	–	–	–	–
Shrewsbury	1770	1,046	–	–	–	–	–	–	–	–	–	–	5.6	–	–	–	2.7	–	–	–	1.6	–
(Holy Cross parish)	1780	1,113	–	–	–	–	–	–	–	–	–	–	3.6	–	–	–	2.0	–	–	–	0.8	–
Ackworth	1757	603	10.3	8.5	9.1	150	–	–	–	–	2.5	2.8	2.6	100	–	–	–	–	1.3	0	0.6	–
	1767	728	8.5	11.0	9.9	67	–	–	–	–	2.6	3.8	3.3	60	–	–	–	–	0.6	1.3	1.0	–
	1772	678	8.5	12.7	10.6	21	–	–	–	–	2.6	4.4	3.5	–	–	–	–	–	0.6	1.4	1.0	–
Ashton-under-Lyne	1773	7,956	–	–	–	–	–	–	–	–	–	–	1.7	–	–	–	–	–	–	–	–	–
Chester	1774	14,713	–	–	5.9	–	–	–	–	–	–	–	4.3	–	–	–	–	–	–	–	0.3	–
Sandwich	1776	609	14.2	12.2	13.1	100	–	–	–	–	6.0	4.6	5.5	113	–	–	–	–	1.4	0.6	1.0	–
Carlisle	1780	7,677	–	–	9.1	–	–	–	–	–	–	–	–	–	–	–	–	–	–	–	–	–
	1788	8,677	–	–	9.1	–	–	–	–	–	–	–	–	–	–	–	–	–	–	–	–	–
Manchester	1773	13,786	–	–	3.4	–	–	–	–	–	–	–	1.9	–	–	–	–	–	–	–	–	–
Maidstone	1782	5,755	–	–	–	–	–	–	–	–	4.2	5.9	5.1	–	–	–	–	–	–	–	0.6	–
Taunton	1791	5,472	–	–	–	–	–	–	–	–	–	–	4.7	–	–	–	–	–	–	–	–	–
Wigton	1791	1,650	–	–	16.3	–	–	–	–	–	3.0	4.8	4.0	50	–	–	–	–	–	–	1.5	–
Bocking	1793	2,943	–	–	–	–	–	–	–	–	3.3	2.1	2.6	–	–	–	–	–	–	–	–	–

Note: These figures have been calculated from the evidence of the nine lists of inhabitants of English communities before 1800 which specify ages (Ealing, Chilvers Coton, Lichfield, Stoke-on-Trent, Corfe Castle, Ardleigh, Grasmere, Buckfastleigh and Ringmore) together with a series of sets of numbers in the population of various English places published by eighteenth-century authors. Figures of the second type are owed to Richard Wall, whose generous assistance is duly acknowledged.

188

interesting exception of Manchester in 1773 at the very dawn of the factory era, seems to have had a consistently high proportion of the elderly.

These statistics, then, might be held to confirm the impression given by the estimates of the expectation of life, which is that a fair number of people reached the higher ages in historic times, and that fertility was consistently lower than the levels now reached in underdeveloped societies in our day. The probable reason for this is not without significance to the overall contrast in marital habits which has been proposed as distinguishing Western European areas from other areas of the world, and which was discussed in chapter 1, that is, a late age of first marriage for women. The figures in the tables might be held to modify the view that the old were never a burden in pre-industrial Europe, which is not easy to sustain in the case of Arezzo in 1427 or of Iceland in 1729, though in both cases there had apparently been exceptional preceding circumstances.

It should be insisted, however, that the absolute reliability of all these figures is questionable, since they come from societies where the reckoning of ages must have been much less accurate than it is today in advanced societies, or even in countries like Indonesia or Tunisia. Older people are known to have exaggerated their ages when they talked to the list-takers of the past, and to have declared themselves at the decadal years to a great extent. This undoubtedly had the effect of inflating the numbers over 60 and probably even more at the advanced ages.

Social development in the past, and the sex ratio, marital status and proportion of the elderly and aged

In tables 5.4 and 5.5 is set out a small selection of figures for the proportion of married, widowed and single amongst the older age groups, by sex. The reason why the number of communities is so few, far fewer than in tables 5.2 and 5.3, is that for England and Wales a concerted search over a decade and more has so far (1976) failed to uncover further documents giving the relevant information. In the case of other countries (for example, Germany) it is known that a great deal more evidence exists, but it has not yet been analysed. Comments on these data therefore must be even more tentative than on the other sets of figures presented here. Nevertheless, it may be worth while to draw attention to some of their features.

Variability is clearly considerable in these statistics, as must be expected for such minute numbers. But the indications, for what they are worth, are that elderly and aged women were no less liable to be widowed than they are in Western countries in our own day. In 1960 50%

TABLE 5.4. *Marital status of elderly and aged persons by sex and age in certain places in England before 1800 (percentages)*

	Aged 60 and above		Aged 65 and above		Aged 70 and above	
	Male	Female	Male	Female	Male	Female
Ealing, Middx. 1599, pop. 427 (16 males, 12 females aged 60 and above)						
Married	62	70	33	33	0	50
Widowed	19	20	67	67	100	50
Single	19	10	0	0	0	0
Chilvers Coton, War. 1683, pop. 780 (24 males, 23 females aged 60 and above)						
Married	74	58	75	40	71	50
Widowed	19	42	25	60	29	50
Single	6	0	0	0	0	0
Grasmere, Westmorland 1683, pop. 310 (11 males, 12 females aged 60 and above)						
Married	75	41	80	60	75	60
Widowed	16	58	20	40	25	40
Single	8	0	0	0	0	0
Lichfield, Staffs. 1695, pop. 2,861 (79 males, 131 females aged 60 and above)						
Married	80	41	81	23	76	19
Widowed	12	58	19	77	24	81
Single	8	1	0	0	0	0
Stoke-on-Trent, Staffs. 1701, pop. 1,627 (65 males, 75 females aged 60 and above)						
Married	62	37	58	25	45	20
Widowed	27	55	31	70	40	73
Single	11	8	11	5	15	7
Corfe Castle, Dorset 1790, pop. 1,239 (76 males, 77 females aged 60 and above)						
Married	58	40	60	37	57	32
Widowed	34	48	38	55	38	68
Single	8	12	2	8	5	0
Ardleigh, Essex 1796, pop. 1,126 (43 males, 20 females aged 60 and above)						
Married	67	50	75	64	70	57
Widowed	33	45	25	36	30	43
Single	0	5	0	0	0	0

Note: Source: age listings held by the Cambridge Group. Not all individuals in these places have marital status recorded. Those of uncertain status have been classified as single.

TABLE 5.5. *Marital status of elderly and aged persons by sex and age in certain places outside England before 1800 (percentages)*

	Aged 60 and above		Aged 65 and above		Aged 70 and above	
	Male	Female	Male	Female	Male	Female
Longuenesse, N. France						
1778, pop. 333 (11 males,						
16 females aged 60 and above)						
Married	64	44	67	31	33	12
Widowed	27	56	22	69	33	88
Single	9	0	11	0	33	0
1790, pop. 387 (18 males,						
11 females aged						
60 and above)						
Married	61	54	67	56	67	50
Widowed	32	46	25	44	33	50
Single	6	0	8	0	0	0
Belgrade, Serbia						
1733–4, pop. 1,357 (28 males.						
Married	69	7	80	7	70	14
Widowed	12	90	13	86	20	72
50 females aged 60 and above)						
Single	19	3	7	7	10	14
Nishinomiya, Japan						
1713, pop. 653 (32 males,						
Married	67	17	50	16	46	0
Widowed	33	83	50	84	54	100
30 females aged 60 and above)						
Single	0	0	0	0	0	0

Note: See table 5.4 note.

of all women were widowed above the age of 65 in Britain, 53% in the United States and 43% in Denmark (Shanas et al. 1968: 12). The same effect is observable for men, if a little less pronounced: the contemporary figures for widowers above 65 are 22% in Britain, 10% for the United States and 23% for Denmark. There is evidently little ground here for believing that widowhood was less common in the English past.

It is interesting, however, that the really sharp contrasts which come in table 5.5 are for two places outside the European West, Belgrade and Nishinomiya, where over 80% of women of 65 and above are given as widowed. A mere 13% of the men lack spouses in Belgrade, an outcome of earlier marriage for women together with a greater age gap between spouses. In Japan the remarriage of widows was perhaps less common, and further research may show that this contrast should not be pressed too far.[7] Almost nothing can be learned from the tables about the probability of being a bachelor or a spinster in later life at these places. This is because the evidence so often leaves unclear the distinction between the unmarried and the widowed.

Table 5.6 provides an account of the actual course of change in the proportion of the elderly in the population for England and Wales on the one hand and France on the other. This covers the whole period of industrialization, from the eighteenth century until 1971. The interesting pattern which these contrasting sets of figures give rise to over time is quite conspicuous in the accompanying figure (5.1).

Two things stand out from these data for England and Wales. One is that the proportion of the elderly seems to have changed very little between the 1840s and the 1900s. The other is that the number of the elderly was probably lower during that period than it had been in preindustrial times, as can be seen by glancing back at table 5.3. So far from bringing about an immediate surplus of the elderly, it would seem that industrialization in England can have had very little effect in that direction for a full century. But change, when it did begin, soon became extraordinarily marked, and it could justly be said that the proportions of the aged have been completely transformed in the sixty years since 1911. Change was greatest in the 1920s, 30s and 60s.

There is a close resemblance in this development over time with the course of mean household size in England, which was also notably constant over the period of industrialization, in fact from the seventeenth century until 1901 (see Laslett 1972b: 139—44 and figs. 4.3, 4.4). Between the 1920s and the 1970s, then, the elderly in England became

---

[7] In Abbehausen, in southern Germany, in 1675, for example, 32 out of 40 women of age 60 and above, likewise 80%, were 'widowed', that is non-married, and only 8 out of 21, or 38% of men, though the marriage pattern there was decidedly not of the Serbian or Japanese type.

TABLE 5.6. *Proportions of elderly persons (% 60 and above) in England and Wales and in France since the late eighteenth century*

Date	England and Wales			France		
	Male	Female	Both	Male	Female	Both
1776	—	—	—	7.2	7.3	7.3
1786	—	—	—	7.8	8.1	7.9
1796	—	—	—	8.6	8.7	8.6
1801	—	—	—	8.7	8.8	8.7
1811	—	—	—	9.0	9.0	9.0
1821	7.3	7.6	—	9.6	9.8	9.7
1831	—	—	—	9.5	10.4	10.0
1841	6.8	7.4	7.2	9.2	10.4	9.9
1851	6.9	7.8	7.4	9.2	11.1	10.1
1861	7.0	7.8	7.3	9.9	11.4	10.7
1871	6.6	7.8	7.4	11.0	11.9	11.7
1881	6.9	7.8	7.3	11.7	12.5	12.1
1891	6.8	7.9	7.2	12.0	13.2	12.6
1901	6.8	8.0	7.3	12.3	13.5	13.0
1911	7.3	8.6	7.9	11.6	13.5	12.6
1921	8.7	10.0	9.3	11.5	14.5	13.7
1931	10.7	12.3	11.5	12.7	15.1	14.0
1936	—	—	—	13.4	16.0	14.7
1946	—	—	—	13.8	17.9	15.9
1951	14.6	17.7	15.9	13.5	18.8	16.2
1961	15.3	17.9	16.2	—	—	—
1968	—	—	—	15.7	21.6	18.8
1971	15.9	21.9	18.7	—	—	—

Note: Calculated from census returns and, for France before 1801, from Pressat 1972 (citing Duvillard).

markedly more numerous, and the disproportion in the number of old women as compared with old men, consistently small in the nineteenth century, suddenly grew. Meanwhile, household size was becoming smaller, so that the percentage of those living in households of one or two persons more than tripled, many of these solitaries and pairs being older people. It might be said that action in the story of social development and aging in England and Wales was long in coming but that when it did arrive, in the lifetime of the aged people still with us today, it was swift and fundamental.

This may be thought to be a surprisingly dramatic story for such a subject as this, and since it is apparently the first time that such a story has been told, it might be natural to suppose that what happened in English society would be typical. The parallel series of figures from France makes it clear that this cannot be so. In table 5.7, moreover, the proportion of aged persons (those over 65 rather than those over 60) at various dates since 1850 in various countries in Europe and North America could be

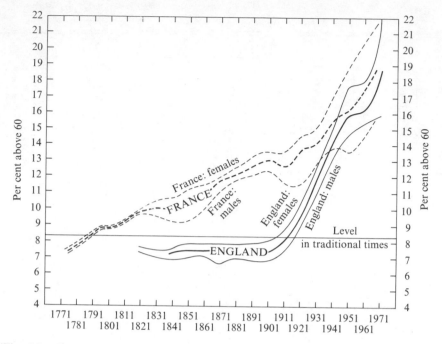

Fig. 5.1 Change over time in proportions of elderly persons: France and England, 1770s – 1971.

used to show that the experience of no industrializing country was typical of all of them in respect of aging.

In France, as the graph makes clear, the proportion of the elderly in the population was not as consistent during the nineteenth century, over the years when industrialization was beginning, as it was in England and Wales, and it was noticeably higher. The difference in the ratio of the proportion of the elderly by sex varied, too. There was a curious rise in this statistic during the years 1821–51, when it could be claimed that France first began to industrialize in earnest, since in that country the process came later than in England. And so the different story continued until the 1950s, when development coincided completely in England and in France for the first time.

This contrasting pattern of development in the two countries was no doubt determined for the most part by their differing histories as to fertility, together with the net effects of migration. It is evident that neither could be taken as representative of Western Europe. England and Wales may conceivably have been at one extreme, where, as in Germany, the proportion of older people remained low until the end of the nineteenth century, and France at the other extreme, where, as in Sweden, the pro-

TABLE 5.7. *Proportions of aged persons (% 65 and above) in various countries since 1850*

Date	England and Wales	France	Germany	Italy	Netherlands	Sweden	U.S.A.	Canada
1850	4.6	6.5	–	–	4.7	4.8	–	–
1900	4.7	8.2	4.9	6.2	6.0	8.4	4.1	5.1
1930	7.4	9.3	7.4	–	6.2	9.2	5.4	5.6
1950	10.8	11.8	9.7	–	7.7	10.3	8.1	7.8
1969/70	13.0	13.0	14.0	11.0	10.0	14.0	10.0	8.0

Note: Calculated from U.N. demographic yearbook.

195

portion was already high by 1900. However this may be, the body of
evidence from very recent decades as to proportions of the elderly and
aged, sex ratios and so on shows a tendency towards convergence in
what we have called high industrial societies, a convergence which it
is interesting to see has been particularly rapid and well marked in the
case of England and France. Their fertility levels, very low fertility levels,
are now very much the same.

The passing of traditional society in England is supposed to have
begun by the 1770s, the earliest decade in our figures, though there is
reason to question how far the process can have gone for the first seventy
or eighty years in changing the lives of the majority of English persons.
It is clear, nevertheless, that for at least half a century elderly people
in England remained as scarce as they had ever been, or even became
scarcer, yet social transformation was going on apace. This demonstrates
once again the point which has been made already, that industrialization
and the demographic transition were quite distinct in time in England.
Yet in France the relationship was not quite the same, and it would seem
that in the United States and elsewhere it was different again, both as to
the proportion of the elderly and the size and fluctuations of that group,
and as to the inception and progress of industrialization. If we considered
countries or areas outside the West, Russia, shall we say, or Japan or
China, we should probably get quite other relationships. Historically,
then, there is no set pattern between the process of industrialization and
the number of elderly persons, whatever may be the case in respect of
countries undergoing industrialization in the late twentieth century.

Table 5.8 has been inserted to show how different the situation can be
now, in countries at various stages of the demographic transition and of
industrialization.

Household position of the widowed, the elderly and the aged in traditional English society

The next four tables in the series attempt to portray the domestic situation of elderly and aged persons in one country, the first to undergo both
modernization and industrialization and the first to be studied from this
point of view. The great difficulty here is to get anything like enough
data to illustrate the principles already laid down about this, the most
important part of our subject. Accordingly, we have begun with a table
analysing lists of inhabitants held by the Cambridge Group which do not
specify ages but do indicate widowhood. While we possess these in tens,
we have less than a dozen English documents in all with data which provide useful age statistics.

Table 5.9 sets out the household position of widowed persons (age

TABLE 5.8. *Proportions of elderly and aged persons in certain industrialized, industrializing and non-industrial countries in the 1960s and 1970s*

	Aged 60 and above				Aged 65 and above				Aged 70 and above				Aged 75 and above				Aged 80 and above			
	M	F	Both	Sex ratio	M	F	Both	Sex ratio	M	F	Both	Sex ratio	M	F	Both	Sex ratio	M	F	Both	Sex ratio
United Kingdom, 1971	15.9	21.7	18.9	69	10.3	15.7	11.1	62	5.8	10.0	8.2	55	3.2	6.1	4.6	46	1.4	3.1	2.3	41
U.S.A., 1970	12.6	15.6	14.1	81	8.5	11.2	9.7	72	5.3	7.5	6.3	68	3.0	4.5	3.7	64	1.4	2.3	1.6	60
Poland, 1971	11.1	14.9	13.1	70	6.9	10.1	8.5	65	3.7	6.1	5.0	5:	1.7	3.2	2.5	51	—	—	—	—
Brazil, 1970	5.0	5.1	5.1	96	—	—	—	—	—	—	—	—	1.7	1.9	1.8	87	—	—	—	—
India, 1971	6.1	6.0	5.9	110	3.3	3.4	3.3	106	2.1	2.1	2.1	104	1.0	1.1	1.0	100	0.6	0.6	0.6	96
Tunisia, 1966	5.8	5.3	5.5	115	3.7	3.3	3.5	116	2.1	2.0	2.1	112	1.2	1.1	1.2	116	0.6	0.6	0.6	108
Indonesia, September 1964—February 1965	4.8	4.2	4.5	110	2.3	2.2	2.3	103	1.5	1.4	1.4	100	0.6	0.7	0.6	93	—	—	—	—

Note: Calculated from U.N. demographic yearbook.

197

TABLE 5.9. *Household position of widowed persons by sex in 61 places in England before 1821*

| | Heading households containing | | | | | In households headed by | | | | Solitary | In institutions | Total |
	Unmarried offspring	Married or widowed son	Married or widowed daughter	Only those not offspring	Sub-total	Son or daughter	Son- or daughter-in-law	Other kin	Other persons			
Widowers												
Number	120	9	5	24	158	12	2	9	18	12	0	211
Per cent	57%	4%	2%	11%	74%	6%	1%	4%	9%	6%	0	100%
Widows												
Number	243	7	5	50	305	48	17	19	41	65	6	501
Per cent	49%	1%	1%	10%	61%	10%	3%	4%	8%	13%	1%	100%
Both												
Number	363	16	10	74	463	60	19	28	59	77	6	712
Per cent	51%	2%	1%	10%	65%	8%	3%	4%	8%	11%	1%	100%

Note: See text for source and for discussion of the category 'widowed'.

not given) in 61 English settlements before 1821, that is, early in the industrializing era and before the demographic transition. The widowed made up some 10% of the population, and though it is not advisable to use widowhood as an accurate indicator of age — indeed, up to half the women aged 45–9 could be widowed in an Elizabethan village — these figures introduce an interesting and important principle. This is that once a man or woman had become a householder or a household-er's wife in England in traditional times, he or she tended to stay at the head of the family, in spite of the vicissitudes of life in that insecure world.

Even these figures are dubious, of course, because of the problem of identification by sex and situation. All men and women living with their children and without a spouse in the household, for example, have to be counted as widowed, so that some numbers of deserted spouses, especial-ly deserted wives, must be present in the data of the table. It is not ab-solutely clear that never-marrieds have always been excluded from the numbers of the widowed. Still we may attach some importance to the percentages which indicate how few of these spouseless persons in the table were living alone or in institutions;[8] to those which show that having a married son or daughter living in the family was rare; and to those which imply that living in a household headed by such married offspring was considerably commoner, but still only affected about a tenth of all widowed people. The other persons in whose households the 'widowed' are found were a miscellaneous lot and included a good pro-portion of unrelated people with whom they were simply lodging. But some amongst them may have been married daughters unrecognized by us.

These uncertainties, it seems to me, cannot disguise the message of the table. Widows and widowers in pre-industrial England lived for the most part where they had been before they became widowed. The loss of a spouse did not always or even usually lead to the breakup of the house-hold: certainly not to its being absorbed into another household. It might, of course, lead to the movement of the bereaved family away from the community, and we saw this happening at Clayworth and Cogenhoe in chapter 2. But we know that those who administered the Elizabethan Poor Law would assist a widow in keeping her family to-gether, though we do not know how often this venture failed. There

[8] Just over 1% of the population of pre-industrial England seem to have lived as soli-taries, and of them a good third (35.2%) are marked as widowed in the 78 lists containing such information. This figure is no doubt too low: about 50% might be nearer the truth. The number of the widowed in institutions is also likely to be under-reported in table 5.9. These facts must be borne in mind when considering the position of widowed per-sons without accompanying family or kin.

may, for instance, have been widowed persons present in these 61 English communities concealed from us because they lived as servants.

Table 5.9 is of value also because it gives a comparative context and some very welcome confirmation of the numerous facts about the household position of the aged persons in pre-industrial England which have been marshalled in tables 5.10, 5.11 and 5.12. If, for instance, 6% of all the widowers and 13% of all the widows can be supposed from the figures in table 5.9 to have been living alone, it is reasonable that we should find that 5% of the widowers over 60 years old in table 5.10 and 16% of the widows of that age should also be found to be solitary.

The difference between men and women was no doubt due to the greater facility with which widowers remarried, and this is one of a number of interesting contrasts between the sexes amongst the elderly in historical communities. We can see from the final column of table 5.11 that four-fifths of all persons of age 60 and older in the six settlements were living as heads of households, including in the number those who lived by themselves. This surely establishes the principle that the elderly as well as the widowed were ordinarily left in charge of the family groups they themselves had brought into being and maintained in their earlier years. But it is noticeable that fewer women than men were in this position, and the effect of widowhood is conspicuous in reducing the proportions of household heads, decidedly more so in the case of males than females. There were in fact actually fewer elderly non-married men than women recorded as heads, in spite of the fact that virtually all of the married men were in charge of the domestic groups they lived in. This seems to have arisen because more widows than widowers lived with their married children, even though widows did not quite so frequently maintain a household along with their un-married offspring as widowers did.[9]

Old men, on the other hand, showed a greater tendency to live as lodgers and in institutions if they lacked spouses. Here we must recognize that some of the individuals were certainly bachelors. Indeed one 80-year-old inhabitant of the hospital at Lichfield in 1695 was called 'maidenly Harry' in the listing document.

The interest of the array of figures in tables 5.10 and 5.11 lies in the contrast which is brought to light between the domestic situation of the elderly in pre-industrial society and their domestic situation in the England and Wales of our own day. We have found it difficult to establish comparison in just the terms which would be most revealing, and

[9] The difference between the percentages of the elderly heading households given here and in the version of this table printed in the *Handbook of aging* arises from the fact that those living alone were reckoned there not to be heads.

TABLE 5.10. *Household position of persons aged 60 and above in six English places before 1800 (data from Ealing, 1599; Chilvers Coton, 1684; Stoke-on-Trent, 1701; Corfe Castle, 1790; Ardleigh, 1796 — see Table 5.4)*

	Males		Females		Both	
	No.	%	No.	%	No.	%
Married persons						
Having in their households spouses and						
their unmarried children	87	51	57	43	144	48
their married children	8	5	6	5	14	5
their grandchildren	12	7	10	7	22	7
their relatives	12	7	8	6	20	7
attached lodgers						
servants	7	4	9	7	16	5
no person other than spouse	44	26	39	29	83	27
Living in the households of						
their unmarried children	0	0	1		1	
their married children	0	0	1		1	
their relatives including grandchildren				3		1
others in unclear relationship	1	1	0		1	
Living as lodgers						
Living in institutions	0	0	1		1	
Sub-total	171	101%	132	100%	303	100%
Non-married persons						
Having in their households						
their unmarried children	34	32	49	26	83	28
their married children	5	5	9	5	14	5
their grandchildren	2	2	3	2	5	2
their relatives or other persons	8	7	23	12	31	11
attached lodgers						
servants only	7	6	5	3	12	4
Living in the households of						
their unmarried children	0	0	0	0	0	0
their married children	2	2	21	11	23	8
their relatives including grandchildren	2	2	5	3	7	2
others in unclear relationship	26	24	25	14	51	17
Living as lodgers						
Living in institutions	16	15	16	9	32	11
Living as solitaries	5	5	29	16	34	12
Sub-total	107	100%	185	101%	292	100%

Note: For sources, see text. Married children include their own spouses and children if present; where grandchildren are specified alone, their parents (the children of the old people) are absent. 'Non-married' means widowed for the most part, but includes some whose spouses were temporarily absent and all never-married persons. Servants and lodgers are relevant only when named, and may be present elsewhere without affecting classification.

TABLE 5.11. *Proportions (%) of persons aged 60 and above in six English places before 1800 heading households or living otherwise (data of table 5.10)*

	Married		Non-married		All males	All females	Both sexes
	Males	Females	Males	Females			
Heads or spouses of heads	100	98	57	64	83	78	80
In households headed by their children	0	2	2	11	1	9	6
other persons	0	0 ⎫					
Lodging	0	0 ⎭	24	16	10	8	9
In institutions	0	0	18	9	6	5	5
Total	100	100	101	100	100	100	100
Proportion living alone					4	11	8
Of which with servants					7/278	5/317	2
entirely solitary					5/278	29/317	6

Note: See text for sources.

the best we can do for the time being is to be found in table 5.12. Here the figures are for the aged rather than the elderly, that is in our usage, those of 65 and above, and only five settlements can be included from traditional England. The resemblances and differences are so interesting that it is to be sincerely hoped that these places are in fact reasonably representative. We shall rather rashly refer to the aged persons in this little group of places as traditional English society, and the carefully selected sample (from Shanas et al. 1968; see tables VI. 16, VI. 17) studied in the 1960s as England today.

Whilst two-thirds of married couples over the age of 65 live together on their own in Britain today, in traditional England this was not the case. Half of the married women were in that position, but rather fewer of the married men. More aged married men in fact lived with spouse and unmarried children than lived with their wives alone in the old social order. In England today only a quarter of aged married persons of either sex have their 'families' of children still at home.

Here we reach the same important point again, that in the traditional world full family life, defined in this way, lasted proportionately longer for most persons than it does in the present world, for those who got married — a very high but uncertain percentage — and for those who became widowed as well. With these tables in front of us, we may dwell a little on the probable reasons for these important circumstances, although at the present time we cannot be very precise in our discussion or entirely confident in the conclusions.

Under the demographic conditions and with the familial rules which prevailed in pre-industrial England numbers of children were quite large, if variable: completed family sizes varying, at different times and places, from four or five to six, seven or eight. Offspring were born relatively late in the childbearing stage both of the husband and of the wife, in contrast (as we saw in chapter 1) with parts of the world where the European marriage pattern did not prevail. Although they left home with remorseless promptness, if not necessarily in age-order, these children went on arriving until well into the 30s or even the 40s of the life span of their mothers. Therefore some of them would still be in the parental household when the parents entered into old age.

Many of the families would be broken by death, but some of the children would remain with their widowed parents. As we observed in considering orphans in chapter 4, remarriage was frequent, and this may have been so particularly for fathers widowed during the mother's childbearing stage, though the facts are still uncertain. As old age proceeded, solitary couples and solitary widowed people grew more common, and living as lodgers or even in institutions began to be the fate of some of the senescent. But two further circumstances helped to ensure that these

TABLE 5.12.   *Household position by sex and marital status of aged persons (65 and above) in England in five places before 1800 compared with Britain in the 1960s*

	Chilvers Coton 1684		Lichfield 1695		Stoke-on-Trent 1701		Corfe Castle 1790	
	Males	Females	Males	Females	Males	Females	Males	Females
Married persons								
Living with								
spouse and unmarried children	3	2	8	6	12	2	7	2
spouse and married children	1	0	3	0	1	1	0	1
spouse only	5	2	8	5	4	3	11	9
others	0	0	1	2	0	1	2	0
Widowed, etc. persons								
Living with								
unmarried children	1	0	3	14	5	8	4	1
married children	0	2	1	10	3	13	2	7
others	1	1	9	16	5	8	7	11
Living alone	0	1	1	10	4	8	3	4

Note: For sources see text.

conditions were confined to a minority. First there was the tendency for a proportion of the surviving grandparents, especially widowed grandmothers, to be taken into the families of their married offspring. Second was the fact that the expectation of life of the old in that society was lower than it is today, certainly not as much lower proportionately as expectation of life at birth, but enough to curtail the final years when familial living might have been more difficult.

In the above rather dogmatic general account of the situation of the old in pre-industrial England nothing has been said of those who never married, but these make no appearance in our tables because we cannot identify them adequately. There are contrasts between the situation now and the situation then which are evident and clearly marked. According to table 5.12 we may have up to double the number of widowed persons living alone in our day than our ancestors did in pre-industrial times. But some parts of the pattern described have to be extracted from our tabular information by comparison and inference.

Table 5.10 shows, for example, that 30% of married males and 36% of married females over 60 were living with spouses only (4% and 7% respectively with servants as well). Table 5.12 reveals that by age 65, 41% of married men and 49% of married women were living with spouses alone. We can therefore infer that during the five years which elapsed between their parents' passing from 60 years to 65 years old the numbers of last remaining children went down quite sharply, and that this left their fathers and mothers on their own. Nevertheless at 65, as table 5.12

| Ardleigh 1796 | | Total | | Percentages | | Britain, 1960s (%) | |
Males	Females	Males	Females	Males	Females	Males	Females
5	4	35	16	46	37	24	24
0	0	5	2	7	5	5	1
3	2	31	21	41	49	67	68
2	1	5	4	7	9	4	7
0	1	13	24	23	20	18	20
2	2	8	34	14	28	23	17
5	5	27	41	48	34	22	18
0	0	8	23	14	19	37	45

makes plain, half as many again are living alone in the Britain that we know today.

The contrast between the contemporary world and the traditional world is well marked in these respects in table 5.12, but there are interesting resemblances as well as differences. Married persons over 65 were only very little more likely, it would seem from this evidence, to be living with their married, as distinct from the unmarried, children, than is the case today. With such wavering statistics, in fact it may well be that there was no difference at all, especially for the males. So much, once again, for the outmoded stereotype of two or more married couples usually being present in the same domestic group in the traditional society of the past.

In traditional England aged married persons seem to have resembled their successors in another important respect. They were members of households other than their children's just about as often as they are today. The heading 'others' in table 5.12 is inclusive; it covers lodging and being in institutions as well as being present as members of family households other than those of your children.

A few — we cannot, unfortunately, say how many — of these others with whom the old were living were kin folk, and represent the whole sum of the *residential* responsibility which related persons, apart from members of the immediate family, undertook for the care of old people. In the case of the 'widowed' (which, it will be remembered, includes the never-married and those deserted by their spouses), the proportions living with these others are quite high, much higher than today. A comparison with table 5.10, which in a sense breaks down this category for the over-60s, seems to imply that this represented lodging to a much greater extent than living with kin (though, which is exasperating to the researcher, we have already seen that the two situations, lodging and living with kin, may not have been always distinguished in that society).

The deserted, and those who had never married, were perhaps the most likely to be living as lodgers, a form of residence which seems to have become more common for people of this sort as they grew older. To find that up to a half of all spouseless old men — that is, 'widowed, etc.' males in table 5.12 — were in this (presumably) entirely *unfamilial* situation, and a third of the women too, is somewhat surprising, even after what has been claimed here about the lack of any responsibility upon the household in that social order to give shelter to distant relatives in need.

It could be said, on the other hand, that one was much less likely to be solitary as an aged widow or widower in earlier times. This seems to have been the case because of the lodging arrangements we have just described rather than because of any greater propensity for widowed people to live with their own children, married or unmarried. The comparison between sharing a household with married children in the traditional world and in our own is rather complicated. Elderly widows now are in this position considerably less often than they were then, but such widowers today are actually much more frequently found with their married children than they were in the pre-industrial settlements in question. The comparison with table 5.10 shows that this practice also seems to have grown as age advanced.

Little, then, seems to be left in favour of any prejudice against the contemporary British family for expelling the really old, or failing to take them in, at least when the comparison is made with the English familial past. Even the advantage, in general, reckoned for widows and widowers in traditional England in table 5.9 and for these over 60 in table 5.10, the advantage of being left to live with unmarried children, seems, from table 5.12, to have been eroded by age 65. Not many more of the spouseless had such offspring still resident than do in our own contemporary world.

When we come to make realistic allowances for the difference between the pre-industrial situation and our own in respect of the numbers of children surviving to the old age of their parents, the numbers of still-living relatives and so on, we will be able to make a more convincing comparison between the two epochs in respect of the aged, even with the present unsatisfactory data. It seems unlikely to me that the tentative conclusions we have drawn from our tables will be overset, even if they have to be revised.

Family cycle and the aged in traditional England

We have described the old in pre-industrial England as having in general been left as they were, and where they were, watching their children grow up and leave home, very seldom to return, and not receiving into their households their own elderly relatives for company or going to live with those relatives for the same reason. The crude, cross-sectional data on which our tables are based cannot tell us about the previous experience of the individuals described. We do not know how many of the few elderly parents found living with their married children had allowed, or encouraged, those children to bring their spouses into the house, or how many had joined those children in their households, abandoning their own family homes. In fact it is unlikely that we shall be able to take the study of the family cycle much further in traditional England unless, or until, we can find more listings with ages specified, especially repetitive listings.

But something can be done when repetitive listings are available even if ages are lacking, provided that the descriptions are accurate and complete. This brings us back once again to the set of materials which we dwelt upon in chapter 2, the listings laboriously composed in April 1676 and May 1688 by the clergyman in the rectory of Clayworth in Nottinghamshire. When taken with his other recordings and with the further documents which survive for the parish over these years, these lists seem to confirm the statements we have made about parents in relation to children growing mature and leaving home. No parental couple, no widowed person even, seems during the period open to view to have been rejoined by a son or a daughter, married or unmarried, coming home to help as health and strength failed. Quite a number of these aging heads of households in Clayworth were being left by their children during the period of time open to observation, and one or two were actually reduced to living on parish relief, or even in the 'common-houses' whilst their children set up home for themselves in the village (see p. 59 above and esp. n. 19). The handful of instances in which married children did live with their parents seem to have come about because a son brought his wife, or a daughter brought her husband, into the house for a year or two or a month or two after marriage. The rule of continued independent residence by the old seems by and large to have been maintained. Even those who were reduced to entering the 'common-houses' may have retained some semblance of living on their own.

But there are significant signs of exception to this rule, and the evidence also hints at the existence of a further practice which likewise implied change of residence for some persons, and which could have been connected with the fear of loneliness in age. The exception applies to the widowed amongst the old, and especially to the women. It seems clear that they were sometimes brought into the households of their married children, of both sexes, and clear too that this practice was connected with the rearing of the grandchildren. (Grandchildren, it may be noticed, are quite often found in the English evidence living with their grandparents rather than with their own fathers and mothers, though some of these children may have been illegitimate). These are the circumstances which seem to account for the figures of widowed parents living with married children set out in tables 5.9—5.12.

The expedient against loneliness was remarriage, which was such a conspicuous feature of the community of Clayworth in 1688 as described in our second chapter. In the Danish census of 1787, 25% of the married men and 22% of the married women had been wedded more than once as early as the age interval 46—50. It seems that if you were in danger of solitary old age, you married again, if you could.[10] This happened in England in spite of the possibility that there may have been some feeling against remarriage. In other countries and cultures it happened even more.

Aging in the English past and aging in the past of other countries

It has been insisted that the notion of a situation of the elderly common both to contemporary pre-industrial societies and to the previous condition of countries like our own is entirely misleading. So also is any assumption that the position of old people was the same in the various societies which represent our own past, the past, that is, of Western Europeans and of the English-speaking peoples and of late-twentieth-century North Americans. Whereas those of English descent can look back on what seems to have been a homogeneous past in respect of aging, other Europeans can do so to a lesser extent and North Americans least of all. Before we conclude this essay in the preliminary analysis of the history of aging we may glance at a little of the evidence just beginning to appear from one or two other past societies, so as to get some

[10] This hypothesis, for it can at present be no more, is one of the issues about remarriage which are being investigated by Janet Griffiths, using Cambridge Group materials, especially the sets of family reconstitution forms for English parishes (for these see p. 244 below). A question requiring an answer is whether it will turn out that men would be willing to marry women past the menopause under circumstances which point to providing against loneliness in later years. The figures for Denmark in 1787 are from Johansen 1976, but he gives no information on the extent to which remarriage was undertaken with a view to companionship in old age. Remarriage in that country apparently took place within a week or two of the death of the spouse, far sooner than in England, but it is not clear that women past the menopause would be involved.

idea of how variable they have been in their treatment of the widowed and the old.

Beginning with France in the seventeenth century, there is, for example, the village of Montplaisant in 1644, with some 350 inhabitants, situated in the Dordogne (South-central). There were only 12 widowed persons there, and 11 of these were heading their own households: the twelfth was a solitary widow. All 4 of the widowers and 4 of the 8 widows were in fact the first named in households which contained their married sons, households which seem to have been complex — some, indeed, very complex. This is a sharp contrast to the English pattern we have examined, though when we reach 1836 we find in Montplaisant fewer multiple households than in 1644. In that later year, however, a singular circumstance appeared. The widowers, 4 out of 5 of them, were living with their married sons, but the widows, 5 out of 9, with their married daughters: no widower is found with his daughter, no widow with her son. Perhaps a chance effect of small numbers, this, but indicating nevertheless how these practices might differ from small community to small community. In northern France at the same time the aged were in the 'English' situation, which (as far as we can yet tell) was by no means confined to England.[11]

Turning from France to Germany, we have two interesting lists of inhabitants giving ages and specifying the familial position of the old. The first, a large village called Abbeheusen in the south with some 1,200 people in 1675, had a pattern of household very like the English, but it seems to have located the old people very differently. Almost a third (23% of the men, 37% of the women, 29% together) of the married elderly had married children living with them, and the non-married elderly lived to an even greater extent in this way (38% of the women, 12% of the men, in all 32%). In spite of this fact the non-married were more often solitary than in England (25% of males, 9% of females, in all 13%). In the second village, from the Baltic area in 1795 (Grossenmeer with 880 people), where more households were complex in their structure, we find no solitary widowed person at all, and a conspicuous difference between the sexes: 10 widowers to 44 widows. Two-thirds of these persons were living with their married children, equally divided between married sons and married daughters, but only 2 of them as heads. These German village arrangements, then, differ markedly from each other and from the English, and differ from Montplaisant, too.

Remarriage must have been even more frequent in Grossenmeer

---

[11] Flandrin (1976:73) notes here that at Breuil-en-Vexin, in another part of northern France, but nearer Paris, no widowed person was solitary, although there were only 7.3% of complex households (p. 241).

amongst the men, and in Montplaisant amongst both sexes, than it was in Clayworth. At Abbeheusen it was less conspicuous. Remarriage seems to have been at its most intense to our knowledge in Lisswege, a Belgian village near Bruges in the early eighteenth century, where a widowed person seems to have been a rarity. In eighteenth-century Denmark the situation was not dissimilar, as we have seen, and here Johansen has demonstrated that about half of a select sample of mid-eighteenth-cen tury villagers in their 60s and 70s whom he has calculated to have had married children actually lived with them (Johansen 1976, covering both sexes, and the widowed as well as the married). These look like levels higher than those which obtained for England, but in his interest-ing analysis of the situation of the aged in his country Johansen comes out quite clearly in favour of the principle we have laid down for England here, that old people tended to remain at the heads of their own households. Going outside the boundaries of Western Europe, we can find villages with even fewer widowed persons, and with even lower levels of residence with unmarried children. At Vändra in Estonia in 1683 (population 967) the only widower recorded was at the head of a household of a married son, and all the 8 widows were living as mem-bers, not as heads, in the households of married sons as well. Households, if household is quite the word, were huge in that settlement and often very complicated. The situation was evidently similar in villages in Latvia in the eighteenth century.

For the settlement of Kölked, in transdanubian Hungary, which ap-peared in our first chapter, we have ages specified for 1816. There were 13 males and 17 females over 60 amongst the population of 636, slightly less than 5%, of whom 6 of the men and 13 of the women were widowed. All the elderly males, married and widowed, were at the head of the households of married sons, and so was 1 of the widows; 5 of the other widows were living in the families of married sons, and the rest of the elderly women were variously disposed. Only 5 of the women were in the 'English' position, that is, in charge of a household containing their unmarried children. Once more, households were often complex in Kölked, but in settlements not far away they were as simple as they have been found to have been almost everywhere in England, with the aged in much the same position as we have described for the English.

The one cultural area outside Europe from which information on the old is beginning to be available for the past is Japan. Here we find exam-ples of a situation which occurs very seldom in our own European data, the situation in which old people, and especially widows, have yielded the headship of the household to their *unmarried* children. Widowhood was commoner in Japan than might have been expected, and remarriage seems to have stopped altogether at the later ages: most old people evidently lived with their married sons. Some of these sons were adopted rather than offspring in the European sense: adoption was a rarity in the West, about which we have very little information.

We do not yet know enough to say whether local variation was common in Japan. Indeed, it must be clear that the sum of our present knowledge goes only to the stage of providing a little of a comparative framework in which to place the English and the Western European pattern of aging. Our own ancestors lived in their own distinctive way in this respect, but it will be a long time before we can say quite how much they differed from the rest of the world. We cannot yet pass any judgement at all on the *common situation* of the aged in non-industrial society generally, amongst humanity as a whole, as has often been done by those who have previously pronounced on aging in relation to social development.

It has been conventional in discussions of aging and the household in the European past, as far as these things have been systematically discussed at all, to insist on two features so far only mentioned in passing, the stem family form of the household and the tradition of retirement. It has recently been shown, for example, that in certain eighteenth-century areas of Austria and Germany, where a stem family arrangement prevailed amongst a sizeable minority of households, the old were allotted a familial situation which gave to retirement an institutional form (see Berkner 1972, 1974). These arrangements meant demotion from the headship and even in a sense expulsion from the family group. This might be said to be a less 'familial' way of treating the aged, or even a more inhumane one, than the practices described for traditional England. But such a pattern, which has also been found in twentieth-century Ireland, did succeed in allotting a position in space to the retired farmer or labourer, a space given the name 'the west room' on Irish farms.

This is not the opportunity to pursue the controversy about the extent to which social scientists have exaggerated the prevalence and importance of these arrangements. The 'west room' of the Irish is now treated with some scepticism by the anthropologists, for example, although research in progress seems to imply that Irish households were rather complex late in the life cycle of their heads, at least in comparison with English households in the 1820s (Carney 1976). Nor have we the space to survey the evidence now being assembled about the position and role of the aged during the long generations which elapsed between the beginning of industrialization and the end of the demographic transition in English historical development. The aged person, it has been commonly assumed, acquired a new role in the early factory era, a role as child-minder.

TABLE 5.13.   *Household position of elderly persons (aged 60 and above),*
Puddletown, Dorset, 1851, 1861 and 1871

	1851 (Pop. 1,297) %	1861 (Pop. 1,229) %	1871 (Pop. 1,351) %
% of married persons (both sexes) living with children at home	69	37	31
Living with spouses only	11	29	44
Living with married children	3	0	0
% of non-married persons (both sexes) living with children at home	38	35	14
Living with married children	9	12	31
Solitary	24	8	20
Lodging	3	28	8

It is becoming known, however (Anderson 1971), that it was not always the parents and parents-in-law of the mill-girl wives who kept the home going during the long shifts at the loom, but friends and neighbours as well, not all of them old. So conspicuously different, moreover, were the factories from what went before that the numerical importance of these arrangements has also been very easy to exaggerate.

The one Victorian English village examined in any detail on the principles laid down here shows an interesting transition in some of the variables from 'pre-industrial' to the 'industrial' situation, as is indicated by the set of partial statistics in table 5.13. There is obviously some instability here, especially as to solitary living and lodging, but it seems clear that children were leaving home earlier as the decades went by in this village and that the old were increasingly going to live with their married children.

One further question only can be broached. How far was it an advantage to the widowed and the old in the traditional world to be kept in the familial situation? Did they in fact have the same appreciation of independence as their successors in our day?

We have one stray result to present in this connection from our English evidence. Amongst the privileged, widowed persons were less, not more, likely to be living with their married children than amongst those below them in the social scale.[12] Those who could afford to do just

[12] This outcome was arrived at by Kurt Back, working at the Cambridge Group in 1974.

what they wanted about their aged parents did not have them at home. They seem to have set them up with their own servants in their own households. Or was it rather that the old gentlemen and old ladies themselves amongst the rich and powerful saw to it that they did not have to live with their married sons and daughters, but maintained their own establishments with their own staffs? This detail is the more significant in that the English gentry, like all privileged classes, were more and not less likely to have their relatives of other kinds living with them in extended or in multiple households. The numbers of the elderly living by themselves except for servants is not negligible in the figures of tables 5.10 and 5.11, and the practice was not entirely confined to the gentry. We can see more modest people providing servants for their aging parents in the evidence from those English villages which can be studied over time.

The conclusion might be that then, as now, a place of your own, with help in the house, with access to your children, within reach of support, might have been what the elderly and the aged most wanted for themselves in the pre-industrial world. This was difficult to secure in traditional England for any but fairly substantial people. It must have been almost impossible in many other cultural areas of the world.

6. Age at sexual maturity in Europe since the Middle Ages

Age at sexual maturation is of obvious interest to historians of the family. It is the point at which offspring begin to be as big in body and as strong as those who gave them birth, a transformation of the situation which had hitherto controlled to such a large extent the relationship between the parent and the child. It determines, therefore, the point at which children reach the crisis of adolescence and begin the process of asserting their independence from their parents and from the family of origin generally. This circumstance was of far greater significance in earlier societies, where physical size and strength counted for much more.

But puberty, as everyone knows, has further emotional and physiological consequences. It marks a stage at which the young adult becomes capable of full sexual intercourse, and, for the women, of experiencing menstruation. Both of these stages of development are often of crucial psychological significance. Moreover, it introduces the possibility of procreation, which immediately implies stringent social control. No society at any period, whatever its resources, can allow individuals to reproduce at will. But puberty is a precondition of marriage itself, as well as of illegitimacy and the other irregularities in procreation which were discussed in some detail in chapter 3. In most societies known to me — certainly in all societies belonging to the Christian tradition, and perhaps in almost every other society, too — sexual maturation is an essential preliminary to marriage for both sexes.

Here is a subject, therefore, which must affect the historian of social structure generally even more than most of those which concern the family group.[1] If children mature late, then presumably parental supremacy endures longer. This has implications which are easy to see for societies organized on patriarchal lines. Furthermore, there are indications that age at sexual maturation may differ between social classes, and this implies a distinction in the fundamental process of personality development between bourgeoisie and workers, or, in the past, between

[1] This essay first appeared in the *Journal of Interdisciplinary History* 2, 1 (1971) and was reprinted in a slightly extended form in T. K. Rabb and R. I. Rotberg (eds.), *The family in history* (1973). Further extensions and modifications have been made here, and some medieval material taken into account.

lords and ladies, gentlemen and gentlewomen, as compared to common folk.[2]

Yet almost nothing numerical is known about age at sexual maturity for any society before the twentieth century, and what fragments of information we have mostly concern only one of the conspicuous developments which occur at this time to one of the sexes. This is menarche, the onset of menstruation or of the 'flowers', as our ancestors more elegantly phrased it. Some statistical information is available on the heights and weights of both sexes in nineteenth-century Europe, and it may be that documents will be found which will push our knowledge of these particulars further back. But, for the moment, it looks as if the history of age at menarche — the mean age at which girls became capable of conception — will have to stand for the whole phenomenon of sexual maturation in men and women.

We have to be satisfied, however, with the small things which we can do in historical sociology, and the little insight we have into the secular trend of age at menarche is certainly intriguing. All of the firm, recent, twentieth-century evidence shows forth a tendency towards progressive decline in the age at which women became mature. J. M. Tanner, who is the established authority on this subject, and one of the few contemporary medical writers who appear to be collecting information on the long-term as well as the short-term trend, estimates that 'menarche in Europe has been getting earlier during the last hundred years by between three and four months per decade'.[3] To its level in Great Britain in the 1960s of about 13.25 years, it has fallen from about 14.5 in the 1920s and 15.5 in the 1890s.

Until recently it seemed fairly well established that this regular decline had gone on at least since the 1830s. Age at menarche had looked like being an interesting indicator of the social changes associated with the whole long process of industrialization, though the figures came from a rather restricted area, especially Scandinavia. A measurement of 17.5 was arrived at for the 1830s, one of a little over 17 for Norway in the 1840s, a further figure of 16.5 for the 1860s, tracing, when the 1890s and the twentieth-century calculations were added,[4] a regular line of descent

[2] See Laslett 1965 (1971 ed.: 89). Inter-class differences in mean age at maturation now appear to be somewhat less than is implied there. But differences in the spread of ages between various social groups in the past seem likely to be quite conspicuous; they are referred to briefly in the addendum to this chapter.

[3] Tanner 1966, with a formidable list of references. The major earlier source of information is G. Backman, 'Die beschleunigte Entwicklung der Jugend. Verfrühte Menarche, verspätete Menopause, verlängerte Lebensdauer', *Acta Anatomica* 4 (1948): 421–80.

[4] Tanner 1966: 532. Cf. Tanner, *Growth at adolescence*, 2nd ed. (Oxford, 1962), 152.

for 145 years. Starting in 1900, records for the United States show a consistently lower age at menarche, which fell to 12.5—13.0 in 1940—5 (white girls). But the twentieth-century slope is roughly parallel between America and Europe, and by the 1970s, the fall had apparently ceased, certainly in the United States.

In recent months, however, this impression of regular, secular decline since industrialization appeared, has been broken (June 1976). Norwegian scholars have revised an important series of figures for their country, which were in any case rather different from those for England at the time, in the 1830s to 1850s. At the moment it is supposed that menarche did not begin its secular fall until the later decades of the nineteenth century.[5] Any earlier information, especially for the eighteenth century or before, which would give us a more distant fix, even for a remote European area, is of signal interest and importance. We know enough to suspect that sexual maturity was not necessarily later in traditional times than it was before recent developments began. But we are deeply ignorant of how much it has varied over time and in relation to other changes.

In this chapter the very imprecise but nevertheless illuminating evidence of an individual document has been used, for the purpose of illustrating what may be done, rather than to present substantive conclusions. It comes from a list of the Christian Orthodox inhabitants of Belgrade, the capital of what was once Serbia, now a part of Yugoslavia, for the year 1733—4. We shall see that estimates of the maximal age at sexual maturity for women recoverable from that document, and other numerical or quasi-numerical evidence going back into the Middle Ages, do not differ very much from those now established for the later nineteenth century.

Although the outcome of actual observation is difficult to obtain and tricky to analyse, literary evidence is available and is beginning to be published. It has been used to suggest that menarche may have come at around 14 in medieval and early modern times, which is a little surprising after the much later ages, in the 16s and 17s, which have until recently been tentatively assumed for the early nineteenth century. All this could be taken to imply that the level actually rose slightly in historical times. Tanner himself quotes interestingly from Shakespeare and from an early seventeenth-century writer named Quarinonius or Guarinonius.

[5] G. H. Bruntland and Lars Walloe, 'Menarcheal age in the 19th century: a re-evaluation', to appear in *Human Biology* (1976). These authors have questioned whether Backman properly understood the Norwegian age expressions in the original sources, and therefore came up with ages for the early nineteenth century which are too high. This would modify the impression of a peak at about that time. On this and other evidence Tanner seems willing to suppose that the secular declining trend did not begin until the late nineteenth century.

But literary evidence of this kind should be handled with great care, even with some suspicion.[6]

Nevertheless, it is proper to start our enquiry by referring to the materials from medieval literature collected and discussed in an interesting note by J. B. Post.[7] They bear more weight as empirical evidence, being the writings of medieval gynaecologists. At their strongest, the statements quoted by Post imply that age at menarche was observed by these physicians to occur in the thirteenth or fourteenth year. Of course, the accuracy of these observations is somewhat impaired by the further claim, which Post quotes from Avicenna and from such splendidly entitled works as *Trotula major* and *Trotula minor*, that menstruation lasts 'until the fiftieth year if the woman is thin; until sixty or sixty-five if she is moist; until thirty-five if moderately fat'.

Though Post suggests that these absurdities about the cessation of menstruation, the menopause, may be due to the paucity of cases, as few women lived into the higher ages, they seem to me to be unfortunately typical of the literary sources, even when medical. Such pieces of evidence are ordinarily incapable of yielding anything which is, properly speaking, numerical and are therefore almost useless for comparative historical purposes, especially when differences of a year or two are in question. They face us with the same difficulties as we found when we considered literature in relation to aging in chapter 5, but are even more exasperating.[8]

The one way to obtain figures would appear to be by working backward from marriage recordings. Since a marriage within the universal Christian Church could only be celebrated if both parties were sexually mature, figures for the age at first marriage for women can be taken as figures for maximal age at menarche. Care must be taken, however, to distinguish between a future promise to marry (a *spousal*, now called an engagement) and marriage itself. A person could become engaged at any age, before puberty or after, and the undertaking was regarded as binding by the Church, like any other promise. This engagement became

[6] Compare Laslett 1976b and references where some attention is given to the notorious case of Juliet's marrying at 13 in *Romeo and Juliet* having been used as an indication of mean age at marriage for women in Elizabethan England; see n. 11 below.

[7] 'Ages at menarche and menopause: some medieval authorities', *Population Studies* 35 (1971): 83—7.

[8] Shorter (1975: 294 n. 53) publishes the results of his surveys of 'topographies médicales' made by French medical men between the mid eighteenth and mid nineteenth century, sources which are decidedly more exact, though still difficult to use for anything but rather gross comparison. His estimates of age at menarche in that country are 15.9 years for the later eighteenth century, 15.7 for the nineteenth century to 1850, and 15.1 thereafter. He also quotes 'clinical surveys' giving 15.7 for 1800—49 and 15.2 for 1850—99.

a valid marriage if sexual intercourse took place, quite apart from a church ceremony, and any *present* undertaking to wed, duly witnessed, bound the partners. A marriage could exist, therefore, which had not been celebrated in church and so, presumably, had never been registered. Nevertheless, both partners to such a union were, by definition, sexually mature at the time it began. But a spousal itself was not a marriage. Indeed, as is well known, inability to copulate in either partner was proper grounds for ending an engagement, or even of annulling a 'marriage'.[9]

If, therefore, the date of a woman's marriage is known it can be assumed that she was sexually mature at the time. But it remains uncertain as to how long she had been mature. Mean age at first marriage as an indication of maximal age at menarche is of little use if it falls above 20. It merely tells us that puberty in that society did not come at a very advanced age indeed. All of which implies that it is information on *teenage marriage* which is really crucial.[10]

But women rarely married before the age of 20 in North-western Europe, at least until recent times. This is what we must expect from the facts superficially surveyed in chapter 1. Whatever may have happened in Renaissance Italy, or in *Romeo and Juliet* (where the heroine married at 13), in English communities only a few years could usually go by when the mean age of brides was as low as the 21st year, and many marry younger than 20. It so happens that this was so for a time in the late sixteenth century in Stratford-on-Avon during which William Shakespeare was living in his native town and took up with Ann Hathaway, whom he married in 1582 when he was 18, though he decided to leave for London in 1586.[11] Family reconstitution has not so far yielded a mean age at marriage as low as that at Stratford for long enough to involve more than a score or so of women either in England or in France. Even in eighteenth-century Canada, where the marriage age came much

---

[9] On spousals, see Laslett 1965 (1971 ed.: 140–5), and on marriage outside the Church, see chapter 3 above.

[10] Strictly speaking, in order to cover illegitimate births (see below) and the case of slaves, who were denied marriage, the age at issue in sexual maturity is that of the initiation of a relationship likely to lead to conception. The question of menarche in American slave girls in relation to the interlude between its occurrence and age at first conception is briefly discussed in ch. 7 below.

[11] The mean age of brides whose birth dates can be confirmed (Ann Hathaway's unfortunately not amongst them) was 20.6 years for the whole decade 1580–9 ($n = 30$), and three girls married at 15, two at 16. It will be noticed that all the marriage ages in question were higher than Juliet's. I owe this information to Michael Martin. It may also be significant that marriage amongst native-born London girls was early about 1600, perhaps as early as at Stratford (information from Vivien Brodsky).

sooner than in the home countries, it was still too high to be of much use in indicating the point at which sexual maturity arrived.[12]

Only for certain counties in the colony of Maryland in the Middle Atlantic area of what was to become the United States of America has a clear example so far been observed of women in an English-speaking population marrying on average below 20 years. This was in the seventeenth and early eighteenth centuries and was true of native-born, not immigrant, women. A mean age at first marriage of 16.4 years has been calculated for 58 women born before 1680 in one county and 17.8 years in another: in a third the figure was 17.9 years for women born before 1700.[13] If what has been claimed about sexual maturity and Christian marriage is true, and if these colonial teenagers were respecting the rules, then we can be certain that a half of them had reached sexual maturity by 18, and probably at up to two years or more earlier.

This suggests that menarche could have come almost as soon in this population as it did in Northern Europe nearly two centuries later. But America is not Europe, and the conditions under which these Maryland brides were living may have been very different from those experienced by their forebears in the Old World. The possibility cannot be excluded, for example, that their plentiful diet brought on maturity in spite of their unfavourable demographic situation. We shall have to return to the issue of the food supply and its importance.

An intensive study of the baptismal registers might add to the impression gained from those of Stratford in Shakespeare's day and from many miscellaneous sources which bear upon the problem, that conception was certainly possible in the teens among the English or French peasantry and townsfolk of earlier times. Little more can be expected of the parochial registers in these countries. Nevertheless, there is an independent documentary source of an 'observational' kind in such census-type documents as have survived from before the nineteenth century. If such a list of inhabitants specified ages and familial relationships, then it is possible to see how many women were married before 20, and how many at the crucial ages were accompanied by children. This last observation enables us, by subtracting the ages of the eldest resident children from those of their mothers, to obtain something like a mean age of first

[12] Jacques Henripin, *La population canadienne au début du XVIIIe siècle* (Paris, 1954).

[13] See Menard 1975: n. 48 —number not given for the second two samples. Research is proceeding on these data, which are confined to Maryland, and larger samples with greater detail can be expected. Mortality was extremely heavy at the time, and a large majority of the brides were orphans, even at these ages (compare p. 169 above). Other documents show age at first conception (see below) of 18.7 years for 20 women and 'just on 17 years for slaves' (numbers not given), using the subtraction method described below and the conventional (not the singulate) mean.

conception for all mothers in the community. But some sort of maximal mean age of sexual maturation is always obtainable from mean age at marriage.

The earliest opportunity so far open for the examination from a list of inhabitants of the age by which women had got married in a Western European country comes as far back as the years 1427–8, in Florence and in Tuscany. It has been shown by Christiane Klapisch from the famous Catasto dating from those years that the mean age of marriage for women in that document was about 17.9 for girls. No less than 31% were married in the towns before the age of 17 (26% in the country), 71% before 18 (65%), 72% by 19 (68%) and 88% by 20 (90%). This information might be used to indicate an age at sexual maturity about the same as that of the girls in seventeenth-century Maryland, but Klapisch has evidence which makes it possible to go into the question in a little more detail. Not only was it the case that some young girls married well before the canonical age of twelve complete years, with the important proviso that they should not live with their husbands until that age arrived, but the bishop of Florence, Saint Anthony, is found declaring in writing that cohabitation could take place up to six months earlier 'provided the girl had reached puberty'.[14] This considerably strengthens the case for supposing that some young women must have been sexually mature at such early ages. But it is also entirely probable that these were the exceptional cases, and that they indicate that the average age must have been later. How much later will be considered in due course.

Subtraction from the mother's age of the age of the first accompanying child was not attempted for these fifteenth-century Tuscan women. If we turn to English evidence of a similar kind coming from the seventeenth century, this is the sort of thing which we find. Among the 780 inhabitants of the agricultural and mining village of Chilvers Coton (also in Shakespeare's county of Warwickshire) there were three married women whose ages are given as below 20. None of these had an accompanying child incontrovertibly her own, though one (aged 18) had two present with her who looked as if they belonged to her husband (aged 50) and had been born to a previous wife. Nevertheless, subtraction from the ages of other, older women shows that one wife living in the village had conceived at 14, two at 15, one at 16, two at 18 and four at 19.[15] Only

[14] Klapisch 1973: table, p. 115.

[15] It is to be expected that the numbers of conceptions below age 20 for the whole group of women should be much higher than those for women actually below that age at the time of the count, since the first figure represents those belonging to all the age cohorts present, and the second those belonging to only one of them. Nevertheless, in view of the probable loss from the sample of children already dead and those who had left home, which must have been considerable, the difference at Chilvers Coton looks

31 out of the 229 cases of women with children are described well enough to be acceptable, and although it may seem surprising that 10 of these women apparently conceived before the age of 20, it must be remembered that the recently married are the most likely to provide the precise information that makes subtraction possible.

These facts from Chilvers Coton illustrate sufficiently the difficulties of such data. Among the 31 whose particulars we can analyse in this way, the mean apparent age at first conception turns out to be well over 22, in spite of 10 cases falling below the age of 20. No estimate for a maximum age of menarche for all women of the village at this time could be based on this handful of observations. If it had been possible to check the census-type document with the parish register, we would at least have had some independently sanctioned dates of first birth, and some reliable marriage ages. But the registers of Chilvers Coton are defective for this period, and, even if we had both good parochial registration and a listing giving ages, the small numbers marrying under 20 in any English village would ensure that no decent maximal figure for age at menarche could be obtained. This is why it is so fortunate that a listing of inhabitants has appeared which clearly belongs to an area and an epoch where mean age at marriage for women was below the age of 20, and below that which obtained in Florence in 1427. Here the possibilities of working out a useful estimate of something like a maximal age at menarche are rather better.

A much more informative and accurate result would of course be obtainable for maximal age at menarche if there existed for the region where this revealing list of inhabitants originates a detailed and consistently maintained parochial register of baptisms, marriages and burials. Family reconstitution based on such a record over a hundred years, shall we say, could establish ages of marriage for women and hence measures of maximal menarcheal age for a chosen sub-period of fifty or even twenty-five years, depending on the size of the population at risk. This is a great deal more than a census-type document will yield, especially one as roughly composed as the one we have to analyse. Reconstitution would also provide ages of first conception, including pre-marital and perhaps extra-marital conceptions. These might point to a significantly

rather large, as it does in Belgrade and in all of the examples we have studied, including official nineteenth-century census documents. The explanation may lie partly in the fact that the very youngest are the least well recorded in all counts of this kind, and in the wish to conceal illegitimate births or births conceived before marriage, a motive which is less important when reporting children's ages later on. More important is the fact that no child born in the year of the count will appear, but all subsequent births which occurred in that year will be referred later on to the year in which the count was made.

lower age at menarche than the maximum indicated by the mean age at first marriage.[16]

The census-type document from Belgrade which the Cambridge Group for the History of Population and Social Structure has been given the opportunity to work upon is, however, of great interest for many purposes, in addition to the present one. With the expected shortcomings and imperfections, it provides the names, most of the ages and sexes, and indications of relationships within the household, of 1,357 Serbian Orthodox Christians living in Belgrade at a date given as 1733–4 by the scholar who had the documents printed. The naming system makes it possible to infer the sexes of nearly all persons and to check the relationship of children to their biological fathers, though not to their mothers.[17] As we have seen in chapter 1, it portrays a familial system sharply distinct from that of the European West, not simply as that system now is, but as it was well before industrial times.

An examination of the distribution of this population by age, sex and marital status shows that its marriage habits were very different from those we have found in England and France at the same period, and in particular in Chilvers Coton in 1684. Whereas in Belgrade nearly 70% of all women in the age group 15–19 were married or widowed, the proportion at Chilvers Coton was under 10%. Stated a little differently, 87% of all women above the age of 15 were married or widowed in Belgrade and 54% in Chilvers Coton. In a group of six pre-industrial English parishes, the proportion married above the age of 15 was only 60%, and a mere 6 out of the 402 women in these villages aged between 15 and 19 were married at all. Proportions for Belgrade are set out in full in table 1.4 and discussed on pp. 27 and 28 above. We may contrast them with the proportion married we have quoted for girls in Tuscany in the fifteenth century and with the figures of table 6.1 below.

This table is the first of the three which together present the numerical evidence from the Belgrade list as it bears on the question of the age of sexual maturation. As might be expected in an unsettled population living in a region characterized by a state of military confusion and low material standards, with presumably a modest level of education throughout the community, the figures are approximate in detail and incomplete overall. Sex information is missing for 13.5% of the people, and

[16] It now seems possible that family reconstitution among a historical population where mean age at marriage was below 20 can be undertaken in Estonia, if not in Serbia. See Palli 1971.

[17] See Laslett 1972c, where a discussion of the provenance and character of the document will be found, as well as a series of analytic tables such as those printed for Clayworth in ch. 1, section IV.

age information for 11.6%. Some of these persons appear, from their positions in their families and the ages of their close kin, to have been eligible for consideration if proper particulars had been present. The peculiarities of the data are plain enough from the figures below, at least in respect of the clustering at various ages.

In table 6.1 the numbers and ages of all women up to the age of 21 are given with information as to their marital status and the presence of children. In table 6.2 mothers only are listed by age from 22 upwards. In table 6.3 the ages of mothers at the birth of their first child are given. These were obtained by subtracting the number of years given for the eldest resident son or daughter from that of his or her own mother.[18]

The rough and arbitrary character of this series of numbers will convince the reader that only general inferences of a fair probability seem permissible. The figures of table 6.3 — the ages at the birth of the first

TABLE 6.1. *Women aged 10—21, by age, marital status and presence of offspring*

	Age	No.	Married		With children	
			No.	%	No.	%
	10	25	0	0	0	0
	11	9	0	0	0	0
	12	19	1	5	0	0
	13	16	0	0	0	0
	14	8	0	0	0	0
Total	10—14	77	1	1%	0	0
	15	9	3	33	0	0
	16	9	5	55	0	0
	17	10	8	80	1	10
	18	15	11	73	2	13
	19	10	10	100	5	50
Total	15—19	53	37	70%	8	15%
Total	10—19	130	38	29%	8	6%
	20	31	30[a]	97	12	39
	21	10	9	90	6	60
Total	10—21	171	77[a]	45%	26	15%
Total	15—21	94	76[a]	81%	26	28%

[a]Includes one widow.

[18] It is not always clear whether a child mentioned after a woman's name is, in fact, her offspring, though in nearly all cases the relationship is made unambiguous by the presence of the words *his* or *her*, or by the naming system which, in Serbian usage, links all offspring to their fathers. The uncertainty is greatest in the case of widows, especially those of more advanced years.

TABLE 6.2. *Mothers aged 22 and over, by age*

Age	No.	Age	No.
22	6	40	14
23	4	43	1
24	1	45	2
25	20	46	1
26	11	47	1
27	2	50	15
28	16	55	1
30	38	58	1
31	1	60	8
32	3	63	1
33	1	65	1
34	4	70	2
35	8	78	1
36	6	80	1
37	2	Total	22–80 = 177
38	3		0–80 = 203[a]
39	1	Of whom widows =	31

[a]Includes total from table 6.1.

TABLE 6.3. *Mothers by age at birth of eldest resident child (from subtraction)*

Age	No.	Age	No.
		22	17
		23	9
		24	9
		25	5
		26	5
		27	9
6	1	28	7
8	3	29	3
10	1	30	5
11	1	31	1
12	2	32	3
13	5	33	1
14	10	35	1
15	13	36	1
16	12	37	1
17	16	38	2
18	16	40	4
19	13	42	2
20	20	44	1
21	3	50	1
Total 6–21	116	6–50	203

child — naturally interest us the most, but some are impossible. Girls of 6 and 8 cannot have had babies.

But before we tackle these and other oddities, let us make what we can of the figures in the first table concerning the number of women married at various ages. They demonstrate that, in so far as women knew their ages and had them accurately recorded by the Christian Orthodox priest who seems to have drawn up the census, some brides were obviously adolescent. A third of all girls of the age of 15, and over half of those of 16, already had husbands.

The singulate mean age at marriage is a measure devised to extract from data of this kind a statistic which can be used for our purposes. If this is calculated on the assumption that all the women whose marital status is left uncertain on the list were in fact single, the result is an age at marriage for women of as low as 14.88 years. On the assumption that all these women were or had been married, the figure is 15.97 years.[19] We may assume, then, that on average these Belgrade girls took husbands between their 15th and 16th birthdays, perhaps a little later but not much. Now these young wives must have been sexually mature if the Christian rules on the point were being observed. Nothing can be said, of course, about the maturation of the six girls of age 15, the four aged 16 and the two aged 17 who were not married, and it is possible that their late development was the reason why some of them were still celibate. Nevertheless, it would seem out of the question to suppose that their backwardness was the sole reason for their being spinsters.

For this would imply that sexual maturity was not simply an essential qualification for marriage, but was universally and immediately followed by marriage. We might reflect for a moment on what this would mean for the young people of fifteenth-century Florence or eighteenth-century Serbia. Every woman would be offered on the marriage market as soon as she became physiologically capable of mating, and taken up with the shortest possible delay. In the case of Belgrade, where husbands

---

[19] The singulate mean age (see John Hajnal, 'Age at marriage and proportions marrying', *Population Studies* 6 (1953): 111—32) is calculated for data which, like that for Belgrade, yield only proportions ever married at particular ages. It has the advantage of making use of such proportions in five-year age-groups, which is considerable protection against the effects of bunching (at age 20 for example, conspicuous here); of making use of the whole range of ages up to the 40s; and above all of avoiding almost all of the effects of bias which conventional averages introduce in such calculations. In an illuminating paper James Trussell of the Office of Population Research at Princeton (mimeograph of 1976, 'The estimation of the mean age of female slaves at the time of first birth') discusses the attributes of this measure, and extends the technique to cover age at first birth. See n. 23 below; I am indebted to Dr Trussell for the sight of his draft paper and for advice.

were on average nearly ten years older than their wives, this conjures up a picture of the men waiting until their late 20s or early 30s to get themselves partners, and then seeking out the youngest nubile girls they could find to marry. No market can be as efficient, even with 'buyers' and 'sellers' as eager as those just described.

However hot and romantic the love life of Renaissance Florence can have been, things surely cannot have gone as far as this. Eugene Hammel of the University of California at Berkeley, a student of present and past Serbian familial life, tells me that nothing in the Serbian social structure or familial custom indicates any tendency towards such extraordinary precipitation.[20] No doubt there was some overlap between the stretch of ages when these girls were becoming sexually mature and the stretch of ages when they were entering marriage. But these considerations can be taken as justifying the assumption that the non-marriers in Belgrade were not markedly later in maturing than those who did marry. In general, it would seem that wives in any age group can be taken as representative in these respects of all women in the age group, with some allowance made in the earliest year — say, up to 16 — but none later.

The considerable numbers of cases studied in our own time show that ages at menarche are normally distributed and that the range between the earliest and latest ages is relatively short. There does not seem to be much discussion of this range in the literature, nor more than a passing reference to the important possibility that it was greater in the case of the poor and undernourished than in that of the rich and well fed, the humble not only maturing later, therefore, but over a wider spread of ages. Tanner simply says that a standard deviation of a value of 1.1 years is characteristic of most series studied.[21] If this value of 1.1, or even a somewhat higher one, is applied to the figures in table 6.1, and the assumption of normal distribution is retained for them, then a further and more specific, though still inexact, numerical indication of the maximal menarcheal age can be obtained.

Since over 95% of all cases in a normal distribution will lie within four standard deviations of a value at the extreme, then it follows that practically all girls in Belgrade became fit to marry within four years after the first recorded age at marriage. Since 12 is the lowest age in the table,

---

[20] Nor do such an attitude and practice seem probable for the young colonists in Maryland in the seventeenth century, where the bridegrooms were presumably much younger than those of Belgrade. A situation like this is conceivable, however, among slaves, if their owners had a financial interest in slave-breeding and if it is supposed that the ordinary conventions of courtship, modesty, respect for extreme youth and so on were absent. See ch. 7 below.

[21] Tanner 1955 (1962 ed.: 154).

then 12—16 would be a first estimate of the range of ages at issue, and 16 itself is our upper estimate for mean age at marriage, a year of age when virtually every girl would have been fully nubile.

This is to place a great deal of weight on a single value, especially as no bride of 13 or 14 is present in the Belgrade table. It is therefore help-ful to know that there were cases in Florence which indicate marriage, if not conception, at this age. Moreover, the general shape of the distri-bution in table 6.1 certainly implies that the ages between 13 and 15 were the years when girls reached marriageability; the years between 17 and 19 look very unlikely.[22] This statement is true, even allowing for the possibility of the unmarried being slower developers and for the half-year which has to be added to the ages in tables 6.1 and 6.2 because they are declared ages, not ages in years and months actually attained.

When we turn finally to the numbers in table 6.3 we are at last in a position to work out single numerical estimates for our statistics, but it has to be said that the figures themselves look so haphazard that the sin-gulate mean and the range just given might be thought of as preferable as results. Beginning with the whole number of mothers — that is, each woman of known age in the sample, accompanied by a child whose age has been subtracted from hers — totalling 203 (set out in tables 6.1 and 6.2), we can work out a further singulate mean, this time for age of mother at first birth, and, by allowing for gestation, age at first concep-tion. These statistics for our data are 19.71 years and 18.96 years. If the whole series could be supposed to be internally consistent, then we could conclude that in the 1730s the Christian women of Belgrade became sexually mature on average between 14 and 15, took husbands on average between 15 and 16 or perhaps a trifle later, and conceived their first babies at about 19, say, between 18.5 and 19.5. The interval of two and a half to three years between marriage and conception could be attri-buted to the known low level of fecundability of women following at-tainment of sexual maturity. It is perhaps too long an interval but is certainly believable.[23]

We can be fairly confident, unfortunately, that such consistency is apparent rather than real, and rely least willingly on the estimate for

---

[22] Some support for the youngest ages being perfectly genuine can be gained even from English evidence. There is the Countess of Leicester who, in 1589, had a child at age 13 (Laslett 1965 (1971 ed.: 91); a girl at Colyton in Devonshire had a bastard in the eighteenth century when she was 13.

[23] Trussell, in his draft of 1976 cited in n. 19 above, talks of an upper bound of some three years on the mean number of years which might elapse between a woman's marrying in her teens and her first conception leading to birth. He states that two to two and a half years would be a more reasonable estimate.

mean age at first conception, since this depends on the subtractions which lead to occasional absurdities. Nevertheless, the age distribution for the Belgrade population as a whole does not fall markedly out of line with similar distributions for other pre-industrial European societies. Mean overall age at Belgrade was 24.5, whereas in the six English communities mentioned above it was 25.73; medians 20.83 and 21.70. For males, the mean at Belgrade was 26.05 (a median of 21.09) and, in the English sample, 25.26 and 20.23; females 23.47 and 20.42 against 26.17 and 22.59. The population was a little younger, and the gap is greatest for women, but the discrepancy is no greater than is found between communities in England. The really disconcerting figures come in table 6.3, with its impossible ages at birth of the first accompanying child. Though it can be shown that all of these cases were probably the results of a woman marrying a widower with children, and though the errors even in this table offset each other, at least to some extent, the statistics from this set of figures are of problematic value and have been treated as such here.

This rough, preliminary exercise in the numerical study of age at maturity in earlier times may imply two principles. The first is that it cannot be assumed of the persons living in traditional societies, where they were immured for so long in their families of origin and kept under discipline for a good part of their lives, that they were necessarily more likely to be reconciled to their situation for physiological reasons. When we contemplate the patriarchal household in Stuart England, colonial America or France under the *ancien régime*, where marriage was so much later than it was in Belgrade, and where — in England especially, but in France and perhaps the colonies as well — so many young people were in subjection as servants (compulsorily celibate like the children), we must think of the long years when young people were capable of fully adult roles, sexual fulfilment and the direction of a family. If fathers were concerned about the chastity of their daughters, it was because they were probably often quite as capable of producing bastards in their middle teens as they are today. Fathers also faced their teenage sons as grown-up persons, as strong as they were themselves in a society where personal, physical violence was more formidable than now.

The second principle is still scarcely established, and it may take many years to decide about it: age at menarche and maturation generally could vary, over time, as well as from social class and place to place. We cannot attempt to go into the reasons for this variation, even if it were within our competence. We may notice that the experts now no longer suppose that climate explains a great deal of the difference in menarcheal age in various parts of the world.

Nothing can be said from this haphazard evidence about the extent to which it was due to genetical heritage, just as the body shape of Latin American peoples is different from that of Asian peoples, for reasons of what was once called race. But Frisch and Revelle have recently published evidence to bear out their view that 'the attainment of a specific body weight at the peak of the adolescent spurt ... may be critical for menarche'.[24] There is no need to accept any particular account of how the process of sexual maturation comes about in women to suppose that it was to a large extent a function of nutrition in the early and especially the earliest years. As historical demographers, we know something already about variations in food supply and their effect on demographic rates, their extreme effects in the crisis of subsistence which the French have delineated, and their long-term effects in the control of population size. It is interesting to have to recognize that differences in nutrition may have caused variations in the internal balance of the domestic group as well, as it definitely must have influenced the physiological relationships between classes. Moreover, let the American readers of this essay reflect on the consequences of the fact that from their very beginnings the American people, especially American children, and even American slaves, have been better fed than Europeans.

Addendum: Further figures from the nineteenth century
and the measurement of variation in
relation to class difference

Research since 1971 shows that this essay by no means represents the first occasion on which early marriage in areas outside Western Europe has been taken as evidence for age at sexual maturity. In the course of his polemic against the dogma that climate was the determining factor in menarcheal age and that hot climates caused women to reach maturity earlier, John Roberton contributed to the *Edinburgh Medical and Social Journal* (1843) a title which can only be called a warning: 'Early marriage so common in oriental countries no proof of early puberty'. Examination of that article, which was reprinted in Roberton's book, *Essays and notes on the physiology and diseases of women* (1851), goes

[24] Rose Frisch and Roger Revelle, 'Variation in body weight and the age of the adolescent growth spurt among Latin American and Asian populations in relation to calorie supplies', *Human Biology* 41 (1969): 185–212. Professor Frisch has summarized her work on age at menarche and set out the implications of nutrition for fecundability throughout the whole span of a woman's childbearing period in Frisch 1975. A critical examination of the hypothesis of a direct relation between menarche and body weight, concluding that it is unacceptable if taken as independent of age, is to be found in W. Z. Billewicz, H. M. Fellowes and C. A. Hytten, 'Comments on the critical metabolic mass and the age at menarche', *Annals of Human Biology* 3, 1 (January 1976): 33–50.

to show that by 'oriental' Roberton meant countries further away than Belgrade. He produces no compelling evidence from the European East that the Christian rule about all brides necessarily being mature at marriage was being extensively ignored. There is a tradition in Serbian history that under the Turkish oppression very young males were sometimes 'married' for property reasons. But there seems to be no evidence that unions of this kind would have been accepted by the Christian Church as indissoluble matrimony. At the present, anyway, the evidence from the Belgrade listing can be accepted.as a provisional indicator, rough and ready as it has to be.

Reference to three of the nineteenth-century British medical men who took part in the discussion of this subject confirms Tanner's judgement of the unreliability of their work in detail, but reveals a situation which is of some interest to the subject as a whole. Evidently, age at puberty was a question which engaged the attention of many people at the time. This was because early maturation and early marriage were associated with the degradation of women and with that tendency toward immorality which Europeans of Western Christianity so much deplored in other parts of the world, above all among 'savages'. There was a deep conviction that climate determined age at puberty, a belief which seems to have originated in an irresponsible remark by Montesquieu in *L'Esprit des Lois*, though Montesquieu may have taken it from a contemporary. It was in refutation of this belief that the same John Roberton, who was surgeon to the Manchester Lying-In Hospital, undertook his researches, starting in the 1820s and publishing them finally in his 1851 book. James Whitehead, also surgeon to that hospital, held the older view and published his figures in 1847, *On the causes and treatment of abortion and sterility*. A further set of figures (collected by Graily Hewitt) was published by Walter Rigden in 1869, and the generosity of Rose Frisch of Harvard allows us to add to them two further sets of data. One is a distribution of *age de la première éruption des règles* collected by M. A. Raciborski (*De la puberté* (Paris, 1844)), and the other a distribution published in the eighth report of the Massachusetts State Board of Health of 1877.[25]

The methods used by the English observers, and presumably by the others, too, were to cross-question the women when they came for examination to the Lying-In Hospital as to when they first menstruated, a method which Tanner condemns.[26] These scholars made no record of the exact date of their observations, and the ages which they recorded are in the form 'first menstruated at the age of 11, 12, 13 etc.' This presumably means the year attained at last birthday, and so has to be increased

[25] I am indebted to Rose Frisch both for these references and for discussion of the whole problem in correspondence.
[26] Tanner 1955 (1962 ed.: 154).

by half a year to enter into comparable calculations, though neither these earlier scholars nor Tanner ever mentions that fact.

With all of these points allowed for, there certainly appear to be grounds for supposing that mean age at menarche was somewhat higher in early-nineteenth-century English cities than it may have been in Belgrade in 1733–4. There may also be some tendency towards a fall in the age of puberty in women detectable in these figures between the 1820s and the 1840s. Roberton's distribution reveals a mean age of 15.7 years and Whitehead's for the 1830s or 1840s a mean of 15.53 (Whitehead may in fact have added the half year); and Rigden's distribution for the 1860s yields a mean age of 14.96 (15.46?). Raciborski's French figures for 1844 have a mean of 14.9 (15.4?), and Bowditch's American figures of 1877 one of 14.7 (15.3?).

More interesting, however, is the shape of the distributions, which are printed for convenience at the end of the addendum. It is obvious at a glance that the spread of the figures is unlikely to be narrow enough to yield a general standard deviation as low as 1.1. Standard deviations for the sets of data are set out below, and in order to be conservative in estimating how much greater the spread might have been in the nineteenth century than it is now, I have calculated values for ages below 20 as well as those for the full distributions. The spread of all five sets of figures is more than half as great again as in contemporary society, even with the extreme values left out at the upper end. Although the contrast in mean age at menarche between our time and that of the young Queen Victoria may be in question, there seems little doubt about the conspicuous difference in the variation.

These results are not incompatible with the general proposition that age at menarche is normally distributed, but statistical examination shows that there is some tendency to depart from this curve: it can be suggested that the shape of the figures results from several, presumably normal, distributions superimposed. This would lend some further support to the belief that in former times the range of ages was rather greater than it is now. Although it is right to be wary of the higher values, it is difficult to see what could have caused a woman to state that she became mature as late as 20 or even subsequently, especially as she was being questioned before the early 40s.[27]

These late ages may, therefore, have some foundation, and when they are included the spread of ages at earlier times appears to be greater still. If the effect is genuine, it could be accounted for by greater differences in nutrition and in general well-being in the population – greater

[27] See A. Damon and C. J. Bajema, 'Age at menarche: accuracy of recall after 39 years', *Human Biology* 46, 3 (1975): 381–4, where half the respondents were accurate to within six months even after so long a period.

class differences, in fact. It might now be thought hazardous for the historical sociologist to think of a rise in menarcheal age as accompanying the early stages of industrialization in Europe in the years up to 1850. But he may still see in its fall since the 1890s, and in the shrinkage of its variance, signs of what might be termed a physiological assimilation between social groups.

Mid-nineteenth-century distributions of age at menarche

	England			France	Massachusetts
	Roberton 1820s	Whitehead 1830s–40s	Rigden 1860s	Raciborski 1840s	Bowditch 1870s
9	—	—	3	—	—
10	10	9	14	4	4
11	19	26	60	10	26
12	53	136	170	20	49
13	85	332	353	29	107
14	97	638	560	38	142
15	76	761	540	41	112
16	57	967	455	20	83
17	26	499	272	20	14
18	23	393	150	12	20
19	4	148	76	—	5
20	—	71	29	4	3
21	—	9	7	—	—
22	—	6	3	—	—
23	—	2	2	2	—
24	—	1	—	—	—
25	—	1	—	—	—
26	—	1	2	—	—
n	450	4,000	2,696	200	575
Standard deviation					
9–20	1.9	1.7	1.8	1.9	1.7
9–26	1.9	1.9	1.9	2.2	1.7

7. Household and family on the slave plantations of the U.S.A.

I

During the extraordinary development of Negro slavery which accompanied the plantation by the Europeans of the West Indian islands and of parts of the American continent, the status of the slave as progenitor and as offspring was variously interpreted. The English-speakers amongst the planters, like the Ancients, held to the principle that the slave could not legally marry. He or she could be neither husband nor wife, son nor daughter, according to the law: no slave union was legally recognized and no slave could be a legitimate child. Indeed, the relationship between owning persons and persons owned, between white and black, was such that a slave could not expect to have that legally sanctioned sexual monopoly in a partner which is a defining characteristic of marriage. The independent status which confers authority on a household head over spouse and offspring had very little on which to rest. Yet slave men and women did make and did maintain marriage-like associations: the word *marriage* perpetually recurs in the discussion of their situation: the plantation recognized 'marriage' even if the law did not. Moreover, slaves most certainly procreated children. It was in the interest of their masters that they should maintain their numbers, and if possible increase.

Here then was present within the meticulously and authoritatively structured society of Western European family groups in America a growing collection of peculiar persons who stood outside the official familial system. Those slaves who could be looked upon as servants because they were living as unmarried individuals within the households of their owners, very much in the way that we have seen all life-cycle servants had always done in English traditional society, fitted the established European familial pattern. It was the plantation workers and all the other extrafamilial individuals whose situation was such an uneasy one in relation to accepted convention. The challenge which this situation posed to established moral values amongst the European whites, especially to their familial values, was becoming intolerable.

Slavery, then, opens up the possibility of probing into the body of behaviour which made up English and West European familial life by demonstrating what happened when family life had no public, legal sanction, and when there was a sense in which all love had to be illicit love. To look on the situation of American slaves in this way is of course to adopt the attitude of their owners and masters and of white society, not that of the blacks themselves. Their conception of domestic living might have been very different. Though we cannot concern ourselves with this important subject, which is beyond the competence of an outside observer, we must notice that the actual living situation of the slaves of the American South differed in another very important way from the living situation of their white compatriots and European contemporaries.

For the domestic group of slaves, the society in which the process of creation and socialization of children took place, could hardly be said to possess economic self-determination. Its nourishment and support did not depend, as it did in the households of the free, on the earnings of its members. They were supplied by the owner. The whole range of circumstances which related the life of the 'family' to its social environment through what we call economics was accordingly lacking. Since economic circumstances of this kind do so much to create the distinction between families of the type we live in and so are important in maintaining the sense of a boundary surrounding each familial unit, the uncertainty of their presence in the case of slaves must have meant that their domestic groups lacked definition.

A wide range of familial functions, including child rearing and the taking of meals, might well go forward in two ways and in two societies. That is to say, they were shared between the wider society of the plantation and the 'families' of the slaves. The collaborative, productive work, on the other hand, that never-ending succession of tasks which associates familial members so closely in all agricultural societies, especially of the peasant type — was organized in a singular unit, that of the plantation itself. In so far as this was true, it was on the plantation, therefore, rather than on the slave domestic group that the economic influences making for solidarity and interdependence were exerted. But the plantation was itself regarded in some ways as a family household, at least by its master and mistress. On the smaller plantations especially, this image of the enterprise as a large patriarchal household must have had some substance to the slaves as well as to the owners. 'The slave holders' insistence on having a "black family" must be taken with deadly seriousness', Genovese declares. Such circumstances required that many, perhaps most, slaves should belong to two familial or quasi-familial institutions. Not only did the 'family' group lack definition for slaves, but it had a plural sense, an overlapping plural sense. A complicated situation indeed.

These complications must be left to the scholars in the United States who are now beginning to recreate the family life and familial system of the North American black slaves.[1] All that will be attempted here is a very limited exercise in comparative familial structure, contrasting the domestic group of a tiny sample of slaves with that of English-speaking white European society as it then was and as it had historically been. The publication of a very remarkable book was the occasion of this exercise, as it has been for so much of the revival of interest in questions concerning American slave society. This book was *Time on the cross*, by Robert Fogel and Stanley Engerman, which appeared in 1974.[2]

Fogel and Engerman make the following overall claims about family and household amongst the slaves of the Southern states. First, that the form of the slave family group during the decades which led up to the Civil War was predominantly nuclear, as in white American society at large, and that most sexually mature individuals lived in monogamous marriage. Slave children under age 14 were brought up to a very large extent in groups each consisting ordinarily of their own father, their own mother and their own brothers and sisters. Second, that the traditional Christian rules governing sexual access to women were main-

[1] See, for example, Orlando Patterson, *The sociology of slavery* (1967), as revised by B. W. Higman (see below) for the West Indies, and for the American South, J. W. Blassingame, *The slave community* (New York, 1972), and the various works of Eugene Genovese, especially *Roll Jordan, roll* (New York, 1974). The revision and development now in progress of the classic works of W. E. B. du Bois (*The Negro American family* (Atlanta, 1908; reprinted New York, 1970)) and E. Franklin Frazier (*The Negro family in the U.S.A.* (Chicago, 1939)) on the slave domestic group and kinship system in the United States, are expected to be advanced by the appearance of H. G. Gutman's book *Afro-Americans: their families during and after enslavement* (forthcoming) and by the research results of Crawford (see below) and others. The rather different marital and familial situation of slaves in Catholic Cuba (where marriage was recognized and the family protected by the priesthood) and in officially Anglican Virginia is brought out in H. S. Klein, *Slavery in the Americas* (1967).

[2] 2 vols., Boston. The present chapter is a development of a paper presented at a conference held in Rochester, N.Y., in October 1974, to discuss that work. Some account has also been taken of a draft of a further volume by Fogel and Engerman, dated July 1975, a commentary on the discussions at Rochester and on some of the large body of writing which has appeared about *Time on the cross*. I am grateful to them for permission to refer to this unpublished piece and to its citations from the outcomes of the research of their associates as it relates to the slave family, and to Robert Fogel for reading and discussing the present chapter. Gutman's extraordinarily unsympathetic but useful and important review of the original book (Gutman 1975a) filled 174 pages of the *Journal of Negro History* and has since appeared in book form. Further discussion, mainly of the free black family during and after the mid nineteenth century will be found in the *Journal of Interdisciplinary History* 6, 2 (Autumn 1975), devoted to the history of the family (the third issue on the topic). Gutman's contribution (1975b), 'Persistent myths about the Afro-American family', and that of C. R. Shiflett, 'The household composition of rural black families in Louisa County, Virginia, in 1880', are particularly relevant to the subject matter of the present chapter, though neither is specifically concerned with slaves.

tained, not only by the slaves themselves, but also (with exceptions) by their white owners and other white persons in control of them or in association with them. Third, that although about a tenth of slave marriages were broken up by sales, the alienation of slave children from their companions in the elementary family usually took place when they were of an age at which separation might be expected to come about in any case.

There are three implications of their position which must be noticed, even though Fogel and Engerman do not pursue them to any great extent. In the first place, the particular characteristics of the black family in our own day in the United States, characteristics often described as its 'weaknesses', cannot be referred for their origin to the slave regime as easily as it was previously supposed. Their beginnings must accordingly be sought in developments which have taken place since the emancipation of the slaves. In the second place, the tendency for the family group to be headed by women alone, living with their children or their grandchildren, or with both, or even with children more distantly related, *without* the presence of husbands or male sexual partners, which is a special feature of contemporary black families, did not necessarily originate in the slave plantation. In the third place the miscegenation between white and black, which is now so widespread, was brought about only to a very small extent by the victimization of black slave women by their owners or by other whites. This third position about racial intermixture will concern us only tangentially.

The arguments of *Time on the cross* have not gone unchallenged, and considerable controversy has arisen about the book, as might be expected. Knowledgeable critics have been reluctant to accept many of its statements about the slave family as demonstrated, and have particularly disputed the claim as to the rarity with which sales divided its members. Herbert Gutman insists, moreover, that there is no positive evidence that slaves lived in nuclear families, and much evidence of an opposite character: 'it is erroneous to assert that slaves lived in stable families' (1975a: 152). The originality and importance of the research methods used by Fogel and Engerman, and the range of the source materials exploited, many of them for the first time, have, however, been readily acknowledged.

We shall have to agree that the challenging positions which these writers try to establish about household and family on the slave plantations of the U.S.A. are somewhat unrealistic as well as ambitious, though they are developed with extraordinary ingenuity from apparently newly discovered documents. The authors imply the analysis of a great body of evidence of a scarce and difficult kind, not by any means all evidence about U.S. slave society only, and maintain that such an analysis must always issue in results which underwrite one particular interpretation. The claim about the nuclear family seems to me to require the demonstration of the following very general and highly exclusive statements, and very much else besides. These statements are:

That this particular familial pattern is the norm for a 'Western' society, and that the domestic groups of black Negro slaves conformed to it at the time in question.

That a sufficiently large proportion of all Negro slave families were of this form for long enough to justify calling the nuclear family a characteristic feature of their way of life when slavery ended.

We need not return here to the questions discussed in chapter 1 about the Western or North-west European familial form, and about how far it has been characteristic of Western culture, including that of the United States, and for how long. If the Fogel and Engerman position is to be assessed, what is evidently needed is a method of analysing the surviving materials on how slaves were associated together for the purposes of procreation, nurture and so on, together with a set of criteria about family structure in general and nuclearity in particular. More important still would be a set of detailed results of applying such criteria to a body of evidence, however restricted that evidence might be.

The same direct documentary methods will be followed in this last chapter as in the preceding chapters of this book. Lists of groups of slaves actually living on plantations[3] will be examined in accordance with the set of analytic conventions being developed for this purpose by the Cambridge Group for the History of Population and Social Structure. The results will then be compared with some of those already briefly reported in chapter 1 for communities, mainly village communities — that is, rural parishes, but other communities, too — of persons living in England and other parts of Europe, West or East, up to the time of the American Civil War. Some attempt will also be made to look at material with considerations in mind which have not so far been found important for European and other societies, criteria for judging, for example, the homogeneity as to their parents of a string of children living together. We shall concentrate our attention on the structure and

---

[3] Reproductions of these lists were generously supplied by Stanley Engerman, who has helped in the analysis of slave family living in every possible way. Documentary details do not seem to be necessary in a preliminary study such as this, and I am so unfamiliar with records of this kind that it would not be easy to undertake adequately. The numbers and contents of the little collection of inventories of slaves which were analysed should be evident from table 7.1 on household composition and from the various references in the text. We analysed the lists in accordance with the conventions in use at the Cambridge Group, and also made out family reconstitution forms (F.R.F.s — see below) for the Good Hope plantation using the register of births and so on which accompanies that listing.

composition of domestic groups rather than on the relationships between them or on kin relations as such. We shall use the criterion of *nuclearity*, in fact, in a rather restricted sense, for strictly comparative purposes only.

The outcome of this exercise, we shall see, is short of being decisive as to the main point. It is not possible to show that the individuals in these groups of slaves were close enough in their familial conduct to the Europeans, and in particular to the Anglo-Saxon, Anglo-American Europeans, to be confident that they belong to the same familial system. The similarities between these slave household groups and those existing in other parts of the white Anglo-Saxon world at the same time do much to suggest that this model of familial behaviour was in the minds of the actors, that is, the black slaves themselves, when they made their decisions about sexual partnerships, parentage and so on. But the anomalies in this body of evidence would make it difficult to dispose of somewhat different interpretations. The fact that the nuclear family, or simple family household, was most certainly in the heads of the slave owners, overseers and those who made out the documents we have to examine, raises the possibility of a bias which we cannot easily allow for. Furthermore, we should do well to restrict all our statements to these documents alone. Any attempt to generalize from these sources to black slave society generally comes up against the fact to which we shall have to return, that these records belong to plantations which could have been exceptional because they were so big.

II

It can be asserted with considerable confidence that the formal structure of the Negro domestic group portrayed in these particular documents was not single-headed, female-headed or, beyond a certain point, matrifocal. What is not revealed by the formal structure, however, that is, by such lists of persons actually living together as domestic groups, is a detectable tendency towards a female principle of continuity in the family group over time, and a slightly anomalous conception of paternity, anomalous, that is to say, in relation to prevalent European norms. This circumstance can only be brought to light by the study of the births, marriages and deaths which relate to the slaves recorded on a list, and unfortunately such a register is available for only one of the documents we have been able to analyse. Though no patent signs of structural incohesiveness show up in the black slave domestic groups we have examined, there are indications of what seems to be an abnormally high proportion of *synthetic* households. A synthetic household is taken to consist of persons co-residing which could not possibly have arisen from a procreative partnership between a man and a woman, and comprising exclusively those partners themselves and their own offspring, together occasionally with spouses of those offspring and grandchildren and so on.

The most striking outcome, as has been hinted, is the very high proportion of double-headed households to be found amongst the Negro slaves. Of the 27 'slave families' living on the Good Hope plantation in South Carolina in 1857 all but two – that is, 93% – were headed by persons called 'Man' and 'Wife', demonstrably the actual parents of most, though by no means all, of the children actually living in those families. This demonstration is possible because Good Hope is the one plantation for which we do have a running record of vital events.

Over nine in ten is an impressive level of double-headed households, since the English standard, as we call it, that is, the proportion of households headed by married couples in the largest sample of communities yet analysed, is 70.4% ± 2.67.[4] The records of five other plantations, which we shall call the Oakley plantations, one dated 1837, the other 1851, show proportions of households headed by 'married' couples of 84%, 62%, 62%, 76% and 82% with a mean of 72% for the 138 domestic groups they comprise.

In these instances, not having vital records, we cannot tell whether the children in the households were in fact the offspring of these 'married couples'. But even the groups of slaves recorded in a further document labelled 'slaves in Laurence County bought for Mr. Dearing, 25 March 1857' were listed for the most part in blocks, each beginning with a man and a woman of an age to be married and to be parents of the children who succeeded them in the list. In fact, all children included in these collections of human livestock seem to have been attached to couples in this way. Though we are not able to be certain of the details of parenthood with such data, we can say that there were as many fatherless children in an ordinary English pre-industrial village as there were infant slaves on these plantations who appear to have lost a parental figure.[5]

---

[4] For the English standard for this variable derived from 70 settlements, 1581 – 1820, see Laslett and Wall (eds.) 1972: chs. 1 and 4, esp. p. 78, and compare table 2.10 above, where figures for Clayworth are set out. Gutman (1975b: table p. 195) finds very similar proportions for double-headed houses as those in our table for slaves, but for large numbers of free black households in various areas, 1850s – 80s. Very much higher levels of double-headed households have occasionally been identified, however, as in seventeenth- and eighteenth-century Belgian, German, Austrian, and Russian villages, or in Estonia in 1684.

[5] See ch. 4 on English orphans. We have not yet collected evidence on the proportion of households with children in England which had female heads, though the figures at Clayworth (see ch. 2) were about 8.5%. This compares with 8–15% in the slave communities here analysed, which may well have had greater numbers of such house-

If our criterion is socialization, that is, experience in the earliest years with all its supposed potential for the later development of character — including the qualities which may be considered to be linked with the strength and stability of the familial group — then we can cautiously infer that these slave children, anyway, the first we have got to know about, were not subjected during their most formative period to parental loss and the breakup of 'marriages' to a greater extent than the children born into English peasant households in traditional times. They were decidedly not living in predominantly female-headed households, maternal or grandmaternal; in these respects the stereotypes are simply false for this particular body of evidence. About what happened later in the life cycle and family cycle, when older children may have been sold away, nothing can be concluded from these data.

The indications in this preliminary sample that the predominantly double-headed households in which these slaves were living were of nuclear form are quite easy to see. In the table below, the proportion in the category 'Simple family households' is by far the largest in all the plantations whose listings by households are sufficiently exact to make it possible to place them under the structural headings established for the purpose.[6]

We have had some difficulty in reducing the materials from the seven slave plantations to the standard form required for the filling out of this table of household composition. This is not only because of the puzzles presented by some of the groups of persons, but also because of the way the information is presented. Slave overseers, or whoever it was who made out these documents, were scarcely as literate as the village constables who often wrote out taxation lists in seventeenth-century England, and much less so than the clergy or fiscal officials of Western Europe in general, or even of the early-nineteenth-century Russian countryside. Accepting this evidence as roughly correct we find that only one of the plantations fails to yield a proportion of simple family households of the same order as the percentage commonly found in English pre-industrial communities, and in that plantation it is noticeable that the proportion of indeterminate households was as high as 40%. According to the documents made out by these plantation officials,

holds than in traditional English society. As for the Dearing list, Genovese claims that 'Masters and overseers normally listed their slaves by households and shaped disciplinary procedures to take full account of family relationships' (1974: 452). This seems inconsistent with Gutman's declaration (1975a: 150) that 'The labor force was never described in familial terms.'

[6] See ch. 1 for the categorization of household structure, and compare tables 1.1–1.3. Using rather different criteria, Gutman (1975b: table p. 196) finds a similar proportion of nuclear families for free blacks.

TABLE 7.1. *Household composition on seven slave plantations compared with English traditional communities*

	English standard sample (30 settlements)	Good Hope plantation 1857 Pop. 175 No.	%	Carlisle Negroes 1831 Pop. 169 No.	%	Oxford plantation 1851 Pop. [103] No.	%	L'Argent plantation 1851 Pop. 123 No.	%	Hariodette plantation 1851 Pop. [99] No.	%	Camperdown plantation 1851 Pop. 133 No.	%	Oakley and Duncan plantation 1851 Pop. 133 No.	%
1. Solitaries	8.5%±1.6	3	9	0	0	7	18	0	0	1	5	0	0	1	2
of which widowed		2	—	—	—	—	—	— [a]	—	— [a]	—	— [a]	—	—	—
2. No family of which	3.6%±1.1	2	6	2	8	—	—	—	—	—	—	—	—	11	19
(a) Siblings		0	—	0	—	—	—	—	—	—	—	—	—	—	—
(b) Other relatives		0	—	2	—	—	—	—	—	—	—	—	—	—	—
3. Simple family households of which	72.1%	26	76	13	52	29	76	23	79	17	77	19	76	40	68
(a) Married couples alone		3	—	1	—	14	—	4	—	1	—	2	—	6	—
(b) Married couples with children		20				7		14		13		12		25	
(c) Widowers with children		1	—	5	—	5	—	4	—	0	—	3	—	4	—
(d) Widows with children		2	—	1	—	3	—	1	—	3	—	2	—	5	—
4. Extended family households of which	11.9%	3	9	0	—	0	0	0	0	0	—	0	0	0	0
(a) Upwards		1	—	—	—	—	—	—	—	—	—	—	—	—	—
(b) Downwards		2	—	—	—	—	—	—	—	—	—	—	—	—	—
(c) Laterally		0	—	—	—	—	—	—	—	—	—	—	—	—	—
(d) Combinations		0	—	—	—	—	—	—	—	—	—	—	—	—	—
5. Multiple family households	3.1%	0	0	0	0	0	0	0	0	0	0	0	0	0	0
6. Indeterminate	0.9%	0	0	10	40	2 [a]	5	6 [a]	21	4 [a]	18	6 [a]	24	7	12
Total households		34	100	25	100	38	99	29	100	22	100	25	100	59	101

[a]Categories 2 and 6 indistinguishable.

241

therefore, and so perhaps generally on plantations of the type which could give rise to such documents, the nuclear family predominated amongst American slaves.

But there are signs that this predominance may not have been of the same kind that has been found in English historical experience. Where the 'no family' households can be distinguished from the 'indeterminate', they are clearly too numerous. We have found only a couple of places in England where the proportion of such households was higher than 6% (one at 11%, one at 12%): this makes the levels on the Oakley and Duncan plantations look entirely excessive, and two others very high. Only one English place has a proportion of solitaries greater than on the Oxford plantation. The plantation figures in fact give an impression of being consistently less regular from plantation to plantation than the English figures do from settlement to settlement, that is (usually), from village to village. When we remember that so many slave households have had to be described as indeterminate – indeed, only two plantations have a proportion of these lower than the maximum for England at 9.4% – we can begin to see why it has to be said that these domestic groups cannot be confidently claimed as clearly belonging to the customary Western nuclear type.

Nothing can be known from these highly restricted and imperfect data about the domestic group cycle amongst the slaves, and without a file of information on the actual history, especially the demographic history, of the groups and of the individuals under study we cannot tell quite what to make even of the evidence we happen to possess, how to resolve the puzzles which appear when we come to look individually at each domestic group. From the one plantation, that of Good Hope in South Carolina, where we do have a register of births and deaths, we can find out a little more when we compare its contents with the names of the slaves actually present in the listing of the plantation in 1857. Some of what we learn is undoubtedly disconcerting, but the first outcome of setting this information alongside what we know of a similar character from within the English traditional social structure is reassuring for those anxious to insist on the stability of slave 'marriages'. With the Good Hope register in hand we can make a comparison with the village of Clayworth (table 7.2).[7] If it can happen that as many slave children were living with their own biological parents and their own

---

[7] The list of inhabitants for Clayworth in 1688 was selected once again, as in chs. 2 and 4, for the completeness of its recordings. It specifies the parentage of all children more fully than any other we hold for England, and is accompanied by an accurately kept register which can be used for checking. But we have seen that the proportion of remarriages in that village in 1688 may have been exceptionally high (see pp. 57–8) and the death rate heavy. Other English villages at other times might have had many fewer

TABLE 7.2.   *Children in Clayworth and children on a slave plantation*

	Clayworth, Notts., England 1688	Good Hope Plantation, Orangeburg, S.C., U.S.A., 1857
Proportion of children named in list born of current union of couples at head of domestic group in which child is found	80%	86%
Born of previous union	18%	8%
Born of father or mother unknown	2%	6%
	100%	100%

biological brothers and sisters as was the case in an ordinary English village in pre-industrial times, then we can surely dispose of the suggestion (for this one plantation, anyway) that such children were always of miscellaneous parentage and were lumped together in 'families' simply for the convenience of maintenance and nurture.

Something in the way of confirmation of this can be found by the examination of the age of every slave child in each string of children in every household group which contained them, using for the purpose the whole body of children in all the documents we dispose of. When this is done, no ties in age at all appear within any one string, except where the children are twins, and it is lucky that twins are marked as such. Absence of ties in age, except in the case of twins, is of course an indication that all the children were born of the same woman. If these strings of children had in fact been synthetic, that is, the result of mixing together miscellaneous offspring, placing them under a married couple and calling the result a household, we could surely have expected some age ties to have occurred.[8]

At this point we reach the end of the somewhat impressionistic evidence which could be used to persuade us that these strings of children

children born of previous unions. In the next most reliable body of evidence, from Ardleigh in Essex in 1796, over 90% of all children appear to have been born of the current union of those at the head of the family of residence. Here we cannot be confident enough of the recordings to be reasonably certain that all stepchildren have been indicated, though the difference from Clayworth may well be due to more favourable demographic conditions in late-eighteenth-century Essex than in seventeenth-century Nottinghamshire. We have taken the Good Hope register on trust. It looks complete and accurate, but having no means of comparing it with others I cannot pronounce it so.

[8] This argument would have been more convincing if the lists had specified age precisely, and not in completed years. It does not seem a straightforward proposition

can only have been the spontaneously arising sets of individuals issuing from the union of the male and female heading the domestic groups in which they are found, thus confirming the generally nuclear-family character of the groups concerned. We now turn to the anomalies, and begin with the family reconstitution forms which can be made out from the register of Good Hope. It turns out that 6 out of these 25 forms show some sort of irregularity — that is, depart in some way from the spontaneous offspring string already discussed, and which is universally exhibited by the F.R.F.s which have been made out for many thousands of families in traditional English society. (By family reconstitution form, or F.R.F., it perhaps ought to be added, is meant the form on which for demographic-analytic purposes a marriage of a man and a woman is recorded, along with the dates of birth of all their children, adding dates of marriage and death (where known) of all the parties. No illegitimate births can appear on F.R.F., because they do not arise from a marriage, and in this technical sense slave unions could not be the subject of F.R.F.s.)

Two of the strings of children on the 6 irregular forms begin with a couple of births from a father unnamed, and continue with the children of a named spouse. One string begins with a child of one man, continues with the child of a man unknown, and then goes on to a series of children of yet a third man. Two have an unnamed father for the first child, and one has the name of the father of the rest. The important point to be recognized is that in no case can these anomalies be explained by the recording of the death of the father in this apparently well-kept register. It would seem, then, that though the children of Good Hope slave households in 1857 did indeed belong to formally nuclear families, they did not all issue in each family group from the same father: there were more step-siblings than there should have been, and the cause of this was not orphanage, but an arrangement the technical name of which might be serial polyandry.

If we look for a reason why this pattern arose, then the obvious suggestion would be that it was due to sale; a young husband was sold off, and had to be replaced — whether at the choice of the owner or overseer or at the choice of the slave 'wife' need not be specified. If this is what happened, the claim as to the rarity of the breakup of family group by sale looks less convincing, even in the case of families in the stage of

to estimate how many ties might have arisen, since it is highly unlikely that synthetically assembled children could have been random as to age: there would undoubtedly have been to some extent inter-related siblings. Even if as many as three children of every five had been siblings, however, we could expect about 1 in 60 of the strings of children to have exhibited ties in age, and there are over 150 groups in our sample.

formation. These facts about the occasional substitution of male spouses might be held to bear out traditional interpretation in another way. For it must be stressed that the principle of continuity of those family groups so affected can only have been the mother of the children. This must be called a matrifocal tendency, which arises whenever there is any depar-ture from the rule that children have to be born from union with one spouse only. The possible extent of these anomalies is increased when it is recognized that 8 out of the 25 strings of children at issue contain less than three names: the type of breach of homogeneity we are discussing cannot be identified in strings of so short a size. Those affected, then, were 6 out of as few as 17 possible candidate strings.

Serial polyandry is not a part of European marriage or familial insti-tutions as usually conceived; it is certainly quite alien to the stringent rules laid down by the Christian Church and obeyed as faithfully in the Catholic areas as it was in the Protestant or the 'Puritan' ones, often, indeed with greater exactness. Nevertheless, the close study of irregular sexual unions leading to illegitimacy which is now under way at the Cambridge Group, in co-operation with scholars elsewhere working on the historical records of a number of countries, shows that something like serial polyandry occasionally occurred. Where a woman had a num-ber of illegitimate children before settling into a marriage, a pattern apparently common in nineteenth-century Germany, for example, but not unknown elsewhere, her final husband was usually the same as the father of their bastards.

In England we should classify such persons, father and mother, as be-longing within that 'sub-society of the illegitimacy-prone' which is brief-ly discussed in chapter 3. But by no means all repetitive bastard-bearers who were ultimately wedded in the approved way chose as husbands the fathers of any or all of their children. Those who finally married and settled down with another man could perhaps be said to be exhibiting serial polyandry. Such examples are extremely rare, and there is no question of a widespread practice. But other irregularities found at Good Hope, a married woman, for example, having a child amongst her other legitimate children engendered by a man not her husband, have also been observed within the bastardy-prone sub-society.[9]

In suggesting that there is some sort of parallel between the behaviour of those persons and that of the slaves of Good Hope, it is not claimed that what so infrequently happened in England was looked upon as any

[9] Subsequent work on English illegitimacy shows that a significant proportion of all British bastards were begotten by masters on their servants, a fact which has inter-esting implications for the issue of miscegeny between white owners or overseers and black female slaves, implications which cannot be taken up here.

sort of precedent amongst the slaves of the plantations. Who could be certain that a connection could ever be established between the two? All that is intended is to point to the existence of people in the English-speaking world at the relevant time who likewise had anomalous marriage practices, and whose behaviour was marked by two further characteristics perhaps also present on the plantations.

One was that though the marriage rules were slightly differently viewed amongst them, marriage itself was nevertheless valued, perhaps highly valued. These English sexual eccentrics got married if they could, usually stayed married and occasionally became the ancestors of an eminently respectable posterity. The other feature was a faintly trace-able tendency towards the persistence over time of this set of attitudes and practices, making of their transmitters a continuing local society.

We have perhaps pressed the interpretation of these wisps of evidence from the Good Hope registers further than is justifiable, and we must not linger much longer. It should be said, however, that this evidence bears the interpretation that some care was being taken to keep the slave children there within the same family group as the mother, and also to ensure that she had living with her a man of an age suitable to be her mate. Such may also have been the reality behind the domestic groups on the other plantations in our little sample. It has to be decided by the authorities on the familial attitudes of the black slaves how far these arrangements were the deliberate actions of the owners or over-seers, or how far they were demanded by the conventions of slave society itself.

There are oddities shown by the rest of the data which may or may not indicate that the birth histories informing them were similar to what we have inferred of the birth histories informing the families recorded at Good Hope. We find on the plantations named in table 7.1, on the Oxford plantation, the Camperdown plantation and so on, quite a proportion of what must be called impossible familial combinations. There are cases where a man is too young to be the father of the eldest child of his 'wife'; cases where the woman is apparently credited with children who would have been born either before she reached the age of childbearing or after she had passed it; cases where there is an age gap of fifteen or twenty years in the string of children, and where it is sometimes revealed by an odd detail that the much younger child was in fact born of one of the older children, a girl, of course, though no 'hus-band' is recorded.[10]

In all these directions — and a fuller discussion with a greater body of

---

[10] It is true that such circumstances are occasionally found in perfectly ordinary English listings. I have not gone so far as to devise tests for deciding whether, as seems evident from comparison by eye, they are more frequent in the data on the slaves.

materials would make it possible to record many more — it is necessary to qualify the judgement that these bodies of persons were living in what ordinary people in our own society today would be prepared to call conventional father—mother—children nuclear families.

There is a further difficulty in these data which has already been hinted at. The documents themselves consist, of course, in lists of persons arranged in blocks, blocks divided from each other by the list-maker. Now we simply do not know whether these divisions correspond to the true residential habits of the persons concerned, or whether they represent the pattern in which they were officially supposed to have lived. We cannot exclude the possibility that the plantation owner or overseer wanted to give the impression to any person who might have access to the documents that this was the form of the domestic organization which was in force amongst the slaves on these plantations, whatever were the real facts. One thing is certain, that these documents were not the handiwork of the people appearing in them, but of the men in control of these people.

III

Nevertheless, they were by no means the only slave owners or administrators who saw their subjects living in simple family households, and the situation we have observed in our chosen set of documents has been found in a number of other contexts. A comparison with what is now becoming known about West Indian slaves and their domestic groups is particularly interesting for our purposes. In 1967 Herbert Klein described how in Cuba the powerfully established Roman priesthood protected Christian ideals of sexuality and procreation among black slaves, and encouraged familial stability. In 1973 Barry Higman came to the conclusion that, on three Jamaican slave settlements in the year 1823, 'although fewer than 25% of the slaves lived with identifiable kin, almost 50% lived in households approximating the nuclear family'. This was in a population whose description was evidently much less specific and revealing than the ones we have considered, and a population which contained a fair number of African-born blacks whose opportunities for settled familial living were presumably less than amongst our subjects. Higman adds this comment on his inference about the nuclear family: 'This has important implications for the understanding of slave family structure. It suggests that the woman-and-children household type was far from dominant, whatever the influence of the mother—child link.'[11]

---

[11] Higman 1973: 534. It has been pointed out, however, that his figures indicate that sexual and housing arrangements may have been independent of each other.

The African-born slaves were apparently somewhat more inclined to live in simple family households than were the Jamaican-born, who more often had their kin in the same household — frequently female-headed. But perhaps the most significant contrast with our data for the American South is that slaves of colour, that is, mulattos or quadroons engendered by white fathers on black slave mothers, 'lived almost exclusively in households dominated by mothers, grandmothers and aunts',[12] with no male present.

For of course there could be no question of white men cohabiting with black slave mates on any plantation, least of all white women with black men. Accordingly, in Jamaica in the 1820s, where white women were so few that European plantation staff could scarcely expect to get married, and had even been forbidden to do so, in the previous century, anyway,[13] 'families', or rather perhaps 'half families', of white fathers were not unlikely occurrences. Such domestic groups were of the utmost rarity in the American South at the time of our documents. There was no shortage of white wives below the Mason—Dixon line, and African-born slaves were few forty years after the slave trade had ended for the U.S.A.

If it is true that for social rules to be rules they have sometimes to be disobeyed, then white men must occasionally, and white women very occasionally, have defied these social and racial taboos. Accordingly, instances of master—slave and mistress—slave cohabitation in the Old South have actually been recorded. In a second study of the slave family household in the West Indies, in course of publication, Higman directly contradicts the assertion of Patterson and others that 'the nuclear family could scarcely exist within the context of slavery'. Using evidence from Barbados in 1796 and Trinidad in 1813 and supplementing that for Jamaica in 1825 with slave marriage recordings, he repeats his claim that simple family households covered a majority of the slave population.

From the rather complex and uncertain body of facts at his disposal he also infers that masters were quite well aware of the domestic groups the blacks were living in, that the larger the plantation the greater the number of family ties amongst the slaves, and that the 'grandmother family' was ordinarily absent. These West Indian plantations were generally very large by the standards of the Old South, and Higman has been able to show that the slaves living on them who were in closest association with the Great House most often displayed the matrifocal

[12] Ibid. p. 536.
[13] Orlando Patterson, *The sociology of slavery* (1967), p. 42. In 1736 white bond servants and overseers as well as slaves were forbidden by law to marry in Jamaica, but in 1826 slave marriages were made lawful under specified conditions.

principle, especially of course where white-fathered offspring lived with their black slave mothers. This, he suggests, may be a reason why it has been so widely supposed that the female-headed household and matrifocality were universal amongst black slave populations.[14]

Though likely to provide, or so it seems to me, the most useful information on the composition of slave families, contemporary lists of slaves in groups are not by any means the only sources open to investigation for the slave states of the U.S.A. Fogel and Engerman report that Stephen Crawford's research into what are called ex-slave narratives, that is, accounts of their experiences given to interviewers during the 1920s and 1930s, can be made to yield original information on the family.[15]

Looking back after sixty or seventy years, over half of these ex-slaves recollected that they had lived before emancipation in two-parent households. But their recollection was that by no means all of these households, not more than four out of five, had been households in which the father was a resident. In the others the father lived elsewhere and was a visitor to his family. Ex-slaves who remembered having lived in one-parent households amounted to over 25% of those interviewed, and of these some three-quarters — that is, about 18% of the total — must have lived in broken families. The reasons for their having been broken are highly significant for our purposes: Fogel and Engerman estimate that in a third of Crawford's cases, sale of mother or father was the cause, and in a fifth (affecting a good twentieth of all the ex-slaves concerned) it was 'because the father was white'. Here the association of matrifocality with miscegenation reappears.

We cannot pursue all the further relevant facts and circumstances which are being recovered by Crawford, and no doubt by others, from these revealing sources. It should not be long before the body of their results appears in print. We must observe, however, that, as Fogel and Engerman point out, proportions of individuals who recollect having lived in one- or two-parent households are not comparable with proportions of slaves listed as living in these ways at some time in the past such as were set out above for our select sample. Accordingly, these two writers have modified Crawford's figures so as to produce table 7.3,

[14] In attributing less, not more, 'regularity' to house slaves, he is in exact contradiction of Dubois's original assertions of 1908; see B. W. Higman, 'Slave family structure in the British West Indies, 1800 — 1834' (1973), typescript of a study that has appeared in the *Journal of Interdisciplinary History* 6, 2 (1975): 265—89. Compare also Fogel 1976. Genovese (1974: 338) shows that there was something of a division between house servants and plantation hands, which would perhaps have been associated with a difference in the composition of their families, though they freely intermarried.

[15] Fogel and Engerman 1975: 28—40, citing the unpublished research of S. C. Crawford. Gutman (1975b) also reports household composition from slave recollections.

TABLE 7.3.   *Distribution of ex-slave households for purposes of comparison with the distribution of households in English and other European villages*

Type of household	Probable distribution of ex-slave households (%)
Two-parent, consolidated	53.6
Two-parent, divided residence	13.0
One-parent	30.6
No family (including solitaries)	2.8

which they suggest can provide a direct contrast with these figures, and also with some of the proportions appearing in table 7.1.

They claim that the first two lines of this table, which can be said to imply that two-thirds of all these households were recollected as double-headed by the respondents, range the sample within the bounds of what is called normal for traditional England on p. 239 above. This is to stretch things a bit,[16] and the contradiction between the figures for 'solitaries' and 'no family' combined given for the slave groups and those both for traditional England and for our select plantations set out in table 7.1 is quite striking, 3% against 12% in England and up to 20% on our plantations. It looks as if the ex-slaves were remembering a situation distinctly different from the one we have been analysing.

One reason for the discrepancy no doubt is that recollection of a distant childhood is not necessarily recollection of a specific situation at a specific time, but rather a general impression over a number of years. If these one-time slaves felt that they ought always to have lived with both their parents as children, or if they had been happiest when they actually lived in such a situation, then we should expect that they would tend to remember it as their whole childhood experience. But there is another probable reason for the inconsistency which is of general importance for our theme. The ex-slaves whose reminiscences are under examination did not represent the range of plantation size: they came disproportionately from the very big and the very small plantations. But they are far less distorted in the distribution of the actual slave population of the American South before 1860 than those appearing in the documents for our select plantations. These belong to very large slave communities only, to the exclusion of all others.

[16] See Fogel and Engerman 1975: 34. The Cambridge Group classification requires an individual to be written down by the list-maker as present in the household in order to count as a member, and it is impossible to say whether such would be the record for the divided-residence slave fathers. In any case not all heads of households are parents in the English materials, so that the two sets of figures are not strictly comparable, after all.

All the seven plantations we have been discussing comprised a hundred persons or so, and two or three of them many more. Yet we learn from the figures reproduced from L. C. Gray's *History of agriculture in the southern United States until 1860* (1933) on p. 144 of vol. 2 of *Time on the cross* that in 1850 not more than 8.50%, and in 1860 not more than 10.0%, of all slaves lived on plantations as large as this or larger. We also learn that nearly half of the slaves in both years lived in groups of between 1 and 20, and a good quarter in groups of less than 10. As for earlier periods, it seems sufficient to quote from the recent account of the Maryland slave population. 'Few planters owned large gangs of slaves in the seventeenth century. Only fifteen of the three hundred owners who left inventories in the four counties between 1658 and 1710 held more than twenty slaves, and only thirty-eight more than ten ... Many slaves lived on plantations with only a few other blacks.' Menard also goes on to show that half the slaves lived in groups of less than 10 and nearly three-quarters in groups of less than 20.[17]

It would be gratuitous to claim that the characteristics of these huge mid-nineteenth-century plantations containing so small a part of the total slave population were necessarily typical of the whole plantation economy during the whole of its history. It also seems rather difficult to believe that the principles of the familial organization which we have been discussing as a model could have operated very effectively on those smaller plantations where so high a proportion of the total number of slaves was living at all relevant times.

Consider a young man or a young woman who attained the age of sexual maturity as a member of a group of 5, 10 or 20 persons only, confined for nearly the entire time to the work-place, which was also the place of residence, and under absolute compulsion never to leave for more than a few hours at a time. How could he or she hope to find and to mate with a suitable partner, and thereafter to 'share a home' with him or her in a way which is universally assumed to be a condition of nuclear family living as we experience it? No wonder the ex-slaves of the 1920s and 1930s recorded their memories of so many divided-residence households.

For settled nuclear family living to be possible for anything like the complete slave population it would seem to me to have been necessary for slave owners on all the smaller plantations to go to great pains and

---

[17] Menard 1975 (see p. 219 above): 34—5. That the family groups on small plantations were likely to have been less 'nuclear' than on large plantations is now beginning to appear from the analysis of household headship. Fogel (1976) states that female-headed households were half as frequent again on plantations with less than 15 slaves than on larger ones, and that plantations of this size, containing a quarter of the slave population in 1860, had nearly half the divided residences.

perhaps considerable expense to provide spouses. Alternatively and additionally, they could have permitted, or even encouraged, the divided-residence arrangements whose importance is now becoming apparent. The father-slave must have had to walk across plantation boundaries. Such circumstances begin to make the difference as to living place in relation to work-place between slave and free labourer rather less than absolute.[18]

If the policy of slave holders was of this description, then it seems that it must have left a considerable body of evidence amongst the materials which have survived from the owners and from the slaves, evidence which could be used to extend the information being derived from interviews. Genovese shows from the great body of materials he has surveyed that most slave holders respected the 'marriages' of their slaves, but this is distinct from pursuing a policy of making it easy for slaves to set up simple family households for themselves. Until the evidence bearing on this point can be taken into account we can only proclaim our ignorance of the 'marital' and familial arrangements for the greater part of the black slave population of the Old South, and our unwillingness to believe that all of them necessarily lived in the fashion which seems to be implied by the documents we have been considering.

IV

Let us now turn to the duration of the familial pattern of slave residence, its duration over time. Fogel and Engerman have made it clear that their generalizations are to be taken to apply to the final generation of slave society in North America, and it is of some importance to insist that the pattern revealed in the documents we have tried to examine could not by itself establish the nuclear family amongst slaves as an ongoing *historical* reality. This would be so even if it could be demonstrated that a large proportion of all slave households conformed to that pattern in, say, the decades of the 30s, 40s, 50s, and 60s of the nineteenth century. When put together, these four decades do not cover two complete developmental cycles of the family group. Why should it be supposed that, because the evidence shows that this was the situation within the slave family on the largest plantations in the final generation of slavery, it was necessarily a part of what might be called 'slave culture'? — that

[18] If indeed this happened amongst the majority of the slave population who worked on the smaller farms, the implications of believing that slaves lived in nuclear families are indeed remarkable. For they begin to transform the picture of an imprisoned slave labouring unit on each plantation, with only *internal* social relationships, into a much more open affair. It seems that the direction of recent work on the issue has been to investigate such a possibility, which is certainly consistent with Crawford's findings.

is, part of the spontaneously arising nexus of social habit over time which can be relied upon to reproduce itself, no change intervening from outside, generation after generation.

This is one of the questions which have to be left to those now engaged upon the recovery of social and familial forms amongst American black slaves. They may conclude that the departures from the white nuclear family which we have described in fact finally derived from the West African society to which the ancestors of these slaves had originally belonged. Or they may be able to prove, as Gurman seems to suggest, that they belonged to an adaptive cultural form unique to this suppressed community, neither a 'survival' nor a 'copy'. In my view, however, it would not be difficult to show how these peculiarities could be accounted for by the alienation of slaves from settled conjugal family units, together with a policy of encouraging slave fertility on the part of slave owners and managers. The groups we have examined might conceivably be used to demonstrate the success of plantation society, magisterial and servile, in maintaining an approximation to a nuclear family form in spite of alienation and all the other counter-influences, including those circumstances which so effectively seem to have blurred the outlines of slave domestic groups and ensured their indefiniteness. The anxiety of the owner and his agents to encourage pregnancy amongst females is written all over these documents and all the others I have seen relating to slave family life. These people may have believed that fostering the nuclear family was the proper policy to this end, and they may have been right.

It is a question of considerable importance to demographers and to anthropologists whether or not the nuclear family structure does lead to higher fertility than other possible family structures. There are those who maintain, along with the great Frédéric le Play and the nineteenth-century familial sociological school, that extended family households are more fertile than nuclear family households in similar social conditions.[19] The commoner view, however, is that the nuclear family system is more efficient in every respect in relation to fertility. Under favourable circumstances it can be observed to be associated with some of the highest fertility rates yet known. There are classic examples of this in the North American continent amongst the Hutterites and amongst

---

[19] Work on this very point is now going forward for the large-scale multiple household of Serbia (Zadruga), of the Baltic states and of Great Russia (Dvor) in the eighteenth and early nineteenth centuries. Demographic theory requires that in extremely unfavourable conditions, with very high mortality indeed, marriage must come so early in order to ensure social survival that complex family households are almost inevitable. People have to procreate as children, in fact, which further emphasizes the importance of age at sexual maturity.

the French Canadians. When it comes to deliberate limitation of fertility, the nuclear family has clearly also shown a quite remarkable pro-
ficiency.

The little that has so far become known about the fertility of slaves
in relation to their domestic situation turns out to be somewhat para-
doxical. Although, as must be expected, women living without mates
had fewer children than those in the ordinary elementary family situation, it seems that fertility was as high in divided-residence households
as it was in consolidated ones. It also appears that the slaves on the
smaller plantations had fewer births than on the larger plantations.[20]
These findings seem inconsistent with the view that the nuclear family
in fact promoted slave reproduction, if it is true, as has been suggested,
that such domestic arrangements were more characteristic of the large
plantations than the small. Such outcomes, together with the fall in successive figures for slave fertility which can be derived from successive
censuses in the late ante-bellum decades — a fall which has been used
to question any proposition about forced breeding amongst them — are,
however, subject to another possible interpretation, if rather a specula-
tive one.

We have attributed to the simple family household in the studies in
this volume a capacity for adaptive control of fertility in relation to circumstance and environment, a control invested, of course, in the spouses
at the head of the household, not in the hands of their owners, should
such exist. If it were correct to assume that households of this type were
growing more common amongst all slaves as the nineteenth century
went on, then we should perhaps also expect their rate of reproduction
to be going down. This view, of course, might imply that more babies
should be born to mothers living in circumstances where these household arrangements were more difficult to establish: on smaller plantations, that is, and where difference of ownership made divided residence
necessary. But if slave owners had a policy with respect to stability in
the families of their slaves (and it must be borne in mind that some
authorities, Gutman included, have denied that this was so), then it
might have been directed towards the more effective rearing of an increasing number of young slaves rather than exclusively towards the
highest possible fertility of slave mothers. What mattered to them was
the maintenance and growth of their labour force and its efficiency.
What also mattered was the set of conventions about family life which

[20] Fogel and Engerman 1975:36—7. They discuss this rather surprising finding in terms
of opportunities and regularity of intercourse, which also seems to be somewhat unrealistic in view of our deep ignorance of all the other circumstances in the lives of slave
couples.

dominated their society, and this must have affected them whatever their personal 'morals', if only because of the criticism of the North.

An interpretation of this kind assumes a growth in the autonomy of the head of the slave household, bringing him to some degree into conflict with his master, who may well have had a greater interest in his reproductive performance than he did himself. It might also be held to imply that a progressive assimilation of the American black into American society at large can be observed to be in progress in his family life even before emancipation. But it must be stressed that these are all hypothetical suggestions only. They must be left undecided, as must indeed the whole question of the relationship between familial composition and fertility.

The same reservation may have to be made in respect of the position which Fogel and Engerman wish to establish about the sexual conduct of slave girls, though there is a prospect that continuing research and improved analysis may eventually decide the issue. This is the principle that a woman should have been a virgin at marriage, or, as was maintained in chapter 3, until the final stage of courtship was reached, when marriage was a near certain outcome. The larger question of miscegenation between white and black certainly bears on the nuclear family, as we have seen, but is likely to be much more difficult to resolve, if it ever can be resolved.

Fogel and Engerman maintain (1975: 24) that there was a clear interval between the time when the average slave girl became capable of full sexual relationships and the time when she began regular childbearing, which must count for marriage in this case. If this could be demonstrated, these young women could be supposed to have resembled their white American contemporaries in the matter of their 'virtue' after puberty and during courtship. The evidence in support of such a view is the age at first birth which Fogel and Engerman believe to have been typical of slave mothers and an assumption, for at present it can be nothing more, that menarche came early, as early as was suggested in our last chapter for Belgrade in the 1730s.

The method so far used to determine age at first birth has been the subtraction from the age of a slave mother listed in the probate inventory of her owner the age of her first accompanying child. Although this evidence seems to have proved itself reliable for other purposes in slave demography, it is not easy to decide how far we can trust an age at first birth of 22.5 years (median 21.3; Fogel and Engerman 1975: 19) derived in this way, especially as other and much lower ages have been advanced, including a singulate mean age at first birth of almost two years younger. It also seems rather risky to base much on the superior diet of slaves as an explanation of why sexual maturity came early amongst them, for all arguments on slave nutrition have been hotly debated.[21]

But there is apparently a good prospect of there coming into the analysis more sets of records of the kind which we have been able to make use of for the Good Hope plantation. With registered birth dates for slave mothers as well as for their children, it should be possible to decide the age at which at any particular date the average slave mother could expect her first conception. The extensive records of the heights of slaves may help in the calculation of age at menarche, since there is a constant relationship between age at onset of height-spurt and time of puberty. If, as seems not unlikely, such methods should succeed in finally fixing menarche in the 15th year, then four years, or even more, might be inferred as the interval which could have elapsed on average between sexual maturity and the beginning of procreation. This is well over the mean interval between marriage and first conception referred to in our last chapter for girls wedded at the ages in question and is too long to be accounted for by considerations about adolescent sub-fecundity or sterility. If, indeed, we ventured to compare the hypothetical history of Serbian adolescent brides in the 1730s suggested tentatively there with this reconstruction of the experience of black slaves in America a century and more later, the advantage might go to the slaves, in the sense that they seem to have spent longer than the Serbs between becoming capable of conceiving and actually doing so.

But Christian women in eighteenth-century Belgrade are a different proposition from white American women of what the Americans themselves still sometimes call the Victorian age. Nevertheless, an outside view must be that slave girls did stay 'unmarried', and perhaps 'intact' in the Victorian sense, for appreciably longer than might be expected if anything like forced breeding was in operation, or if the rule of marriage after courtship had no importance in their behaviour. Perhaps more important for historical sociology is the fact that there should be a prospect of more detailed information, even fairly certain information, on the physiological development of these enslaved women of the past — more, that is, and more reliable, than we seem ever likely to obtain about

---

[21] Ibid p. 87 etc. and the citation of works by Sutch and others criticizing the statements of *Time on the cross* about diet. Gutman (1975a) cites probate and other plantation records which he reckons show a mean age at first birth of well under 20, and also the U.S. Census of 1880 (details of a group of ex-slave women) implying one of 18 to 18.9 years. James Trussell, in an unpublished study (see ch. 6, n. 19 above), comments on the biasses which enter into all such calculations and estimates a singulate mean which is some two years lower than the Fogel and Engerman figure. This is still just a little higher than the singulate mean age at first birth calculated in ch. 6 above for Belgrade in 1733–4. A more accurate estimate, which seems certain to be forthcoming, awaits the recovery and analysis of further data.

other women. The possession of human beings as property, valuable property, in a highly developed society, already in almost all respects what we think of as a modern society, seems to have ensured the survival of an abundance of physiologically significant detail for the historical sociologist to use — one more of the paradoxes about prolonged survival of the institution of chattel slavery in the United States of America.

V

As we survey one by one the characteristics of family life amongst the slaves who lived in such numbers within the society of American Europeans a little over a century ago, it is not, I think, too fanciful to say that our own familial habit reveals itself to us as a historical reality, sharper and still sharper in its silhouette. We can recognize its presence in every one of the subjects and situations we have surveyed in this volume, and its sudden, disconcerting default when we come to contemplate what happened amongst slaves.

The breakup of society of man, wife and child before due time by such a thing as the enforced departure of any of its members grates upon our consciences. Slaves provide the only example of such a dissolution yet found in the familial history of the West, even if there are faint traces of the sale of wives amongst the English peasantry — when this occurred it is best looked upon as a primitive form of divorce — and even if children could sometimes go out as servants before their tenth birthday. In our own generation of loosely structured sexual habits, substitution of sexual partners and ever-increasing confusion of links between parents and offspring, we still expect every child in a family group to be born of the couple at its head, or of their once legitimate spouses. We can be brought to recognize that orphanage, stepchildhood and stepparenthood must have been very common in the Western family in the past: this was the object of chapter 4 of this volume. But it is a different matter to have to contemplate the fact that a slave child need never have had a socially recognized father at all, and that this had nothing to do with dying. Only the wretched foundlings taken in by hospitals established for the purpose in traditional Europe were in such a situation, and even here it is surprising how often the parentage of these infants was revealed in a note pinned to their baby clothes.

In our day we have elaborately enlightened views on illegitimacy; so much so that it may soon become quite difficult to find out from public records to whom this unwelcome and undeserved stigma should be attached. Nevertheless, it is satisfactory in a way to find out that over the centuries of English history illegitimacy levels were on the whole low, and a shock to learn that amongst slaves neither legitimacy nor illegitimacy officially existed, that it could not have mattered if a string of slave children belonging to an existent partnership were of various fatherhoods or motherhoods. We are still interested in questions of sexual behaviour which modulate the shape and extent of the family group, perhaps inordinately interested in spite of our newly won permissiveness. It makes a difference to people to get to know that a parent or a grandparent or even a more remote ancestor was illegitimate, or even so much as conceived outside marriage, although the facts of courtship in an earlier society can be shown to bring such occurrences into the European familial tradition. This is the reason why the extent to which 'unmarried' Negro slaves preserved their virginity has to be looked upon as a matter worth investigating: it certainly concerned their black descendants when the issue was raised for the first time in public from historical evidence in 1974.

The discussion of the composition of households is perhaps a more abstract matter, in spite of the deep-seated prejudice in favour of believing in the large-scale, complex household as a standard feature of former society. Indeed it has been claimed elsewhere (Laslett in Laslett and Wall (eds.) 1972: xi, 63) that the form of the family household has never held the normative position in patterns of behaviour that monogamy and its regulations have always done. It affects us, all the same, it speaks to our notion of what a family should be and what it has been in the past, when we find that single-headed households were more common amongst the peasantry than seemed at all possible, and not the universal rule amongst slave populations that recent opinion would have us believe. We feel something like complacence also when we are informed that aging slaves in the West Indies tended to live with their 'married partners' more often than the younger ones, or that in the second generations slave offspring seemed to have dwelt with their parents until marriage, and lived as near them as possible after that.

It might be said that all the familial facts about slavery flow from the one outrageous anomaly, that slavery consists in the ownership of men by men. This makes it more instructive to be able to claim that all the themes of this book intertwine in the slowly emerging story of what happened when the Western nuclear family came up against the existence of an enslaved minority, with its different familial traditions and its entirely anomalous position in the social structure. Aging is touched upon least when we analyse the family life of slaves, though the facts just cited do bear upon it; and there is one subject which has been a major concern in the preceding pages which has yet to be brought in. This is the subject of the turnover of membership in the local community which appeared so prominently in chapter 2. It was the servants, it will be remembered, who were shown to have had most to do with the tendency for settled English and northern French villages to change their composition as to persons at such a surprising rate.

A good half and more of the servants, who could themselves be a tenth or an eighth of the whole population, were shown to have changed the jobs they were in and the villages where they lived every succeeding year. This cannot usually have been in the interests of their masters, and it seems undeniable that the agricultural entrepreneur won an important victory when he found that Negroes could have immobility forced upon them, that the traditions of English law and English social practice as to freedom of movement as well as of the person could be abrogated for the blacks. In this sense it seems possible to say that a first description of slavery within the historical Western social structure established in the New World was that slaves were servants forbidden to move.

Those who stay where they are mate and engender their children with other persons in the same place or living very near it. As generation succeeds generation it must follow that a society of these persons develops an intense and complicated set of kin relationships. In spite of the alienation by sale of individual slaves, in spite of the trek westwards from the Old South of Virginia, the Carolinas and Georgia to the New South of Texas and the Mississippi Delta, and allowing for the complication of divided residence across plantations, it seems to me indisputable that the slave population of the United States must have had a kinship density far exceeding that of the whites of that region or of the rest of the country. Perhaps this says very little in a country so given, as the early-nineteenth-century United States was, to regional movement and so subject to emigration.

But it also seems reasonable to expect that American slave society by the year 1850 had a network of kinship consistently better developed than that which existed amongst the peasantry of pre-industrial Western Europe. The landholders, land workers and craftsmen of eighteenth-century England and northern France must have had considerably greater freedom of choice in marriage than ever slaves can have had. They also moved, not often very far, but certainly far enough for many of them to get beyond the reach of contact with their kin.[22]

[22] The subject of kinship and its density, as was made clear in chs. 1 and 2, is a peculiarly difficult one for historical sociologists, and we have little as yet in the way of hard evidence about how closely the inhabitants of a pre-industrial village were related to each other. The work referred to there suggests that the situation was extremely variable and that primary kin relations (filial and conjugal) could involve up to three-quarters of all the conjugal family units in a community, but that this proportion could also fall below a half. Microsimulation methods may soon, we hope, make it possible to study relation-

It is one thing to have your kin folk near you as the slaves did, but it is another thing to know how they are related to you and to regulate relationships with them so that a system of kinship shall come into being, proliferate and be transferred from generation to generation. We must appeal once again to the students of the society of the American black slave to find out for us how far the slave individuals knew who their ancestors and relatives were, how far they arranged their unions so as to produce a particular pattern of relationship and descent, how far, in fact, they had a distinct familial and kinship system of their own.[23]

Whatever that system may turn out to be, however far it can be shown to consist in what black slaves themselves had in their heads as distinct from what their owners thought was right for them, one thing should be clear from the present discussion. Family for the slave cannot have been quite the same thing as it was for those who owned them. It is in such contrasts and comparisions as these, comparisons of likes with apparent likes and comparisons between quite dissimilar things, that the future of historical sociology will rest. The study of family life and illicit love in former generations has a great deal yet to do, and the contemplation of the slave plantations of the Southern states should help us to decide what next should be undertaken.

Footnote 22 (continued)

ships beyond the primary, and further analytic work may yield more revealing measures. The importance of kin links is becoming evident in nineteenth-century American cities and in industrial communities, and it should not be assumed that migration always reduces the importance of a kin nexus. It must sever many links, but migrants often go to places where kin have preceded them, and their links with those particular kin are often of great economic importance.

[23] In his two publications of 1975 (see n. 2 above) and his paper for the Sixth International Congress on Economic History, Copenhagen, August 1974, 'Kinship groupings on Southern plantations in the United States', Herbert Gutman demonstrates that evidence for such a familial and kinship system certainly exists. He insists, for one thing, that first-cousin marriages were strictly prohibited by the slaves themselves, a convention which distinguishes them sharply from their owners, who intermarried freely, and one which reveals a clear awareness of kin relations amongst the black people. Professor Gutman was kind enough to send me copies of a number of slave genealogies demonstrating this and other features of slave familial and kin relations, for which I should like to thank him. The full account will presumably appear in his forthcoming book.

Bibliography

Books published in London unless otherwise stated

Anderson, M., 1971 *Family structure in nineteenth century Lancashire*, Cambridge
    1972 'Household structure and the industrial revolution', in Laslett and Wall (eds.)
    1972: 205—14
Andorka, Rudolf, 1975 'Peasant family structure in the eighteenth and nineteenth centuries', *Ethnographia* (Budapest) 86, 2—3: 341—65
Ariès, Philippe, 1960 *L'enfant et la vie familiale sous l'ancien régime*, Paris; 2nd ed.,1973.
    Trans. Robert Baldick as *Centuries of childhood*, 1960
Baker, David, 1973 *The inhabitants of Cardington in 1782*, Bedfordshire Historical Record
    Society, vol. 52
Beauvoir, Simone de, 1970 *La vieillesse*, Paris. Trans. Patrick O'Brian as *Old age*, 1972
Berkner, L. K., 1972 'The stem family and the developmental cycle of the peasant household: an eighteenth-century Austrian example', *American Historical Review* 77: 398—
    418
    1974 'Inheritance, land tenure and family structure in lower Saxony at the end of the
    seventeenth century', paper for the International Conference of Economic History,
    Copenhagen, September 1974
Birren, James E. (ed.), forthcoming *Handbook of aging and the social sciences*, vol. 1, ed. E.
    Shanas and R. Binstock, New York
Blayo, Yves, 1970 'La mobilité dans un village de la Brie vers le milieu du XIXe siècle',
    Population (Paris) 25: 573—605
    1975 'La proportion de naissances illégitimes en France de 1740 à 1892', *Population*
    (Paris) 30: 65—70
Bouchard, Gérard, 1972 *Le village immobile: Sennely-en-Sologne au XVIIIe siècle*, Paris
Carney, F. J., 1976 Dissertation in progress for the University of Pennsylvania using the
    Census of Ireland of 1821
Carter, H. and Glick, P. C., 1970 *Marriage and divorce*, Cambridge, Mass.
Chambers, J. D., 1972 *Population, economy and society in pre-industrial England*, ed. W. A.
    Armstrong, Oxford
Coale, A. J. and Demeny, P., 1966 *Regional model life tables and stable populations*, Princeton,
    N. J.
deMause, Lloyd (ed.) 1974 *The history of childhood*, New York; London, 1976
Drake, Michael, 1969 *Population and society in Norway, 1735—1865*, Cambridge
    1973 *Applied historical studies: an introductory reader*
Drake, Michael (ed.), 1974 *Historical data and the social sciences*, course books for the Open
    University, Milton Keynes
Du Bois, W. E., 1908 *The Negro American family*, Atlanta, Ga.; reprinted New York, 1970
Flandrin, Jean-Louis, 1976 *Familles: parenté, maison, sexualité dans l'ancienne société*, Paris
Fogel, Robert W., 1976 'Cliometrics and culture: some recent developments in the historiography of slavery', mimeograph, April
Fogel, Robert W. and Engerman, Stanley L., 1974 *Time on the cross*, 2 vols., Boston
    1975 'Why the U.S. population grew so rapidly: fertility, population and household

structure', ch. 3 of 'Further evidence on the economics of U.S. slavery', mimeograph, July

1976 'Explaining the relative efficiency of slave agriculture in the ante-bellum South', mimeograph, February

Frazier, E. Franklin, 1939 *The Negro family in the U.S.A.*, Chicago

Frisch, Rose, 1975 'Demographic implications of the biological determinants of female fecundity', *Social Biology* 22: 17—22

Genovese, Eugene D., 1974 *Roll Jordan, roll*, New York

Glass, D. V., 1973 *Numbering the people*, Saxon House, Farnborough

Gutman, Herbert, 1975a Extended review of *Time on the cross*, *Journal of Negro History* 60 (January): 53—227. Published as *Slavery and the numbers game*, New York

1975b 'Persistent myths about the Afro-American family', *Journal of Interdisciplinary History* 6, 2 (Autumn): 181—210

Hair, P. E. H., 1966 'Bridal pregnancy in England in earlier centuries', *Population Studies* 20: 233—43

1970 'Bridal pregnancy in earlier centuries further examined', *Population Studies* 24: 59—70

Hajnal, J., 1965 'European marriage patterns in perspective', in D. V. Glass and D. E. C. Eversley (eds.), *Population in history:* 101—43

Hammel, E. A., Hutchinson, D., Lundy, R. and Wachter, K., 1975 'Socsim: a demographic microsimulation program', mimeograph, Institute for International Studies, Berkeley, Calif.

Hammel, E. A. and Laslett, P., 1974 'Comparing household structure over time and between cultures', *Comparative Studies in Society and History* 16: 73—110

Hansen, Hans Oluf, 1971 'Tabulation of the Icelandic population of 1729', mimeograph

Hartley, Shirley Foster, 1975 *Illegitimacy*, Berkeley, Calif.

Higman, B. W., 1973 'Household structure and fertility of Jamaican slaves', *Population Studies* 27, 3: 527—50

1975 'Slave family structure in the British West Indies', *Journal of Interdisciplinary History* 6, 2 (Autumn): 265—89

Johansen, H.-C., 1976 'The position of the old in traditional society', mimeograph, University of Odense

Katz, Michael B., 1976 *The people of Hamilton, Canada West: family and class in a mid-nineteenth-century city*, Cambridge, Mass.

Klapisch, Christiane, 1973 'L'enfance en Toscane au début du XVe siècle', *Annales de Démographie Historique:* 99—122

Klein, H. S., 1967 *Slavery in the Americas*

Klep, P. M. M., 1973 'Het huishouden in Westelijk Noord-Brabant: struktuur en ontwikkeling 1750—1849', *A. A. G. Bijdragen* 18: 23—91

Kussmaul-Cooper, Ann, 1975 'The mobility of English farm servants in the seventeenth and eighteenth centuries', mimeograph

Laslett, Peter, 1963 'Clayworth and Cogenhoe', with John Harrison, in H. E. Bell and R. L. Ollard (eds.), *Historical essays presented to David Ogg:* 157—84

1964 'Market society and political theory', review of C. B. Macpherson, *Political theory of possessive individualism*, *Historical Journal* 7: 150—4

1965 *The world we have lost;* 2nd ed., 1971. Trans. C. Campos as *Un monde que nous avons perdu*, Paris, 1969

1966 'Social structure from listings of inhabitants', in Wrigley (ed.) 1966: 160—208

1967a 'The extent of bastardy in Restoration England', mimeograph, Center for Advanced Study in the Behavioral Sciences, Palo Alto, Calif.

1967b 'History and the social sciences', *Encyclopaedia of the Social Sciences*, ed. D. Sills, New York: 434–40

1968 'Le brassage de la population en France et en Angleterre au XVIIe et au XVIIIe siècles', *Annales de Démographie Historique*: 99–109

1971 'Age at menarche in Europe since the early eighteenth century. Evidence from Belgrade in 1733/4', *Journal of Interdisciplinary History* 2, 2: 221–36. Reprinted in Rabb and Rotberg (eds.) 1973 : 28–47

1972a 'Introduction: the history of the family', in Laslett and Wall (eds.) 1972: 1–89

1972b 'Mean household size in England since the sixteenth century', in Laslett and Wall (eds.) 1972: 125–58.

1972c 'Houseful and household in an eighteenth-century Balkan city. A tabular analysis of the listing of the Serbian sector of Belgrade in 1733–4', with Marilyn Clarke, in Laslett and Wall (eds.) 1972: 375–400

1972d 'La famille et le ménage: approches historiques', *Annales E. S. C.*: 847–72

1973 'Introduction', *The earliest classics* (works by John Graunt and Gregory King with a manuscript notebook of King's), Pioneers of Demography series, Gregg International (now D. C. Heath), Farnborough

1974 'Parental deprivation in the past', *Local Population Studies* 13 (Autumn): 11–18

1975 'The family and industrialisation', paper to be published in German by *Arbeitskreis für Sozialgeschichte*, Heidelberg

1976a 'Philippe Ariès and *la famille*', *Encounter* (February): 80–3

1976b 'The wrong way through the telescope; a note on literary evidence in sociology and historical sociology', *British Journal of Sociology* 26, 3 : 319–42

Laslett, Peter and Oosterveen, Karla, 1973 'Long-term trends in bastardy in England', *Population Studies* 27: 255–86

Laslett, Peter and Wall, Richard (eds.), 1972 *Household and family in past time*, Cambridge

Le Bras, Hervé, 1973 'Parents, grands-parents, bisaieux', *Population* (Paris) 28, 1: 9–38

Leffingwell, Albert, 1892 *Illegitimacy and the influence of seasons upon conduct*

Levine, David and Wrightson, Keith, 1975 'The social context of illegitimacy in early modern England', mimeograph

Löfgren, Orvar, 1974 'Family and household among Scandinavian peasants', *Ethnologia Scandinavica*: 1–52

Macfarlane, Alan, 1970 *The family life of Ralph Josselin*, Cambridge

Maddox, Brenda, 1975 *The half-parent*

Menard, Russell R., 1975 'The Maryland slave population, 1658–1730: a demographic profile of blacks in four counties', *William and Mary Quarterly*, 3rd series, 32: 29–54

Mitterauer, Michael, 1973 'Zur Familienstruktur in ländlichen Gebieten Österreichs im 17. Jahrhundert', in H. Helcmanovski (ed.), *Beiträge zur Bevölkerungs- und Sozialgeschichte Österreichs*, Vienna: 167–222

Palli, Heldur, 1971 'Historical demography of Estonia in the seventeenth and eighteenth centuries', in J. Kahk and A. Vassar (eds.), *Studia historica in honorem Hans Kruus*, Tallinn: 205–21

1974 'Perede strukturist ja selle uurimiset' [Study of household structure], *Proceedings of the Soviet Academy of Estonia*, 23, 1: 64–76

Patterson, Orlando, 1967 *The sociology of slavery*

Piazzini, Aldo, 1974/5 'Caratteristiche della struttura della famiglia in due zone della campagna Fiorentina nella seconda metà del XVIII secolo, in base agli "stati anime"', honours thesis, University of Florence

Plakans, Andrejs, 1975a 'Peasant farmsteads and households in the Baltic littoral, 1797', *Comparative Studies in Society and History* 17: 2–35

1975b 'Seigneurial authority and peasant family life', *Journal of Interdisciplinary History* 6, 4: 629—54

Pressat, Roland, 1972 *Demographic analysis,* Chicago and London

Rabb, T. K. and Rotberg, R. I. (eds.), 1973 *The family in history,* New York

Registrar-General of England and Wales *Annual report* of 1843, 1844, 1847 etc. *Statistical review* of 1966 etc.

Richards, M. P. M. (ed.), 1974 *The integration of the child into a social world,* Cambridge

Shochet, G. J., 1969 'Patriarchalism and mass attitudes in Stuart England', *Historical Journal* 13 : 413—41

1975 *Patriarchalism and political theory,* Oxford

Schofield, R. S., 1970 'Age specific mobility in an eighteenth century rural English parish', *Annales de Démographie Historique:* 261—74

Shanas, E., Townsend, P., Wedderburn, D., Milhøj, P., Friis, H. and Stehouwer, J., 1968 *Old people in three industrial societies*

Shorter, Edward, 1971 'Illegitimacy, sexual revolution and social change in modern Europe', *Journal of Interdisciplinary History* 2, 2 (Autumn) : 237—72

1975 *The making of the modern family,* New York; London, 1976

Shorter, Edward, van de Walle, E. and Knodel, J., 1971 'The decline of non-married fertility in Europe', *Population Studies* 25, 3 (November): 375—93

Smith, Richard Michael, 1974 'English peasant life-cycles and social—economic networks', Ph.D. dissertation, Cambridge University

Spufford, Margaret, 1974 *Contrasting communities: English villages in the sixteenth and seventeenth centuries,* Cambridge

Tanner, J. M., 1955 *Growth at adolescence,* Oxford; 2nd ed., Oxford, 1962

1966 'The secular trend towards earlier physical maturation', *Tijdschrift voor Geneeskunde* 44: 531ff

Todd, Emmanuel, 1974 'Kinship and geographical mobility in pre-industrial Europe', dissertation, Trinity College, Cambridge

1975 'Mobilité et cycle de vie en Artois et en Toscane au XVIIIe siècle', *Annales E. S. C.,* no. 4: 726—44

Wikman, K. Rob V., 1937 'Die Einleitung der Ehe. Eine vergleichend ethno-soziologische Untersuchung über die Vorstufe der Ehe in den Sitten des Schwedischen Volkstums', *Acta Academica Aboensis Humaniora* 11 : 1—384

Wrigley, E. A., 1966 'Family limitation in pre-industrial England', *Economic History Review* 19:82—109. Reprinted in M. Drake (ed.), *Population in industrialization,* 1969: 157—94

1969 'Baptism/marriage ratios in late seventeenth century England', *Local Population Studies* 3 : 15—17

1972 'Mortality in pre-industrial England: the example of Colyton, Devon, over three centuries', in D. V. Glass and Roger Revelle (eds.), *Population and social change:* 243—72

1973 'Clandestine marriage in Tetbury in the late seventeenth century', *Local Population Studies* 10: 14—21

1974 'Fertility strategy for the individual and the group', in C. Tilly (ed.), *Historical studies in changing fertility,* in press

Wrigley, E. A. (ed.), 1966 *An introduction to English historical demography*

Index